THE WAY OF MINDFULNESS

BHIKKHU SOMA

RAYS OF THE DHAMMA SERIES

SECOND REVISED AND ENLARGED EDITION

Printers:
CEYLON DAILY NEWS PRESS
LAKE HOUSE, COLOMBO

"Rays of the Dhamma" Series No. 1

Bhāsaye jotaye dhammaṁ

THE WAY OF MINDFULNESS

being a translation of the Satipaṭṭhāna Sutta of the Majjhima Nikāya ; its Commentary, the Satipaṭṭhāna Sutta Vaṇṇanā of the Papañcasūdanī of Buddhaghosa Thera ; and excerpts from the Līnatthapakāsanā Ṭīkā, Marginal Notes, of Dhammapāla Thera on the Commentary

by

BHIKKHU SOMA

with a Word to the General Reader, an Introduction and Explanatory Additions

AJIRĀRĀMA COLOMBO

2492 1949

DEDICATED

TO

The Venerable Mahā Nāyaka Thera
Paeḷāēṇē Siri Vajirañāṇa of Vajirārāma,
Colombo, Ceylon

and

The Venerable Mahā Thera Pāṇḍava
of Taungwainggyi Shwegyin Kyaung
Taik, Moulmein, Burma

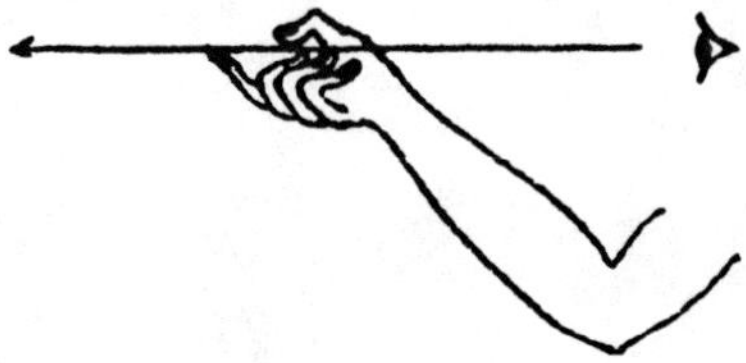

As a fletcher straightens his shaft, the wise man straightens the restless, fickle mind, hard to watch and to restrain.

—*Dhammapada*

Bhikkhus, those with whom you feel, those who deem you worth listening to, your friends, your associates, your kinsfolk and your blood-relations should be spurred on to, advised, and made firm in the cultivation of the Four Arousings of Mindfulness.

SATIPAṬṬHĀNA SAṀYUTTA

The two drawings in this book are
by Mr. P. T. James Vithanavasang of
Nālandā Vidyālaya, Colombo.

CONTENTS

INTRODUCTION TO THE FIRST EDITION

Directing attention to the four truly genuine stages of Sainthood in this universe, the Buddha says: "Here, O Bhikkhus, are the First Ascetic [Sotāpanna], the Second Ascetic [Sakadāgāmi], the Third Ascetic [Anāgāmi], and the Fourth Ascetic [Arahat]; empty of Ascetics are the other ways of thought. Resound thus, O Bhikkhus, your swelling diapason of just rejoicing." [Cūla Sīhanāda Sutta].

Later, the Buddha states why he affirms that nowhere, outside his System of Deliverance, are genuine Saints to be found. It is because the Goal, Perfection [Niṭṭha; here a synonym for the attainment of the Arahat] is "One, not Multiple," and the views of man are many. In a Buddha's system of Deliverance there are no "Views"; instead, there is right understanding of things as they really are.

All Doctrines outside Buddhism fall under one of these two: the Existence view and the Non-existence view. Those who adhere to either of these views are hostile to the adherents of the other. But none of them "understand, in accordance with truth, the arising and the decline of these two views." Lusting, hating, deluded, craving, clinging, untaught, easily annoyed, easily roused to enmity,—"all these, obsessed with pleasures and attachments, attain not to Deliverance from birth, decay and death, sorrow, pain, lamentation, grief, and despair. They are not freed from suffering," says the Teacher.

All these blind folk suffer from Craving, based on four kinds of attachment: Clinging to Sensuality, Clinging to mere Opinion, Clinging to Ceremonial Observances, and Clinging to Belief in a Soul. "There are many religious folk," teachers and followers, says the Buddha, "who profess themselves masters of these attachments; yet they do not exhibit such mastery."

The Teacher goes on to tell us that even when the first three kinds of Clinging are mastered, the last,—"Clinging to Belief in a Soul is a hurdle too difficult for any but a Buddhist to surmount. These good religious folk "indeed do not rightly comprehend this one thing," declares the Buddha, and thus their doctrines are incapable of leading any to final Deliverance from Suffering.

"But the Tathāgata, O Bhikkhus, the Arahat, the Fully Enlightened One, declares himself fully aware of all forms of Clinging, and he makes known to perfection the Science of the same. In a doctrine and discipline [Dhamma-vinaya] of this sort, O Bhikkhus, what joy there is in the Teacher is to be proclaimed perfect ; what joy there is in the Teaching is to be proclaimed perfect ; what observance of Virtue there be is proclaimed perfect ; what pleasure and happiness there be amongst fellow-disciples is proclaimed perfect. And for what reason ? Because, verily, O Bhikkhus, these things are truly so in this well-declared doctrine and discipline, clearly explained, leading to the Deliverance, conducive to the Peace taught by a Supreme Sambuddha."

In the subject now presented to the reader, " The Discourse on the Arousing of Mindfulness [Satipaṭṭhāna Sutta]," I myself prefer to call it " The Discourse on Penetrating Mindfulness," the Peerless Teacher gives an aspirant details of how to use the weapon of Mind if he wishes to make an end of the Bonds of Suffering.

" This is the **sole way**, O Bhikkhus, leading to the purification of beings.........to the Realization of Nibbāna," declares the Blessed One. And this " sole way," this one and only way is **revealed only in the Buddha-dhamma and nowhere else**, which is why other systems of " religion ", however much they may claim to own saints, are actually unaware of what even constitutes true Sainthood. True Gold can be obtained only from a gold-bearing source, though others who dig may vainly point to their gold-seeming ores of baser metals which, however useful they may be, will ever be rejected by him who would fashion a crown for earth's princes.

The reader will note a certain abruptness, almost jerkiness of expression, in the text. This is even more so in the commentary. This effect is brought about partly by the concise way in which a complex subject, of many details, is treated. But actually the text reflects the course of the Aspirant's progress in watchful thinking, even as verses in a gallop rhythm can picture the speeding rider and the steady beat of a horse's hooves.

He who begins this practice of Satipaṭṭhāna finds that indeed he needs must rein in his thoughts sharply and often. No racing steed can equal thought which, now here, looking at the Temple Bo Tree, is in a moment at Buddhagayā's Shrine, and next instant visualizing the poplars in an English Park. But, as a rider slides as it were into the way of its doing, on a bicycle, or a trotting horse,—so in this practice the Yogi gradually falls in with " its way " till, after a while, its working seems smooth and clear.

The Translator is a Bhikkhu well qualified for the task. For him it was a happy labour of love, and a tribute to his Teachers in that secluded many celled Ārāma in far Burma, where he, and another young Bhikkhu from Lankā, held out to the last in a long course of instruction in Satipaṭṭhāna method. A Mahā Thera, as well-known there as he was qualified in learning and temperament, supervised the course. The Discipline was strict, but just ; and the Teacher firm, compassionate and a seer beyond the normal. The lodging and diet were simple to a degree. The Mahā Thera's own teacher of old, master of meditation and expert in practical teaching for all that he was a layman, was deputed to instruct the yogins. Like all older Burmans, he had aforetime himself been a wearer of the yellow robe ; his experience was vast and his learning profound.

The Course started with a crowd of Aspirants many of whom were pious layfolk ; but, as the weeks passed and endurance gave way, the class of pupils was sadly thinned out. Some, after a time, gave up the effort. Others, perhaps through a difference in preparation or temperament, completed the course early. Others again went on and on with the training until, at last, the two earnest ones from Lankā were left to face the calm Teacher whose evenness of mind was in no way disturbed by the recurring phenomenon of dwindling enthusiasm or numbers in those courses of hard life and abstruse thought. The training was beyond price. Keener at the close than even at the start of that course, our Translator today is yet happily and earnestly following that trail.

These are indeed difficult times for layman and Bhikkhu alike. The seven year maximum has not yet passed ; and indeed we are woefully weak for the Sutta's "seven days" minimum for results,—that is Arahantship, or failing that, the Anāgāmi stage of Sainthood. Yet the strenuous will press on—

> " Remembering the Saints of other days,
> And recollecting how it was they lived,
> E'en though today be but the after-time—
> One yet may win the Ambrosial Path of Peace."
>
> Saritvā pubbake yogī tesaṁ vattam anussaraṁ
> Kiñcāpi pacchimo kālo phuseyya Amataṁ Padaṁ
>
> Theragāthā 947

Cassius A. Pereira

Nugegoda,
8th August, 1941

ACKNOWLEDGMENTS

In bringing out this second and enlarged edition of a book published seven years ago I received encouragement from the Ven. Mahā Nāyaka Thera Paeḷāēṇē Siri Vajirañāṇa of Vajirārāma who with great kindliness and sympathy gave me all the help I needed in the translation of the Discourse, Commentary and Marginal Notes.

Four sabbrahmacāris (brothers in the holy life) have to be thanked particularly. They are the Ven. Bhikkhus Kheminda, Nyāṇapoṇika, Puññānanda and Kassapa. The word to the general reader was written on the advice of the Ven. Bhikkhu Kassapa ; the whole commentary was critically read by the Ven. Bhikkhu Nyāṇapoṇika and I have made changes and left out several unimportant passages on seeing the cogency of his arguments; the Ven. Bhikkhu Kheminda has gone through practically every part of the book and assisted me by his opinion on several points; and the Ven. Bhikkhu Puññānanda has read the proofs.

I must also thank Mr. & Mrs. Nalin Moonesinghe who generously undertook to print this book on the Buddhaword so that the Teaching of Happiness may become a little more accessible than it now is in regard to at least certain important parts of it connected with the practice of concentration and wisdom.

Let every kind of help given to the work of resetting the Buddhaword in this little book be a conditioning force for the future weal of the helpers.

A WORD TO THE GENERAL READER

There is a Diamond City set high above the plains. It is a City which has everything of worth. Possessed of complete power and freedom it is perfectly secure. From its gates facing the cardinal points radiate four straight shining roads which appear as if they were the veins of the diamond out of which the City is built. These roads stretch to the ends of the earth and are known as the Fourfold Way to the City. Both City and the Way to it are indestructible. To have merely a glimpse of the City is to become wise and contented ; to live in it is to be plunged in the peace and happiness of immortality.

Periodically, a change takes place over the face of the earth and people lose sense of the Way. But the memory of the City persists in men's minds like the fugitive fragrance of a forgotten flower. Time after time, when for long ages the Way is lost to men, there arises a person of heroic mould who hears about the City and determines to reach it. He explores every place where the Way is likely to be, after gleaning whatever information is available to him regarding the direction in which the City could possibly exist. Undaunted by failure, he carries on his quest till he finds the Way, and sees the City. Then he makes known his discovery to his fellowmen and they travel on the Way and bear witness to the truth of his word.

The instructions of the last discoverer of the Way are still with us and form a map with copious explanations, and many persons all over the world are studying the map and are treading the Way as of old. From the instructions we learn that the Way is not easy to journey on because it traverses territories hostile to those who wish to reach the City of Light. The king of the hostile territories is very powerful. He knows that if one goes to the Diamond City that one passes out of his sway. He wants to have as many subjects as possible who would obey him, and whenever one travels along the Way to the City he obstructs that one's progress. Sometimes with terrorizing magical illusions of fire, flood, tempests, armies, ferocious beasts, and angry demons, but more often with temptations of beauty, pleasure, security, and power, does the king try to deflect the traveller from the Way.

But the man of set purpose cannot be frightened or tempted. He keeps his feet steadily on the Way and his mind on journeying to the City. Such a determined person is helped by invisible beings. He is clad in invincible armour and equipped with an all conquering sword. He is always calm and clear-headed and his sight is keen enough to see through the illusions and snares of the hostile one. Standing on the unyielding Way, sure of foot, and wielding his mighty weapon, he routs all enemies and journeys onwards unhurt and free, and reaches the City.

The Diamond City is Nibbāna. The Four Roads that issue from its gates are to be taken as the Fourfold Way of Mindfulness. The glimpsing of the City is the attainment of purity in the four stages of sanctification in the Buddhadhamma. One lives in the City when one passes away entirely from future birth and death as a fullfledged Saint, an Arahat, and is finally liberated from suffering. The discoverer of the Way who reaches the City first after it is lost to men for a long time is a Buddha. Those who listen to a Buddha, follow in his footsteps and reach the Goal are his Noble Disciples.

The persons who are now trying to tread the Way according to the instructions of the last Buddha are the people who practise mental culture and inner development.

The Fourfold Way and the City are both in us. It is through the mind that the Way runs and it runs to the Everest point of clear consciousness from which we behold the Vision Splendid of Knowledge and Purity which makes us free. The invisible beings that help are our own mental controlling forces, our own mental powers and skills, the bright side of our nature. The hosts of evil are our own lusts, hatreds, and weaknesses, and the leader of these hosts is ignorance which rules the dark side of our character.

The diamond of the Way on which we stand to fight the evil in us is virtue that always supports. The invincible armour is concentration which keeps us calm and clear-headed and the mighty weapon is wisdom born of the penetrative insight by which we see things as they are.

The Fourfold Way of Mindfulness consists of meditation on the Body, Feeling, Consciousness and Mental Objects which make up the individual. Who knows these knows himself and knowing himself becomes skilful in **the use** of the things which he possesses. Such a person becomes free from fears and tremblings and from all bondages because he sees that there is nothing in him which can subjugate or overpower him. Rather everything in him is under his sway because he knows to use all that belongs to him properly, effectively and advantageously, and is never at a loss to act rightly for the attainment of the highest good.

The Buddha's instructions concerning the Way have been compared to a map with detailed explanations. That map is the Threefold Collection of his teaching, the Tipiṭaka. In the Tipiṭaka the Buddha draws the attention of people to the Way much in the same manner that a merchant proclaims the virtues of his wares. And just as on hearing the words of the merchant people who have money buy from his stock what they like and people who cannot afford to buy have a look at the goods and learn to appreciate the stuff, so on hearing the words of the Master some pay the price and buy his immortal goods but those who have not the money listen to the teaching and learn to value it. And it may well happen that when those who are now poor acquire the coin of energy they may all the quicker make up their minds to buy the Buddha-merchandise because of their having learned to know its worth earlier.

Learning to value the Teaching even without real practice of it is important. It is a kind of habituation of the mind to the qualities of the Truth, the implanting of conditions which could be of help to one in the future, and a preparation for one to practice the teaching when one is more favourably placed than now with regard to energy and resolution.

Buddhists of old regarded this "implanting of conditions" for the future as wholesome and tried to help all they could on this Way. Their beneficence in this respect was not limited to human beings. Even animals which were amenable to their influence were the objects of their sympathy. The legend of the young parrot found in the commentary but not included in the translation is a simple story simply told in which the "implanting of conditions" for future weal is brought out. It runs as follows: In the Kuru country, a band of players used to go about training a young parrot in the course of their journeys. Once when they had stayed at a place near a nunnery and were departing they let go their parrot. The novices of the nunnery got hold of the parrot and looked after it and gave it the name Buddharakkhita.

It is said that on a certain occasion when the young parrot was hopping around the abbess the following conversation took place:

The Abbess: "Buddharakkhita!"

The Parrot: Yes, lady.

The Abbess: Do you reflect on any subject of meditation?

The Parrot: No, lady.

The Abbess: It is not fit, friend, to live near homeless ones a lax person. Indeed some kind of reflection is desirable. As you however will not be able to do any other go on repeating the word, "bones" (one of the thirty-two subjects of meditation on the body).

Now that young parrot, listening to the abbess, went about repeating the word: "bones."

One morning while the parrot was sunning itself on the top of the gateway, a hawk swooped down and carried it away. The parrot began to squeak. The novices heard the cries of distress. After informing the abbess that they wished to save Buddharakkhita, they pursued the bird of prey, threw clods and stones at it and freed the parrot. Then having brought the parrot they placed it before the abbess.

The Abbess : Buddharakkhita, what did you think when the hawk seized you ?

The Parrot : I thought only this : A heap of bones goes having seized another heap of bones. In some place indeed the heap of bones will scatter. Thus I thought, lady, only of the heap of bones.

The Abbess : Very good, Buddharakkhita. That will be to you a condition for future weal.

The person who reads with sympathy and an open mind enough of this Way of Mindfulness to know what it is, though he may not have any desire to practise it, will, even by his bare conceptual grasp empty of true discernment driving to realisation, and so comparable to the parrot's repetition of the word, " bones ", be habituating himself to appreciate the Way to some extent, and be sowing in his consciousness the seed of mindfulness of the Way which will help him to happiness in the future. Deriving itself from the Buddha, the great seer, the Buddhist perspective is vast in its sweep and leads to the penetration of actuality. In that perspective all that is outside Nibbāna, all life, is seen to be unending, unceasing, in its process, and this knowledge enables those who are still on the lower planes of the perfections to plan unhurriedly, vastly and efficiently for the aeons ahead. Verily, a hopeful view !

INTRODUCTION

The Goal and the Way

The Buddha's Goal of Emancipation is attained with the extirpation of all craving and spiritual ignorance. Who wins it gains lasting mental strength and contentment. It is the source of real peace and equanimity.

Unfreedom consists of subjection to hate, lust and ignorance. Virtuous conduct wipes out hate ; the calm of skilful concentration casts out lust ; and wise understanding of the world within oneself dispels ignorance. The Way of Mindfulness does all this ; it is designed for the attainment of fullest inner freedom.

This is the only satisfying way for the seeker of truth when the diffuseness [papañca] of the external world with its thin layer of culture, comfort and allurement, ceases to be interesting and is found to lack true value. The seeker knows to a certainty that what he wants is to be found in the realm of the spirit. There alone he feels he could reach the vision of oneness [ekatta] of the enduring [dhuva] by transcending the diversity [nānatta] of change [aniccatā]. And what he wants is inward integrity, intactness, inviolability, based on the unshakable deliverance of the mind from the sway of all conditioned phenomena. To this the Way of Mindfulness leads by showing him how to penetrate into the singleness of nature [ekasabhāva] of the Supreme Void [Agga Suñña], Nibbāna, which is permeated with the one taste [ekarasa] of liberation [vimutti].

General distinctions and divisions of the Way

The Buddha's Way of Emancipation has eight leading constituent factors : Right Understanding, Thought, Speech, Action, Livelihood, Effort, Mindfulness and Concentration. Real knowledge is made up of the first two factors ; real conduct, of the next three ; and real meditation comprises the last three. According to the number of constituents the Way is eightfold. But by taking into consideration the constituent which is thought necessary for progress at all times it is called the Way of Mindfulness. The Way has two distinct stages : one of mundane preparation and another of supramundane fulfilment. When mindfulness and the other factors that go along with it are found in a state of supramundane consciousness, there comes into being the Supramundane Way of Mindfulness ; and when they are present in any other state of consciousness, the Mundane Way of Mindfulness is said to exist.

The Way of Mindfulness reaches the first stage of supramundane fulfilment with what is technically known as "entry into the stream" or the arrival at the unswerving path to the Goal. Before that there could be serious deviations, but not from that point where the First Direct Glimpse of the Goal is obtained. One enters the Stream by overcoming self-delusion, doubt as regards the Buddha, the Teaching and the Saints, and the casting out of belief in rites and ceremonies. A Streamwinner cannot murder, steal, do sexual wrong, utter falsehood deliberately, and partake of drinks and drugs that intoxicate. The second stage is reached with the thinning of sensuality and ill-will ; the third, with the complete abandoning of these two evils ; and the last stage, with the ending of craving, pride, restlessness and ignorance through speckless Saintship [arahatta], the attainment of the crest of perfection.

The Discourse on the Arousing of Mindfulness deals with the preparatory part, the Mundane Way of Mindfulness which is of immediate practical value to worldlings still in the valleys of the spirit far from the supramundane peaks.

Wise actions of worth, persistently practised, and unremitting renunciation involving often many a bleeding wrench and tear are necessary to complete the path of mundane preparation and that of supramundane fulfilment. If for low things, things of ephemeral value, a little power, fame and comfort, men often have to pay heavily can they expect to get the Highest Good lightly? Verily only with the Highest Effort and the development of the best in us can the Highest Good be won ; never with feeble mean effort or with our second-best powers. The wrecks of spiritual ventures with which our own lives are strewn are standing monuments of reproach to and warning against the inanity of lax endeavour in lofty enterprises.

The Meaning of Mindfulness

Mindfulness is a process, an event and an arising and a passing away momentarily like any other mental property. Although it is a basic power, a shelter and a refuge of the mind, the role it plays in the drama of transition from Ignorance to Knowledge differs considerably according to the other properties of mind with which it works.

For instance in association with Right Understanding and its group which comprises "wisdom, intense knowledge, discrimination, research, investigation of things, consideration, close examination, pondering over, learning, skilfulness, keen-wittedness, analysis, reflection, vision, sagacity, the discernment that leads aright, penetrative insight and clear comprehension," it is rational. And when it is combined with Right Concentration and its cognates such as "mental steadfastness, serenity, immovability, quietude, non-distraction, and pacification," it is intuitive.

But the intuitive or rational role does not preclude mindfulness from communicating its regulative impulse of moderation to the mind, at all times. It is the property which makes for proper proportion in the response of the mind to mental objects.

Mindfulness as memory is indicated by such terms as a n u s s a t i = calling to mind ; p a ṭ i s s a t i = remembrance ; d h ā r a ṇ a t ā = bearing in mind; sāraṇatā = recollection. In this connection the process of mindfulness is compared to the Treasurer of a King who reminds the King of the Royal Possessions in detail, daily, at night and in the morning.

The mindfulness of the aspirant to the Highest Goal of Liberation from Suffering reminds him of Virtue, Concentration and Wisdom, which constitute the possessions of the Good Life in the Dispensation of the Buddha. The value of the recollective activity of mindfulness is seen in the increasing awareness of the essentials of holy living in the aspirant's mind, and the growing strength of purpose for realising these within himself.

Above that stands mindfulness as the activity that takes care of the mind and protects it. It is compared to a waggoner who ties the oxen to the waggon's yoke, greases the axle, and drives the waggon, making the oxen go gently. In this activity mindfulness looks to the smooth working and movement of the mind and takes notice of the processes both skilful and not, taking place in the consciousness.

In its more complex forms it is the selective and integrative action of the mind. The selective activity has been compared to the work of the Chief Adviser of a King. As the Adviser is instrumental in distinguishing the good, from the bad, and in getting the good and avoiding the bad, so mindfulness distinguishes the worthy from the unworthy things, avoids the unworthy and obtains the worthy.

The integrative character of mindfulness is like the Minister-of-all-work of a King. He is wanted in putting through every project of the King. He is commissioned to organise and combine the workers and execute the tasks. Mindfulness is also like that Minister. It is the organizing activity of the mind necessary for the development of wholesome states of consciousness. It combines the various other qualities which compose those states, puts them to their appropriate tasks and keeps them in proper working order. By the strength of integrating mindfulness a conscious state of skill functions harmoniously and becomes a well-knit unity. This activity of mindfulness makes the work of the aspirant complete at every stage of his progress.

Integrating mindfulness sees all lacks and deficiencies, brings in the needed qualities and suitably applies them. It is called the highest wisdom of mindfulness [parama satinepakka], and constitutes the core of the Mindfulness that is Included in the Real Way [Ariya Magga Pariyāpanna Sati], of the Way Factor of Mindfulness [Sati Magganga] and of the Enlightenment Factor of Mindfulness [Sati Sambojjhanga]. It is Right Mindfulness [Sammāsati] in the full sense of the term.

From the foregoing it can be seen that it is mindfulness that holds things together in the mental flux, brings them up, and prevents them from floating away, getting submerged, forgotten and lost. Without mindfulness there will be no reconstitution of already acquired knowledge and consciousness itself would break to pieces, become fragmentary, and be unable to do properly the work of cognition. Further, without mindfulness that is become wisdom, the highest kind of mindfulness which includes clear comprehension, cognition will be superficial ; there will not be the knowledge of things gained from different relations and different angles—the work of discernment and discrimination peculiar to selective activity—or any really constructive understanding—the yield of integration—and so penetrative vision into the full significance of spiritual things will not be reached.

When one is strongly mindful one plants one's consciousness deep in an object like a firm post well sunk in the ground, and withstands the tempestuous clamour of the extraneous by "a sublime ignoring of non-essentials." But this does not mean that in such a one interest is narrow and the outlook wrongly restricted. Strong mindfulness ignores the unnecessary, by sticking to the centre of the business in hand, and extends its view to important peripheral conditions, with a widespreading watchfulness resembling that of the sentinel on a tower scanning the horizon "for the glint of armour". By such a balance between width and depth mindfulness steers clear of the extremes of lopsided vision and practice.

In the sense of overcoming mental conflict, and in the sense of getting rid of all unclarity, all incapacity to judge aright and indefiniteness due to mental unquiet, mindfulness is a controlling faculty [indriya]. The controlling faculty of mindfulness makes for the absence of confusion [asamussanatā] and produces lucidity of thought, sound judgment, and definiteness of outlook. Mindfulness accompanied by keen understanding appears as the controlling faculty of mindfulness.

Mindfulness accompanied by sustained energy is mindfulness considered as a spiritual power [bala] and is the quality of earnestness [appamāda] which destroys the wavering of negligence [pamāda]. Negligence is the wandering of the mind in objects of fivefold sense-pleasure, repeatedly : it is the absence of thoroughness, of perseverance, and of steadfastness in doing good ; the behaviour that is stuck in the mud of worldliness ; the casting aside of the desire to do what is right ; the casting aside of the duties which belong to one ; the absence of practice, development, and increase of wholesome qualities ; the lack of right resolve, and the want of application. Earnestness is the opposite of all that negligence connotes. According to meaning earnestness is, verily, the non-neglect of mindfulness [Atthato hi so satiyā avippavāso]. Indeed, earnestness is the name for mindfulness that is always active, constantly at work. Earnestness may also be explained, as it has been by some, as the four mental aggregates of feeling, perception, consciousness, and formations proceeding with the application of mindfulness and clear comprehension [Satisampajaññayogena pavattā cattāro arūpino khandhā appamādo].

All that the Buddha taught from the time of his enlightenment to his passing away into the Element of Immortality has been summed up in the sentence : "Strive with Earnestness", the last words of the Master. Earnestness runs through the whole of the Buddhaword and embraces everything there. It is like the elephant's footprint which is able to contain the footprint of any other animal. Therefore did the Blessed One say : "All wholesome things are founded on earnestness, converge on earnestness, and earnestness is to be considered as the most excellent of them."*

Mindfulness in this sense is found to be the chief characteristic of all skilful actions leading to bliss here and hereafter and tending to one's own and to others' profit. It is the force which pushes one to right practice, after one has given careful thought to the Buddha's Teaching.

The Moral Basis of the Way

Life as it is understood in the Dispensation of the Buddha is unsatisfactory until one can through moral joy, meditative tranquillity and wise understanding reach mental invulnerability to suffering. The Way of Mindfulness is understanding and tranquillity illumined by a bright moral character. Without a blameless happy life of virtue it is not possible to tranquillize the heart or make the intellect keen and clear for spiritual perfection. The spiritual man is a person of so sensitive and heightened a consciousness that he finds even slight moral guilt burdensome, and so he cannot help avoiding all traces of it by a strict adherence to virtue. Otherwise owing to remorse at his backslidings and preoccupation with them he will not find the right inner environment and climate for developing the placidity and insight which produce the power of perfect equanimity necessary for changing over from mental slavery to freedom. The cheerful joyous atmosphere which virtue gives is more necessary to the aspirant to Nibbāna than anything else to keep him spiritually alive and kicking.

Although the Discourse on the Arousing of Mindfulness does not speak of virtue directly, in detail, and is principally concerned with the calming of the mind and wise understanding, the presence of the virtue-foundation is implied, since the instruction on mindfulness is intended for the "purification of beings", and there is no purification in the Dhamma which does not begin with the "purification of virtue" [sīla visuddhi], and it is only after establishing himself in virtue [sīle patiṭṭhāya] that the wise man develops concentration, and wisdom and attains liberation. Further, there is enough in the commentary and the scholium to it, to prove the importance of virtue to the aspirant, and to show how tranquillity and understanding help in the protecting, the preserving, and the perfecting of virtue.

The Way of Mindfulness moves towards the Equanimity of the Fully Quieted Mind along the firm and sure ground of active virtue. Because of this virtuous basis it is a reliable way to highest security, free from the bogs, swamps, and sloughs of vice and the dangerous futility of inaction.

The Element of Analysis

Analysis is a salient feature of the method of arriving at knowledge in the Buddhadhamma. The Buddha is the Master of Analytic Knowledge and his doctrine is called the Teaching of Analysis [Vibhajjavāda]. The Way of Mindfulness is therefore naturally replete with the application of the principles of analysis. The sentient being is radically searched through manifold analysis to see if anything in him is unanalysable. Only that which is relative is analysable; only that which is conditioned and dependent on something else. The absolute, the unconditioned and the independent are not analysable. Is there anything absolute in the sentient being or is everything in the sentient being relative? The answer has to be found out, by the aspirant, after being convinced by valid thought and experience, in order to reach the First Glimpse of the Goal. By training to think along the lines indicated in the Way he will be able to conclude with certainty what the nature of sentient individuality really is. On the immovable basis of such correct knowledge rests the final realisation of supramundane perfection.

The Unifying Quality of the Way

The aim of analysis in the Way of the Buddha is to attain a correct understanding of the component parts of sentient existence and their relations for rightly grasping the unique totality of the individual that emerges from those relations. Only a Buddha, however, has the ability to gauge the uniqueness of individual totality consummately. But the important thing to be noted here is that a just and generally accurate perception of the significance of the totality as a thing distinct from every other and possessing a character that clearly is not to be merely described or defined by the parts is the result of the team-work of the forces of wisdom and concentrated vision. Analysis of the parts lays bare the constituent components. Analysis of the relations gives a sense of the totality. All the differences that make for uniqueness are seen as due to subtle distinctions of relations. And the uniqueness of the personality, individuality, and entirety of a living being depends on the countless number of everchanging relations, their infinite variety, subtle nuances, and endless possibilities in each separate life-flux. The analytic nature of the Way leads one finally to the vision of the sentient being as a uniquely related totality that transcends the parts and has a character all its own. The sense of totality to which the logic of analysis leads is realised as true in the intensity of the absorptive or unifying activity of concentrative thought.

The Yoking of Insight and Concentration

Here, the Development of Penetrative Insight [Vipassanā] combines with that of Tranquillizing Concentration [Samatha], and each functions in a way that does not outstrip the other. Both gain uniformity of force. Through the overdoing of analysis there could be flurry. And indolence creeps in through too much of tranquillity.

Searching analysis is predominantly intellective, and is the work of insight. Wholehearted acceptance is principally intuitive and springs from the placidity of concentration. In the sense of yoking [yuganandhaṭṭhena] and of not letting (either) become overwhelming [anativattanaṭṭhena] contemplative balance is reached. That balance is manifested as the sober, serene, steadfast acceptance of the truth which analysis reveals.

The Middle Way

This is a middle way. It does not overlook any valuable knowledge or experience of the spirit and does not edge sideways but goes straight forward, intent on the Real, free from all biases. Though it looks within it is aware of what is without. Along such a way one could transcend the narrow vision of a barricaded individuality and the indefinable looseness of view of a dissipated and disintegrated spirit.

This Middle Way of Mindfulness is clearly not based on revelation, dogmas, and vacuous beliefs like those in a Supreme Creator God and an Eternal Soul, irrational in the extreme. What is irrational is not the Teaching of the Buddha though it be found in Buddhist Scriptures. On the contrary " Whatever is well said is the Word of the Buddha," even when it is not the Master's own utterance, because the Blessed One acknowledges Truth wherever and by whomsoever spoken.

The Arousing of Mindfulness

To raise up the person to a keen sense of awareness in regard to an object and to bring into activity, to call forth, and stir up the controlling faculty, the power, the enlightenment factor and the way factor of mindfulness is the Arousing of Mindfulness designed.

Every Arousing of Mindfulness in regard to body, feeling, consciousness or a mental object can be considered as a beginning of the road to insight. And so these " arousings " are, in a sense, " starting-points ". Further with the Arousing of Mindfulness one wakes up heedfulness, intentness and carefulness, and is in a state of mental preparedness in regard to any work in hand.

These Arousings of Mindfulness are many as regards objects but are one in the sense of taking place in a single way of quietude charged with insight that leads to Nibbāna.

The different objects of mindfulness

All the four different objects of mindfulness : body, feeling, consciousness and mental objects, have to be understood before one reaches sanctitude. According to character, temperament and cognising slant one can make however only one of these the preliminary object of contemplation. It is often the case that owing to a lack of proper understanding of oneself one has to try all objects before one gets to know what suits one best for the preliminary work. The choice is made more difficult by the fact that most of us have no clear cut natures and are a mixture of a little of every possible human characteristic. In these circumstances there is no alternative to the method of trial and error. But the earnest ones will find their way with persistence and sustained effort.

By character there are two types determined by the excess of sensuous qualities of craving, or of the asensuous qualities of abstract beliefs that make up their personality. The craving type is generally extravert ; the other is generally introvert. According to temperament there are those whose mental functioning is slow, those who are languid mentally and those who are mentally keen, the nervous type. But here it must be understood that the terms languid and nervous have no necessary connection with calm and excitement. The nervous often keep cool when the languid fluster. The nervous type is sensitive, but strong and vigorous and keen. The nervous think forcefully and clearly. The languid are sluggish, inert, and weak, unclear, discursive, and often mixed-up in thought. Cognising slant is either intuitive or intellective.

According to character and temperament the body-object is recommended for the languid extravert and the feeling-object for the nervous extravert. For the languid introvert the consciousness-object is recommended, and for the nervous introvert, mental objects.

According to cognising slant and temperament the body-object is pointed out for the mentally slow who belong to the intuitive kind which makes concentration its vehicle for progress, and for the mentally keen of this kind the feeling-object. For the mentally slow who belong to the intellective kind which makes insight its vehicle the consciousness-object is recommended, and to the mentally keen of this kind the mental object.

Further, contemplation on the body destroys the delusion of beauty ; that on feeling destroys the delusion of pleasure ; contemplation on consciousness dispels the delusion of permanence ; and that on mental objects, the delusion of the soul.

On Reading the Discourse and the Commentary

The person who wishes to practise meditation according to the instruction of the Buddha on the Arousing of Mindfulness should first read the Discourse with the commentary on the Synopsis and get a fair idea of the trend of the teaching. Today, there are still people as of old who learn the Discourse by heart as a preparation to practice. Such memorizing is helpful to certain types. But it is not essential. What is essential is to think long and deep on the instruction, until one gets the hang of its application to daily life. Only by repeated reflection on all the implications of it can the Discourse be made an effective instrument of mental culture.

The core of the instruction is in the sections dealing with the modes of deportment and clear comprehension. These are intended for all types of aspirants. The commentary on these sections is very important and should be carefully studied. The whole practice of mindfulness depends on the correct grasp of the exercises included in the two parts referred to here.

One should then look through the rest of the exercises in the Discourse with the help of the commentary to find a preliminary object of concentration or subject of meditation that accords with one's character, temperament and cognising slant mentioned earlier. If, for instance, one is an extravert mentally languid or a person whose cognizing slant is intuitive and is temperamentally slow of mind, the contemplation on breathing could well suit that one as a preliminary object.

If one finds the explanation given in the commentary to the Discourse on Mindfulness on any preliminary object one chooses insufficient, one should read the exposition of it in the Path of Purity [Visuddhi Magga]* of our commentator. One may, if a teacher of Buddhist meditation can be found, also consult him and ask for elucidation of any difficult points connected with meditative practice.

Necessary too to be read by all are the portions of the commentary on the contemplation of Feeling and Consciousness and those on the Hindrances, the Sense-bases and the Factors of Enlightenment (in the contemplation on Mental Objects) which give information on the obstacles and aids to concentration on the preliminary object.

General hints on the practice of mindfulness

In concentrating on any preliminary object, say the breath, if any feeling, or thought that interferes with concentration arises, then one should contemplate on that interfering phenomenon in a manner that accords to the exposition on Feeling, Consciousness, the Hindrances, or the Sense-bases, in the commentary, until the interference disappears and revert to the preliminary object.*

Similarly, when attending to the preliminary object any overactiveness or slackness present should be overcome by the method taught in the exposition on the Factors of Enlightenment in the commentary and then there will be steady work possible on the object of concentration. It is useful to bear in mind that either the favourable or the unfavourable qualities increase by pondering over them and decrease by the turning away of attention from them.

In beginning to practise mindfulness one has to become aware of one's actions, speech and thought and drive these towards good as a cowherd his charge to healthy pastures. It is helpful to get into the habit of preparing the mind before proceeding to act, and to pause a while before initiating new activities. By such practice one learns to act deliberately, consciously, and with circumspection, and not on the spur of the moment, and so does everything prepared to face all consequences, and with a proper sense of responsibility.

Wholetime practice of mindfulness consists in the carrying out of each of the three following activities of contemplation at the proper time : attention on the preliminary object of concentration, reflection on the modes of deportment and clear comprehension. When one is not attending to the preliminary object for one good reason or another, one should be reflecting on the modes of deportment or be doing clear comprehension.

Wholetime practice of mindfulness could be carried out by all. There will however be differences in the degree of intensiveness of the practice according to the " busy-ness " of the individual. The more one is busy with external activities, the less will the time at his disposal be for attending on the preliminary object, and also for steady reflection on deportment and for penetratively clear comprehension. One should therefore try to cut and also slow down as much as one can, rightly and reasonably, one's external activities.

Periodic special training

It would greatly benefit most people to go in for the training in mindfulness in an intensive way from time to time in a suitable place, under the direction of a good meditation-master, if such a person is available, and instil into themselves the habits of recollection, carefulness, discrimination and consideration. In Siam and especially in Burma there are meditation monasteries (kamaṭān kyaungs) to which recluse and layman go in search of solitude, periodically, to learn to walk along this Way, under the guidance of a teacher of meditation (kamaṭān saya).

In a meditation monastery every trainee is given a separate cell and provided with simple food and drink for which provision has to be made earlier. During the period of practice the trainee can speak only with the meditation-master. No reading, repetition of formulae or the use of a rosary is permitted. The trainee has to be mindful from the time he wakes up to the time he falls asleep, and put himself chiefly to the practice of concentration on the preliminary object. Rarely does such a period of practice extend beyond a month.

The aim of the meditation-master is straightforward. It is to prepare the mind of the pupil for direct personal experience of the truth. He does this by making the pupil occupy himself with the doing at the proper time of bare mindfulness through reflection on the modes of deportment and concentration on the preliminary object first. By bare mindfulness one becomes aware of oneself and one's actions are observed systematically. By such observation the most important thing achieved is the very great reduction of the conceptualizing tendency of the mind, the source of imaginings [maññanā] and delusions [vipallāsa]. When imaginings and delusions are for the most part absent in mind the veil of *maya* is removed to an extent which enables the pupil to appreciate **the nature of the thing**, dhamma sabhāva, and he passes naturally on to clear comprehension which sets a-foot the process of analysis leading to right understanding. Thereafter, attention on **the nature of the thing** which the pupil contemplates opens to his view the universal characteristics of mundane existence : impermanence, suffering and insubstantiality. When that view purifies the pupil's character for good, the Goal to which the Way of Mindfulness leads is reached.

Concluding remarks on the Way

Who reflects on his movements and clearly comprehends states of activity and rest as taught in the commentary has his mind turned towards self-mastery. The preliminary object however is the basis of the practice and is the resort of the aspirant or the main object and ground of contemplation.

The Way of Mindfulness is the objective way of viewing anything whatsoever. It reckons just what is present and stopping the garrulity of one's own mind lets the objects speak for themselves and unfold their character. Also, by its patient pursuit of the meaning of things, its readiness to see every side of any thought or experience, and by its breadth and tolerance, it predisposes the mind to receive the impressions of truth, induces inner pliancy and the mood of spiritual receptivity necessary for highest intuition.

Since mindfulness is the only way for anyone who wishes inner happiness men of old, irrespective of the school of thought to which they belonged underlined the importance of the Buddha's teaching on this point. In his " Friendly Letter, " Nāgārjuna says : " The Happy One (Sugata) said that the only way to be walked on is mindfulness directed bodywards ; therefore keep to it resolutely; for if mindfulness is wanting all good (dharma) decays." And Śāntideva in his Bodhicaryāvatāra says : " If the mind, the tusker maddened with passion, is bound completely with the rope of mindfulness, then, all perils disappear and all blessings come into being."

THE DISCOURSE ON THE AROUSING OF MINDFULNESS

The origin of the Discourse on The Only Way

Thus have I heard.

At one time the Blessed One was living in the Kurus, at Kammāsadamma, a market-town of the Kuru people.

Then the Blessed One addressed the bhikkhus as follows: "This is the only way, o bhikkhus, for the purification of beings, for the overcoming of sorrow and lamentation, for the destruction of suffering and grief, for reaching the right path, for the attainment of Nibbāna, namely, the Four Arousings of Mindfulness."

The Four Arousings of Mindfulness

"What are the Four?"

"Here, bhikkhus, a bhikkhu lives contemplating the body in the body, ardent, clearly comprehending (it) and mindful (of it), having overcome, in this world, covetousness and grief; he lives contemplating the feelings in the feelings, ardent, clearly comprehending (them) and mindful (of them), having overcome, in this world, covetousness and grief; he lives contemplating consciousness in consciousness, ardent, clearly comprehending (it) and mindful (of it), having overcome, in this world, covetousness and grief; he lives contemplating mental objects in mental objects, ardent, clearly comprehending (them) and mindful (of them), having overcome, in this world, covetousness and grief."

Mindfulness on Breathing

"And how, o bhikkhus, does a bhikkhu live contemplating the body in the body?"

"Here, o bhikkhus, a bhikkhu gone to the forest, to the foot of a tree, or to an empty place, sits down, bends in his legs crosswise on his lap, keeps his body erect and arouses mindfulness in the object of meditation, namely, the breath which is in front of him."

"Mindful, he breathes in, and mindful, he breathes out. He, thinking, 'I breathe in long,' understands when he is breathing in long; or thinking, 'I breathe out long,' he understands when he is breathing out long; or thinking, 'I breathe in short,' he understands when he is breathing in short; or thinking, 'I breathe out short,' he understands when he is breathing out short."

" 'Experiencing the whole body, I shall breathe in,' thinking thus, he trains himself. 'Experiencing the whole body, I shall breathe out,' thinking thus, he trains himself. 'Calming the activity of the body, I shall breathe in,' thinking thus, he trains himself. 'Calming the activity of the body, I shall breathe out,' thinking thus, he trains himself."

"Just as a clevei turner or a turner's apprentice, turning long, undeistands: 'I turn long;' or turning short, understands: 'I turn short;' just so, indeed, o bhikkhus, a bhikkhu, when he breathes in long understands: 'I breathe in long;' or, when he breathes out long, understands: 'I breathe out long;' or, when he breathes in short, he understands: 'I breathe in short;' or, when he breathes out short, he understands: 'I breathe out short.' He trains himself with the thought: 'Experiencing the whole body, I shall breathe in.' He trains himself with the thought: 'Experiencing the whole body I shall breathe out.' He trains himself with the thought: 'Calming the activity of the body I shall breathe in.' He trains himself with the thought: 'Calming the activity of the body I shall breathe out.' "

"Thus he lives contemplating the body in the body internally, or he lives contemplating the body in the body externally, or he lives contemplating the body in the body internally and externally."

"He lives contemplating origination-things in the body, or he lives contemplating dissolution-things in the body, or he lives contemplating origination-and-dissolution-things in the body. Or indeed his mindfulness is established with the thought: 'The body exists,' to the extent necessary for just knowledge and remembrance, and he lives independent and clings to naught in the world. Thus, also, o bhikkhus, a bhikkhu lives contemplating the body in the body."

The Modes of Deportment

"And further, o bhikkhus, when he is going, a bhikkhu understands: 'I am going;' when he is standing he understands: 'I am standing;' when he is sitting, he understands: 'I am sitting;' when he is lying down, he understands: 'I am lying down;' or just as his body is disposed so he understands it."

"Thus he lives contemplating the body in the body internally, or he lives contemplating the body externally or he lives contemplating the body in the body internally and externally."

"He lives contemplating origination-things in the body, or he lives contemplating dissolution-things in the body, or he lives contemplating origination-and-dissolution-things in the body. Or indeed his mindfulness is established with the thought: 'The body exists,' to the extent necessary for just knowledge and remembrance, and he lives independent and clings to naught in the world. Thus, also, o bhikkhus, a bhikkhu lives contemplating the body in the body."

THE FOUR KINDS OF CLEAR COMPREHENSION

"And further, o bhikkhus, a bhikkhu, in going forwards (and) in going backwards, is a person practising clear comprehension; in looking straight on (and) in looking away from the front, is a person practising clear comprehension; in bending and in stretching, is a person practising clear comprehension; in wearing the shoulder-cloak, the (other two) robes (and) the bowl, is a person practising clear comprehension; in regard to what is eaten, drunk, chewed and savoured, is a person practising clear comprehension; in defecating and in urinating is a person practising clear comprehension; in walking, in standing (in a place), in sitting (in some position), in sleeping, in waking, in speaking and in keeping silence, is a person practising clear comprehension."

"Thus he lives contemplating the body in the body internally, or he lives contemplating the body in the body externally, or he lives contemplating the body in the body internally and externally."

"He lives contemplating origination-things in the body, or he lives contemplating dissolution-things in the body, or he lives contemplating origination-and-dissolution-things in the body. Or indeed his mindfulness is established with the thought: 'The body exists,' to the extent necessary for just knowledge and remembrance, and he lives independent and clings to naught in the world. Thus, also, o bhikkhus, a bhikkhu lives contemplating the body in the body."

THE REFLECTION ON THE REPULSIVENESS OF THE BODY

"And further, o bhikkhus, a bhikkhu reflects on just this body hemmed by the skin and full of manifold impurity from the soles up, and from the top of the hair down thinking thus: 'There are in this body hair of the head, hair of the body, nails, teeth, skin, flesh, fibrous threads (veins, nerves, sinews, tendons), bones, marrow, kidneys, heart, liver, pleura, spleen, lungs, contents of stomach, intestines, mesentery, faeces, bile, phlegm, pus, blood, sweat, solid fat, tears, fat dissolved, saliva, mucous, synovic fluid, urine.'"

"Just as if, o bhikkhus, there were a bag having two openings, full of grain differing in kind, namely, hill-paddy, paddy, green-gram, cow-pea, sesamum, rice; and a man with seeing eyes, having unloosed it, should reflect thinking thus: 'This is hill-paddy; this is paddy; this is green-gram; this is cow-pea; this is sesamum;

this is rice.' In the same way, o bhikkhus, a bhikkhu reflects on just this body hemmed by the skin and full of manifold impurity from the soles up, and from the top of the hair down, thinking thus : ' There are in this body hair of the head, hair of the body, nails, teeth, skin, flesh, fibrous threads (veins, nerves, sinews, tendons), bones, marrow, kidneys, heart, liver, pleura, spleen, lungs, contents of the stomach, intestines, mesentery, faeces, bile, phlegm, pus, blood, sweat, solid fat, tears, fat dissolved, saliva, mucous, synovic fluid, urine.' "

" Thus he lives contemplating the body in the body, internally, or he lives contemplating the body in the body, externally, or he lives contemplating the body in the body, internally and externally."

" He lives contemplating origination-things, in the body, or he lives contemplating dissolution-things, in the body, or he lives contemplating origination-and-dissolution-things, in the body. Or indeed his mindfulness is established with the thought : ' The body exists,' to the extent necessary for just knowledge and remembrance, and he lives independent and clings to naught in the world. Thus also, o bhikkhus, a bhikkhu lives contemplating the body in the body."

The Reflection on the Modes of Materiality (Elements, Dhātu)

" And further, o bhikkhus, a bhikkhu reflects on just this body according as it is placed or disposed, by way of the modes of materiality, thinking thus : ' There are, in this body, the mode of solidity, the mode of cohesion, the mode of caloricity, and the mode of oscillation.' "

" O bhikkhus, in whatever manner, a clever cow-butcher or a cow-butcher's apprentice, having slaughtered a cow and divided it by way of portions, should be sitting at the junction of a four-cross-road, in the same manner, a bhikkhu reflects on just this body, according as it is placed or disposed, by way of the modes of materiality, thinking thus : ' There are in this body, the mode of solidity, the mode of cohesion, the mode of caloricity, and the mode of oscillation.' "

" Thus he lives contemplating the body in the body internally, or he lives contemplating the body in the body externally, or he lives contemplating the body in the body internally and externally."

" He lives contemplating origination-things, in the body, or he lives contemplating dissolution-things, in the body, or he lives contemplating origination-and-dissolution-things in the body. Or indeed his mindfulness is established with the thought, ' The body exists,' to the extent necessary for just knowledge and remembrance, and he lives independent and clings to naught in the world. Thus also, o bhikkhus, a bhikkhu lives contemplating the body in the body."

CEMETERY CONTEMPLATION 1

"And further, o bhikkhus, if a bhikkhu, in whatever way, sees a body dead one, two, or three days; swollen, blue, and festering, thrown into the charnel ground, he thinks of his own body thus: 'Verily, this body of mine too is of the same nature as that body, is going to be like that body, and has not got past the condition of becoming like that body.'"

"Thus he lives contemplating the body in the body, internally, or he lives contemplating the body in the body, externally, or he lives contemplating the body in the body internally and externally."

"He lives contemplating origination-things in the body or he lives contemplating dissolution-things in the body, or he lives contemplating origination-and-dissolution-things in the body. Or indeed his mindfulness is established with the thought, 'The body exists,' to the extent necessary for just knowledge and remembrance, and he lives independent and clings to naught in the world. Thus, also, o bhikkhus, a bhikkhu lives contemplating the body in the body."

CEMETERY CONTEMPLATION 2

"And, further, o bhikkhus, if a bhikkhu in whatever way sees whilst it is being eaten by crows, hawks, vultures, dogs, jackals or by different kinds of worms, a body that had been thrown into the charnel ground, he thinks of his own body thus: 'Verily this body of mine, too, is of the same nature as that body, is going to be like that body, and has not got past the condition of becoming like that body.'"

"Thus he lives contemplating the body, in the body, internally, or he lives contemplating the body in the body, externally, or he lives contemplating the body in the body internally and externally."

"He lives contemplating origination-things in the body or he lives contemplating dissolution-things in the body, or he lives contemplating origination-and-dissolution-things in the body. Or indeed his mindfulness is established with the thought, 'The body exists,' to the extent necessary for just knowledge and remembrance, and he lives independent, and clings to naught in the world. Thus, also, o bhikkhus, a bhikkhu lives contemplating the body in the body."

Cemetery Contemplation 3.

"And, further, o bhikkhus, if a bhikkhu, in whatever way, sees a body thrown in the charnel ground and reduced to a skeleton together with (some) flesh and blood held in by the tendons, he thinks of his own body thus : 'Verily, this body of mine too is of the same nature as that body, is going to be like that body, and has not got past the condition of becoming like that body.' "

"Thus he lives contemplating the body in the body, internally, or he lives contemplating the body in the body, externally, or he lives contemplating the body in the body, internally and externally."

"He lives contemplating origination-things, in the body, or he lives contemplating dissolution-things, in the body, or he lives contemplating origination-and-dissolution-things, in the body. Or indeed his mindfulness is established with the thought, 'The body exists,' to the extent necessary for just knowledge and remembrance, and he lives independent, and clings to naught in the world. Thus, also, o bhikkhus, a bhikkhu lives contemplating the body, in the body."

Cemetery Contemplation 4.

"And further, o bhikkhus, if a bhikkhu, in whatever way, sees a body thrown in the charnel ground and reduced to a blood-besmeared skeleton without flesh but held in by the tendons, he thinks of his own body thus : 'Verily, this body of mine, too, is of the same nature as that body, is going to be like that body, and has not got past the condition of becoming like that body.' "

"Thus he lives contemplating the body in the body internally, or he lives contemplating the body in the body externally, or he lives contemplating the body in the body internally and externally."

"He lives contemplating origination-things in the body, or he lives contemplating dissolution-things in the body or he lives contemplating origination-and-dissolution-things in the body. Or his mindfulness is established with the thought, 'The body exists,' to the extent necessary for just knowledge and remembrance, and he lives independent and clings to naught in the world. Thus also, o bhikkhus, a bhikkhu lives contemplating the body in the body."

Cemetery Contemplation 5.

"And, further, o bhikkhus, if a bhikkhu in whatever way sees a body thrown in the charnel ground and reduced to a skeleton held in by the tendons but without flesh and not besmeared with blood, he thinks of his own body thus : ' Verily, this body of mine, too, is of the same nature as that body, is going to be like that body, and has not got past the condition of becoming like that body.' "

" Thus he lives contemplating the body in the body, internally, or he lives contemplating the body in the body externally, or he lives contemplating the body in the body internally and externally."

" He lives contemplating origination-things, in the body, or he lives contemplating dissolution-things in the body, or he lives contemplating origination-and-dissolution-things in the body. Or his mindfulness is established with the thought, ' The body exists,' to the extent necessary for just knowledge and remembrance, and he lives independent and clings to naught in the world. Thus, also, o bhikkhus, a bhikkhu lives contemplating the body in the body."

CEMETERY CONTEMPLATION 6.

" And, further, o bhikkhus, if a bhikkhu, in whatever way, sees a body thrown in the charnel ground and reduced to bones gone loose, scattered in all directions—a bone of the hand, a bone of the foot, a shin bone, a thigh bone, the pelvis, spine and skull, each in a different place,—he thinks of his own body thus : ' Verily, this body of mine, too, is of the same nature as that body, is going to be like that body, and has not got past the condition of becoming like that body.' "

" Thus he lives contemplating the body, in the body internally, or he lives contemplating the body, in the body, externally, or he lives contemplating the body in the body internally and externally."

" He lives contemplating origination-things in the body, or he lives contemplating dissolution-things in the body, or he lives contemplating origination-and-dissolution-things in the body. Or his mindfulness is established with the thought, ' The body exists,' to the extent necessary for just knowledge and remembrance, and he lives independent and clings to naught in the world. Thus, also, o bhikkhus, a bhikkhu lives contemplating the body in the body."

CEMETERY CONTEMPLATION 7.

" And, further, o bhikkhus, if a bhikkhu, in whatever way, sees a body thrown in the charnel ground and reduced to bones white in colour like a conch, he thinks of his own body thus : ' Verily, this body of mine, too, is of the same nature as that body, is going to be like that body, and has not got past the condition of becoming like that body.' "

" Thus he lives contemplating the body in the body, internally, or he lives contemplating the body in the body, externally, or he lives contemplating the body in the body internally and externally."

" He lives contemplating origination-things in the body, or he lives contemplating dissolution-things in the body, or he lives contemplating origination-and-dissolution-things in the body. Or his mindfulness is established with the thought, ' The body exists,' to the extent necessary for just knowledge and remembrance, and he lives independent and clings to naught in the world. Thus, also, o bhikkhus, a bhikkhu lives contemplating the body in the body."

Cemetery Contemplation 8

" And, further, o bhikkhus, if a bhikkhu, in whatever way, sees a body thrown in the charnel ground and reduced to bones more than a year old heaped together, he thinks of his own body thus : ' Verily, this body of mine, too, is of the same nature as that body, is going to be like that body, and has not got past the condition of becoming like that body.' "

" Thus he lives contemplating the body in the body, internally, or he lives contemplating the body in the body, externally, or he lives contemplating the body in the body internally and externally."

" He lives contemplating origination-things in the body, or he lives contemplating dissolution-things in the body, or he lives contemplating origination-and-dissolution-things in the body. Or his mindfulness is established with the thought, ' The body exists,' to the extent necessary for just knowledge and remembrance, and he lives independent, and clings to naught in the world. Thus, also, o bhikkhus, a bhikkhu lives contemplating the body in the body."

Cemetery Contemplation 9

" And, further, o bhikkhus, if a bhikkhu, in whatever way, sees a body thrown in the charnel ground and reduced to bones gone rotten and become dust, he thinks of his own body thus : ' Verily, this body of mine, too, is of the same nature as that body, is going to be like that body, and has not got past the condition of becoming like that body.' "

" Thus he lives contemplating the body in the body, internally, or he lives contemplating the body in the body, externally, or he lives contemplating the body in the body internally and externally."

" He lives contemplating origination-things in the body, or he lives contemplating dissolution-things in the body, or he lives contemplating origination-and-dissolution-things in the body. Or his mindfulness is established with the thought, ' The body exists,' to the extent necessary for just knowledge and remembrance, and he lives independent and clings to naught in the world. Thus, indeed, o bhikkhus, a bhikkhu lives contemplating the body in the body."

The Contemplation of Feeling

" And how, o bhikkhus, does a bhikkhu live contemplating feelings in feelings ? "

" Here, o bhikkhus, a bhikkhu when experiencing a pleasant feeling understands : ' I experience a pleasant feeling ' ; when experiencing a painful feeling he understands : ' I experience a painful feeling ' ; when experiencing a neither-pleasant-nor-painful feeling he understands: 'I experience a neither-pleasant-nor-painful feeling ' ; when experiencing a pleasant worldly feeling, he understands : ' I experience a pleasant worldly feeling'; when experiencing a pleasant spiritual feeling he understands : ' I experience a pleasant spiritual feeling ' ; when experiencing a painful worldly feeling he understands : ' I experience a painful worldly feeling ' ; when experiencing a painful spiritual feeling he understands : ' I experience a painful spiritual feeling ' ; when experiencing a neither-pleasant-nor-painful worldly feeling he understands : ' I experience a neither-pleasant-nor-painful worldly feeling ' ; when experiencing a neither-pleasant-nor-painful spiritual feeling, he understands : ' I experience a neither-pleasant-nor-painful spiritual feeling.' "

" Thus he lives contemplating feelings in feelings, internally, or he lives contemplating feelings in feelings, externally, or he lives contemplating feelings in feelings internally and externally."

" He lives contemplating origination-things, in feelings, or he lives contemplating dissolution-things, in feelings, or he lives contemplating origination-and-dissolution-things in feelings. Or his mindfulness is established with the thought : ' Feeling exists,' to the extent necessary for just knowledge and remembrance and he lives independent and clings to naught in the world."

" Thus, indeed, o bhikkhus, a bhikkhu lives contemplating feelings in feelings."

The Contemplation of Consciousness

" And how, o bhikkhus, does a bhikkhu live contemplating consciousness in consciousness ? "

" Here, o bhikkhus, a bhikkhu understands the consciousness with lust, as with lust ; the consciousness without lust, as without lust ; the consciousness with hate, as with hate ; the consciousness without hate as without hate ; the consciousness with ignorance as with ignorance ; the consciousness without ignorance as without ignorance ; the shrunken state of consciousness as the shrunken state ; the distracted state of consciousness as the distracted state ; the state of consciousness become great as the state become great ; the state of consciousness not become great as the state not become great ; the state of consciousness with some other mental state superior to it as the state with something mentally higher ; the state of consciousness with no other mental state superior to it as the state with nothing mentally higher ; the quieted state of consciousness as the quieted state ; the state of consciousness not quieted as the state not quieted ; the freed state of consciousness as freed ; and the unfreed state of consciousness as the unfreed."

"Thus he lives contemplating consciousness in consciousness, internally, or he lives contemplating consciousness in consciousness, externally, or he lives contemplating consciousness in consciousness internally and externally."

"He lives contemplating origination-things in consciousness or he lives contemplating dissolution-things in consciousness, or he lives contemplating origination-and-dissolution-things in consciousness. Or his mindfulness is established with the thought : 'Consciousness exists,' to the extent necessary for just knowledge and remembrance, and he lives independent and clings to naught in the world."

"Thus, indeed, o bhikkhus, a bhikkhu lives contemplating consciousness in consciousness."

The Contemplation on Mental Objects. 1. The Five Hindrances

"And how, o bhikkhus, does a bhikkhu live contemplating mental objects in mental objects ?"

"Here, o bhikkhus, a bhikkhu lives contemplating the mental objects in the mental objects of the five hindrances."

"How, o bhikkhus, does a bhikkhu live contemplating mental objects in the mental objects of the five hindrances ?"

"Here, o bhikkhus, when sensuality is present, a bhikkhu with understanding knows : 'I have sensuality,' or when sensuality is not present he with understanding knows : 'I have no sensuality.' He understands how the arising of the non-arisen sensuality comes to be ; he understands how the abandoning of the arisen sensuality comes to be ; and he understands how the non-arising in the future of the abandoned sensuality comes to be. When anger is present, he with understanding knows : 'I have anger.' He understands how the arising of the non-arisen anger comes to be ; he understands how the abandoning of the arisen anger comes to be; and he understands how the non-arising in the future of the abandoned anger comes to be. When sloth and torpor are present he with understanding knows: 'I have sloth and torpor.' He understands how the arising of non-arisen sloth and torpor comes to be; he understands how the abandoning of the arisen sloth and torpor comes to be; and he understands how the non-arising in the future of the abandoned sloth and torpor comes to be. When flurry and worry are present he with understanding knows: 'I have flurry and worry.' He understands how the arising of non-arisen flurry and worry comes to be; he understands how the abandoning of the arisen flurry and worry comes to be; and he understands how the non-arising in the future of the abandoned flurry and worry comes to be. When scepsis is present he with understanding knows: 'I have scepsis.' He understands how the arising of non-arisen scepsis comes to be; he understands how the abandoning of the arisen scepsis comes to be; and he understands how the non-arising in the future of the abandoned scepsis comes to be."

"Thus he lives contemplating mental objects in mental objects, internally, or he lives contemplating mental objects in mental objects, externally, or he lives contemplating mental objects in mental objects internally and externally."

"He lives contemplating origination-things in mental objects, or he lives contemplating dissolution-things in mental objects, or he lives contemplating origination-and-dissolution-things in mental objects. Or his mindfulness is established with the thought, 'Mental objects exist,' to the extent necessary for just knowledge and remembrance and he lives independent and clings to naught in the world. Thus, indeed, o bhikkhus, a bhikkhu lives contemplating mental objects in the mental objects of the five hindrances."

2. The Five Aggregates of Clinging

"And, further, o bhikkhus, a bhikkhu lives contemplating mental objects in the mental objects of the five aggregates of clinging."

"How, o bhikkhus, does a bhikkhu live contemplating mental objects in the mental objects of the five aggregates of clinging?"

"Here, o bhikkhus, a bhikkhu thinks: 'Thus is material form; thus is the arising of material form; and thus is the disappearance of material form. Thus is feeling; thus is the arising of feeling; and thus is the disappearance of feeling. Thus is perception; thus is the arising of perception; and thus is the disappearance of perception. Thus are the formations; thus is the arising of the formations; and thus is the disappearance of the formations. Thus is consciousness; thus is the arising of consciousness; and thus is the disappearance of consciousness'."

" In this way, he lives contemplating mental objects in mental objects, internally, or he lives contemplating mental objects in mental objects, externally, or he lives contemplating mental objects in mental objects internally and externally."

" He lives contemplating origination-things in mental objects, or he lives contemplating dissolution-things in mental objects, or he lives contemplating origination-and-dissolution-things in mental objects. Or his mindfulness is established with the thought, 'Mental objects exist,' to the extent necessary for just knowledge and remembrance, and he lives independent, and clings to naught in the world. Thus, indeed, o bhikkhus, a bhikkhu lives contemplating mental objects in the mental objects of the five aggregates of clinging."

3. The Six Internal and the Six External Sense-Bases

" And, further, o bhikkhus, a bhikkhu lives contemplating mental objects in the mental objects of the six internal and the six external sense-bases."

" How, o bhikkhus, does a bhikkhu live contemplating mental objects in the mental objects of the six internal and the six external sense-bases ? "

" Here, o bhikkhus, a bhikkhu understands the eye and material forms and the fetter that arises dependent on both (eye and forms) ; he understands how the arising of the non-arisen fetter comes to be ; he understands how the abandoning of the arisen fetter comes to be ; and he understands how the non-arising in the future of the abandoned fetter comes to be. He understands the ear and sounds and the fetter that arises dependent on both (ear and sounds) ; he understands how the arising of the non-arisen fetter comes to be ; he understands how the abandoning of the arisen fetter comes to be ; and he understands how the non-arising in the future of the abandoned fetter comes to be. He understands the organ of smell and odours and the fetter that arises dependent on both (the organ of smell and odours) ; he understands how the arising of the non-arisen fetter comes to be ; he understands how the abandoning of the arisen fetter comes to be ; and he understands how the non-arising in the future of the abandoned fetter comes to be. He understands the organ of taste and flavours and the fetter that arises dependent on both (the organ of taste and flavours) ; he understands how the arising of the non-arisen fetter comes to be ; he understands how the abandoning of the arisen fetter comes to be ; and he understands how the non-arising in the future of the abandoned fetter comes to be. He understands the organ of touch and tactual objects and the fetter that arises dependent on both (the organ of touch and tactual objects) ; he understands how the arising of the non-arisen fetter comes to be ; he understands how the abandoning of the arisen fetter comes to be ; and he understands how the non-arising in the future of the abandoned fetter comes to be. He understands consciousness and mental objects and the fetter that arises dependent on both (consciousness and mental objects) ; he understands how the arising of the non-arisen fetter comes to be ; he understands how the abandoning of the arisen fetter comes to be ; and he understands how the non-arising in the future of the abandoned fetter comes to be."

" Thus, o bhikkhus, a bhikkhu lives contemplating mental objects in mental objects, internally, or he lives contemplating mental objects in mental objects, externally, or he lives contemplating mental objects in mental objects internally and externally."

" He lives contemplating origination-things in mental objects, or he lives contemplating dissolution-things in mental objects or he lives contemplating origination-and-dissolution-things in mental objects. Or his mindfulness is established with the thought, ' Mental objects exist,' to the extent necessary for just knowledge and remembrance, and he lives independent and clings to naught in the world. Thus, indeed, o bhikkhus, a bhikkhu lives contemplating mental objects in the mental objects of the six internal and the six external sense-bases."

4. The Seven Factors of Enlightenment

" And, further, o bhikkhus, a bhikkhu lives contemplating mental objects in the mental objects of the seven factors of enlightenment."

" How, o bhikkhus, does a bhikkhu live contemplating mental objects in the mental objects of the seven factors of enlightenment ?"

" Here, o bhikkhus, when the enlightenment factor of mindfulness is present, a bhikkhu with understanding knows : I have the enlightenment factor of mindfulness ; or when the enlightenment factor of mindfulness is absent, he with understanding knows : I have not the enlightenment factor of mindfulness ; and he understands how the arising of the non-arisen enlightenment factor of mindfulness comes to be and how the completion by culture of the arisen enlightenment factor of mindfulness comes to be. When the enlightenment factor of the investigation of mental objects is present, he with understanding knows : I have the enlightenment factor of the investigation of mental objects ; when the enlightenment factor of the investigation of mental objects is absent, he with understanding knows : I have not the enlightenment factor of the investigation of mental objects ; and he understands how the arising of the non-arisen enlightenment factor of the investigation of mental objects comes to be and how the completion by culture of the arisen enlightenment factor of the investigation of mental objects comes to be. When the enlightenment factor of energy is present, he with understanding knows : I have the enlightenment factor of energy ; when the enlightenment factor of energy is absent, he with understanding knows: I have not the enlightenment factor of energy ; and he understands how the arising of the non-arisen enlightenment factor of energy comes to be and how the completion by culture of the arisen enlightenment factor of energy comes to be. When the enlightenment factor of joy is present, he with understanding knows: I have the enlightenment factor of joy ; when the enlightenment factor of joy is absent, he with understanding knows : I have not the enlightenment factor of joy ; and he understands how the arising of the non-arisen enlightenment factor of joy comes to be and how the completion by culture of the arisen enlightenment factor of joy comes to be. When the enlightenment factor of calm is present, he with understanding knows : I have the enlightenment factor of calm ; when the enlightenment factor of calm is absent, he with understanding knows : I have not the enlightenment factor of calm ; and he understands how the arising of the non-arisen enlightenment factor of calm comes to be and how the completion by culture of the arisen enlightenment factor of calm comes to be. When the enlightenment factor of concentration is present, he with understanding knows : I have the enlightenment factor of concentration ; when the enlightenment factor of concentration is absent, he with understanding knows : I have not the enlightenment factor of concentration ; and he understands how the arising of the non-arisen enlightenment factor of concentration comes to be and how the completion by culture of the arisen enlightenment factor of concentration comes to be. When the enlightenment factor of equanimity is present, he with understanding knows : I have the enlightenment factor of equanimity ; when the enlightenment factor of equanimity is absent, he with understanding knows : I have not the enlightenment factor or equanimity ; and he understands how the arising of the non-arisen enlightenment factor of equanimity comes to be and how the completion by culture of the arisen enlightenment factor of equanimity comes to be."

"Thus he lives contemplating mental objects in mental objects, internally, or he lives contemplating mental objects in mental objects, externally, or he lives contemplating mental objects in mental objects, internally and externally."

"He lives contemplating origination-things in mental objects, or he lives contemplating dissolution-things in mental objects, or he lives contemplating origination-and-dissolution-things in mental objects. Or his mindfulness is established with the thought, 'Mental objects exist,' to the extent necessary for just knowledge and remembrance, and he lives independent and clings to naught in the world. Thus, indeed, o bhikkhus, a bhikkhu lives contemplating mental objects in the mental objects of the seven factors of enlightenment."

5. THE FOUR TRUTHS

" And, further, o bhikkhus, a bhikkhu lives contemplating mental objects in the mental objects of the Four Real Truths."

" How, o bhikkhus, does a bhikkhu live contemplating mental objects in the mental objects of the Four Real Truths ? "

" Here, o bhikkhus, a bhikkhu understands: ' This is suffering,' according to reality ; he understands : ' This is the origin of suffering,' according to reality ; he understands : ' This is the cessation of suffering,' according to reality ; and he understands : ' This is the road leading to the cessation of suffering,' according to reality."

" Thus, he lives contemplating mental objects in mental objects, internally, or he lives contemplating mental objects in mental objects, externally, or he lives contemplating mental objects in mental objects internally and externally."

" He lives contemplating origination-things in mental objects, or he lives contemplating dissolution-things in mental objects, or he lives contemplating origination-and-dissolution-things in mental objects. Or his mindfulness is established with the thought, ' Mental objects exist,' to the extent necessary for just knowledge and remembrance, and he lives independent and clings to naught in the world. Thus, indeed, o bhikkhus, a bhikkhu lives contemplating mental objects in the mental objects of the Four Real Truths."

ASSURANCE OF ATTAINMENT

"Verily, o bhikkhus, should any person make become the Four Arousings of Mindfulness in this manner for seven years then by him one of two fruitions is proper to be expected : Knowledge (Saintship) here and now, or if some form of clinging is yet present, the state of Non-Returning (the Third Stage of Supramundane Fulfilment)."

" O bhikkhus let alone seven years. Should a person make become these Four Arousings of Mindfulness, in this manner, for six years.........for five years.........four years.........three years ....two years.........one year, then by him one of two fruitions is proper to be expected : Knowledge here and now, or if some form of clinging is yet present, the state of Non-Returning."

" O bhikkhus, let alone a year. Should any person make become these Four Arousings of Mindfulness, in this manner, for seven months, then by him one of two fruitions is proper to be expected: Knowledge here and now, or if some form of clinging is yet present, the state of Non-Returning."

" O bhikkhus, let alone seven months. Should any person make become these Four Arousings of Mindfulness in this manner for six months.........five months.........four months.........three months ....two months.........a month.........half-a-month, then, by him one of two fruitions is proper to be expected: Knowledge here and now, or if some form of clinging is yet present, the state of Non-Returning."

" O bhikkhus, let alone half-a-month. Should any person make become these Four Arousings of Mindfulness in this manner for a week, then by him one of two fruitions is proper to be expected: Knowledge here and now, or if some form of clinging is yet present, the state of Non-Returning."

" Because of this was it said: 'This is the only way, o bhikkhus, for the purification of beings, for the overcoming of sorrow and lamentation, for the destruction of suffering and grief, for reaching the right path, for the attainment of Nibbāna, namely, the Four Arousings of Mindfulness."

Thus spoke the Blessed One. Satisfied the bhikkhus approved of his words.

THE COMMENTARY TO THE DISCOURSE ON THE AROUSING OF MINDFULNESS WITH MARGINAL NOTES

THE SECTION OF THE SYNOPSIS

EVAṀ ME SUTAṀ = " Thus have I heard " the Discourse on the Arousing of Mindfulness [Satipaṭṭhāna Sutta]. " I " refers to the Elder Ānanda, cousin of the Buddha. At the first Buddhist council held in the Sattapaṇṇi Cave at Rājagaha under the presidentship of the Great Disciple of the Buddha, the Elder Mahā Kassapa, the Collection of the Discourses [Sutta Piṭaka] was recited by the Elder Ānanda.

EKAṀ SAMAYAṀ BHAGAVĀ KURŪSU VIHARATI = " At one time the Blessed One was living in the (country of the) Kurus." Although the territory of the Kuru princes, their homeland, was a single contiguous domain, by taking into consideration its many villages and market-towns, it was commonly referred to by the use of the plural form " Kurus."

In the time of the legendary king Mandhātu, say the commentators, inhabitants of the three continents, Pubba Videha, Apara Goyāna, and Uttara Kuru, having heard that, Jambudīpa*, the birthplace of Sammāsambuddhas,** Paccekabuddhas,*** the Great Disciples of the Buddhas, Universal Monarchs and other beings of mighty virtue, was an exceedingly pleasant, excellent continent, came to Jambudīpa with the Universal Monarch Mandhātu who was making a tour of all the continents, in due order, preceded by his Wheel Treasure. And at last when Mandhātu bodily translated himself by means of his psychic virtue to the Tāvatiṁsa devaloka, the heaven of the Thirty-three, the people of the three continents who accompanied him to Jambudīpa begged of his son for territory to live in, as they said they had come carried by the great power of Mandhātu, and were now unable by themselves to return to their own continents. Their prayer was heard and lands were granted to each of the three groups of people of the three continents. The places in which these people settled got the names of the original continents from which they had emigrated. The settlement of people from Pubba Videha came to be known as Videha, of those from Apara Goyāna, as Aparanta, and of those from Uttara Kuru as Kururaṭṭha.

KAMMĀSADAMMAṀ NĀMA KURŪNAṀ NIGAMO = "At Kammāsadamma a market-town of the Kuru people." Some explain the word Kammāsadamma, here, spelling it with a "dh" instead of a "d". Since Kammāsa was tamed here it was called Kammāsadamma, the place of the taming of Kammāsa. Kammāsa refers to the cannibal Kammāsapāda, the one, with the speckled, black and white or grey coloured, foot. It is said that a wound on his foot, caused by a stake, healed, having become like a piece of wood with lines of fibre of a complex pattern [cittadāru sadiso hutvā]. Therefore, he became well-known as Kammāsapāda, Speckled Foot. By whom was Speckled Foot tamed? By the Great Being, the Bodhisatta. In which Birth-story [Jātaka] is it stated? Certain commentators say: "In the Sutasoma Birth-story". But the elders of the Great Minister at Anurādhapura, the Mahā Vihāra, say that it is stated in the Jayaddisa Birth-story. Verily, Kammāsapāda was tamed, weaned of his cannibalism, by the Great Being, in the circumstances mentioned in the Jayaddisa Birth-story. The following statement occurs in that story:

To free my sire did I renounce my life,
When born as very son of the king,
Jayaddisa, Pañcāla's sovran chief,
And make even Speckled Foot have faith in me.*

Some [keci] however explain spelling the word thus: Kammāsadhamma. It is said that the traditional Kuru virtuous practice [Kuruvattadhamma] became (black or diversified or) stained [kammāso jāto] in that place. Therefore, it was called Kammāsadhamma. The market-town established there, too, got the same name.

Why was it not said KAMMĀSADAMME KURŪNAṀ NIGAME using the locative? Because, it is said, there was no monastery (or dwelling place) at which the Blessed One could stay, in that market-town. Away from the market-town, however, there was a huge dense jungle in a delightful region watered well. In that jungle, the Blessed One lived, making the market-town his place for gathering alms.

EKĀYANO AYAṀ BHIKKHAVE MAGGO = "This is the only way, o bhikkhus." Why did the Blessed One teach this Discourse? Because of the ability of the people of the Kurus to take in deep doctrine.

The inhabitants of the Kuru country—bhikkhus, bhikkhunis, upāsakas, upāsikās—by reason of their country being blessed with a perfect climate and through their enjoyment of other comfortable conditions were always healthy in body and in mind.

They, made happy with healthy minds and bodies, and having the power of knowledge, were capable of receiving deep teachings. Therefore, the Blessed One, perceiving their ability to appreciate this profound instruction, proclaimed to them this Discourse on the Arousing of Mindfulness which is deep in meaning, having set up the subject of meditation, in Arahatship, in twenty-one places. For even as a man having got a golden basket should fill it with divers flowers or indeed having got a golden casket should fill it with precious jewels of the seven kinds, the Blessed One, having got a following of the Kuru-land people, dispensed, it is said, deep doctrine. Likewise, on that very account, there, in the Kurus, the Blessed One, taught other deep teachings: the Mahā Nidāna Sutta, Mahā Satipaṭṭhāna Sutta, Sāropama Sutta, Rukkhūpama Sutta, Raṭṭhapāla Sutta, Māgandiya Sutta, and the Āneñjasappāya Sutta.

Further in that territory of the Kuru people,* the four classes—bhikkhu, bhikkhuni, upāsaka, upāsikā—generally by nature were earnest in the application of the Arousing of Mindfulness to their daily life. At the very lowest, even servants, usually, spoke with mindfulness. At wells or in spinning halls useless talk was not heard. If some woman asked of another woman, "Mother, which Arousing of Mindfulness do you practise?" and got the reply, "None at all," then that woman who replied so was reproached thus: "Your life is shameful; though you live you are as if dead," and taught one of the kinds of Mindfulness-arousing. But on being questioned if she said that she was practising such and such an Arousing of Mindfulness, then she was praised thus: "Well done, Well done! Your life is blessed; you are really one who has attained to the human state; for you the Sammāsambuddhas have come to be.

WITH A PERFECT CLIMATE.........COMFORTABLE CONDITIONS. *This includes such items as wholesome food and drink essential for maintaining mind and body unimpaired.*

"The only way" = The one way [Ekāyanoti ekamaggo]. There are many words for "way". The word used for "way" here is "ayana" ("going" or road). Therefore, "This is the only way, o bhikkhus [Ekāyano ayaṁ bhikkhave maggo]" means here: "A single way ("going" or road), o bhikkhus, is this way; it is not of the nature of a double way [Ekamaggo ayaṁ bhikkhave maggo na dvedhāpathabhūto]."

Or it is "the only way" because it has to be trodden by oneself only [ekeneva ayitabbo]. *That is without a companion. The state of being companionless is twofold :* without a comrade, after abandoning contact with the crowd, and in the sense of being withdrawn (or secluded) from craving through tranquillity of mind.

Or it is called " ekāyana " because it is the way of the one [ekassa ayana]. "Of the one " = of the best ; of all beings the Blessed One is the best. Therefore, it is called the Blessed One's Way. Although others too go along that way, it is the Buddha's because he creates it. Accordingly it is said : " He, the Blessed One, is the creator of the uncreate path, O Brahmin." It proceeds (or exists) only in this Doctrine-and-discipline and not in any other. Accordingly the Master declared : " Subhadda, only in this Doctrine-and-discipline is the Eightfold Way to be found." And further " ekāyana " means : It goes to the one [ekaṁ ayati]—that is, it (the way) goes solely to Nibbāna. Although in the earlier stages this method of meditation proceeds on different lines, in the later, it goes to just the one Nibbāna. And that is why Brahmā Sahampati said :

> Whose mind perceiving life's last dying out
> Vibrates with love, he knows the only way
> That led in ancient times, is leading now,
> And in the future will lead past the flood.*

As Nibbāna is without a second, that is, without craving as accompanying quality, it is called the one. Hence it is said : " Truth is one; it is without a second."

Why is the Arousing of Mindfulness intended by the word " way " ? Are there not many other factors of the way, namely, understanding, thinking, speech, action, livelihood, effort, and concentration, besides mindfulness ? To be sure there are. But all these are implied when the Arousing of Mindfulness is mentioned, because these factors exist in union with mindfulness. Knowledge, energy and the like are mentioned in the analytically expository portion [niddese]. In the synopsis [uddese], however, the consideration should be regarded as that of mindfulness alone, by way of the mental disposition of those capable of being trained.

Some [keci], however, construing according to the stanza beginning with the words, " They do not go twice to the further shore [Na pāraṁ diguṇaṁ yanti]"** say, "One goes to Nibbāna once, therefore it is ekāyana." This explanation is not proper. Because in this instruction the earlier part of the Path is intended to be presented, the preliminary part of the Way of Mindfulness proceeding in the four objects of contemplation is meant here, and not the supramundane Way of Mindfulness. And that preliminary part of the Path proceeds (for the aspirant) many times ; or it may be said that there is many a going on it, by way of repetition of practice.

In what sense is it a "way"? In the sense of the path going towards Nibbāna, and in the sense of the path which is the one that should be (or is fit to be) traversed by those who wish to reach Nibbāna.

Regarding " the only way", there is the following account of a discussion that took place long ago :

The Elder Tipiṭaka Culla Nāga said : " The Way of Mindfulness-arousing (as expounded in our Discourse) is the (mundane) preliminary part (of the Eightfold Way)."

His teacher the Elder Culla Summa said : " The Way is a mixed one (a way that is both mundane and supramundane)."

The pupil : " Reverend Sir, it is the preliminary part."

The teacher : " Friend, it is the mixed Way."

As the teacher was insistent, the pupil became silent. They went away without coming to a decision.

On the way to the bathing place the teacher considered the matter. He recited the Discourse. When he came to the part where it is said : " Verily, o bhikkhus, should any person make become the Four Arousings of Mindfulness in this manner for seven years," he concluded that after producing the consciousness of the Supramundane Path there was no possibility of continuing in that state of mind for seven years, and that his pupil, Culla Nāga, was right. On that very day, which happened to be the eighth of the lunar fortnight, it was the Elder Culla Nāga's turn to expound the Dhamma. When the exposition was about to begin, the Elder Culla Summa went to the Hall of Preaching and stood behind the pulpit.

After the pupil had recited the preliminary stanzas the teacher spoke to the pupil in the hearing of others, saying, " Friend, Culla Nāga." The pupil heard the voice of his teacher and replied : " What is it Reverend Sir ? " The teacher said this : " To say, as I did, that the Way is a mixed one is not right. You are right in calling it the preliminary part of the Way of Mindfulness-arousing." Thus the Elders of old were not envious and did not go about holding up only what they liked as though it were a bundle of sugarcane. They took up what was rational ; they gave up what was not.

Thereupon, the pupil, realising that a point on which an expert of the Dhamma like his learned teacher had floundered fellows of the holy life in the future were more likely to be unsure, thought : " With the authority of a citation from the Discourse-collection, I will settle this question." Therefore, he brought out and placed before his hearers the following statement from the Patisambhidā

Magga : " The preliminary part of the Way of Mindfulness-arousing is called the only way."* And, in order to elaborate just that and to show of which path or way the instruction in our Discourse is the preliminary part, he further quoted the following also from the Paṭisambhidā Magga : " The Excellent Way is the Eightfold Way ; four are the truths ; dispassion is the best of things belonging to the wise ; besides that Way there is no other for the purifying of vision. Walk along that Way so that you may confound Death, and put an end to suffering."**

SATTĀNAṀ VISUDDHIYĀ = " For the purification of beings." For the cleansing of beings soiled by the stains of lust, hatred and delusion, and by the defilements of covetise called lawless greed and so forth. All reach the highest purity after abandoning mental taints. By way of physical taints, however, there is no cleansing of impurities taught in the Dhamma.

By the Great Seer it was not said
That through bodily taints men become impure,
Or by the washing of the body they become pure.
By the Great Seer it was declared
That through mental taints men become impure,
And through the cleaning of the mind they become pure.

Accordingly it is said : " Mental taints soil beings ; mental cleaning sanctifies them."***

SOKAPARIDDAVĀNAṀ SAMATIKKAMĀYA = " For the overcoming of sorrow and lamentation." If this Way is developed it will lead to the casting out of sorrow similar to that experienced by the Minister Santati and the casting out of lamentation similar to that of Paṭācārā. With analytical knowledge did Santati reach arahatship after hearing this stanza :

Purge out the things belonging to the past ;
Let there be naught to rise in future times.
If what's 'twixt past and future you don't grasp,
You will be one who wanders forth serene.****

Paṭācārā reached the fruition of the first stage of saintship after hearing the following :

For one who is by death oppressed there is
No safety seen in children, father, friends,
Or others close to one. A shelter true
Amongst one's kinsfolk one does never find.*****

Since there is nothing called spiritual development [bhāvanā] without laying hold on something whatsoever in material form, feeling, consciousness and mental objects [kāya vedanā citta dhammesu kiñci dhammaṁ anāmasitvā] they (Santati and Paṭācārā) too overcame sorrow and lamentation just by this Way of Mindfulness.

For the hearers [sāvaka], namely, the disciples of the Buddha, there is no attainment of the Real Path [Ariya Magga] possible, except by practising the subject of meditation [kammaṭṭhāna] of the Four Truths [Catu Sacca]. Spiritual development usually called meditation is the development of wisdom [paññā bhāvanā]. Just the contemplation of material form (corporeality), of feeling, consciousness or mental objects constitutes the cultivation of the Arousing of Mindfulness.

DUKKHA DOMANASSĀNAṀ ATTHANGAMĀYA = " For the destruction of suffering and grief." For the cessation of bodily suffering and mental grief. Verily this way made to become by contemplation is conducive to the destruction of suffering similar to that of the Elder Tissa and of grief similar to that of Sakka.

Tissa, the head of a family at Sāvatthi, renouncing forty crores of gold, became a homeless one, and dwelt in a forest far from other human beings. His sister-in-law sent a robber band of five hundred to scour the forest in order to find him, and ordered them to kill him when he was found.

She sent them, it is said, in five batches of a hundred each in succession. After entering the forest and searching for the elder they in due course came to the place in which he lived and sat round him.

When the robbers surrounded him, the elder spoke thus : " Lay disciples, why have you come ? " They replied : " To kill you." Then the elder said : " On a security, give me my life for just this one night." Said the robbers : " O recluse, who will stand surety for you in a place like this ? " The elder, thereupon, took a big stone, broke the bones of his legs and said : " Lay disciples, is the security of value ? " They leaving the elder went to the end of the ambulatory and lighting a fire lay on the ground.

The elder contemplating on the purity of his conduct after suppressing his pain attained saintship, at dawn, having fulfilled the recluse's regimen in the three watches of the night. Giving expression to his feelings he said :

> " A surety let me raise breaking both my legs ;
> To die with lustful mind I loathe and shrink."
> Having thought thus I saw things as they are,
> And with the dawn I reached the saint's domain.

There is another story. Thirty bhikkhus taking the subject of meditation from the Blessed One went into residence, during the rains, in a forest-dwelling, agreeing amongst themselves to practise the duty of the recluse, during all the three watches of the night, and to avoid one another's presence.

One by one those monks who began to doze early in the morning after doing the recluse's duty during the three watches of the night were carried away by a tiger. Not one of those carried away did even utter the words : " I am taken by a tiger." When thus fifteen bhikkhus had been devoured, on uposatha day (the day of the Meeting of the Order for recitation of the Rules), after it was asked (by the elder) " Friends, where are the others ? " and it became known that they had been devoured by a tiger, it was agreed that anyone seized by the tiger, thereafter, should utter the words : " I am taken." Then a certain young bhikkhu was seized by the tiger in the same circumstances in which the others were seized earlier. That young bhikkhu said : " Tiger, Reverend Sir." The other bhikkhus carrying sticks and torches went in pursuit of the tiger.

The tiger having taken the young bhikkhu up to a rocky place, a broken edge over a hollow spot inaccessible to the bhikkhus, began to devour its prey from the feet upwards. The pursuing bhikkhus said : " Good man, there is nothing that could be done by us. The extraordinary spiritual attainment of bhikkhus is to be seen in such a place (as that in which you are)."

That bhikkhu even prostrate in the tiger's mouth suppressed his pain and developing the wisdom of insight attained the four paths and fruits of sanctitude together with analytical knowledge. Then he uttered this ecstatic utterance :—

> Virtuous was I keeping to my vows
> And wise with growing insight was my mind
> That had to concentration well attained.
> Yet, because I slacked for just a while,
> A tiger took my frame of flesh and blood,
> Unto to a hill and then my mind did quake.
> Devour me as you please, o tiger, eat,
> This body of mine which is bereft of thought ;
> Within the thought of quiet strongly held
> A blessing will my death become to me.

And then there is the story of the elder Pītamalla who in the time he was a layman took the pennon for wrestling in three kingdoms. He came to Tambapaṇṇī Isle, had audience of the king and received royal assistance. Once while going through the entrance to the Screened Sitting Hall he heard the following passage from the " Not-your " chapter of Scripture : " Material form, o bhikkhus, is not yours ; renounce it. That renunciation will, for a long time, be for your welfare and happiness." And he thought : "Neither material form, indeed, nor feeling is one's own," and making just that thought a goad, he renounced the world. At the Great Minister, the Mahā Vihāra, at Anurādhapura, he was, in due course, given the lower ordination and the higher. When he had mastered the two Codes of Discipline [Dve Mātikā], he went to the Gavaravāliya Shrine with thirty other bhikkhus and did the duty of the recluse. While meditating in the open at night there once, he was moving on his knees on the ambulatory when his feet were unable to carry him, and a hunter mistaking him for a deer struck him with a spear. The elder removed the spear which had gone deep into the body and stopping the wound with a wad of grass, sat down on a flat stone. Making of his misfortune an opportunity for setting energy afoot, he developed insight and attained saintship with analytical knowledge. After he had reached the state of arahatship, in order to apprise his fellow-bhikkhus of his achievement, he made a sign by clearing his throat and uttered this saying of joy at final liberation from suffering :

> The Word of the Fully Awakened Man, the Chief,
> Holder of Right Views in all the world is this :
> Give up this form disciples ; it is not yours.
> Fleeting truly are component things
> Ruled by laws of growth and decay ;
> What is produced to dissolution swings ;
> Happy it is when things at rest do stay.

Then those fellow-monks of the Elder Pītamalla who had come to see him said : "Reverend Sir, if the Buddha were living he would have expressed his approval of your effort, by stretching out his hand over the ocean and stroking your head."

THREE KINGDOMS=*Paṇḍu, Coḷa, Goḷa. Because he was in the habit of carrying a yellow pennon about his body and also because he adorned himself with that pennon when taking part in wrestling matches he was well-known as Pītamalla, the yellow wrestler. After his renunciation of the world too, he was known as the elder Yellow-wrestler. He came to Tambapaṇṇī Isle—Ceylon—having got the information that wrestlers were honoured and hospitably received in the island.*

So, in this manner, this way is conducive to the destruction of suffering of those like the Elder Tissa.

Sakka, king of the gods, after seeing the five portents, afraid of death and grief-stricken, came to the Buddha and asked a question ; at the close of the answering of that question by the Buddha, Sakka was established in the first stage of sainthood.

Eighty thousand other gods were established together with Sakka in the same stage of sanctity. And the life of Sakka again was restored to just its original state *through his rebirth once more as the king of the gods*.

Further it is said that Subrahmā the god was partaking of the delights of paradise in the company of a thousand heavenly nymphs. There, five hundred of the nymphs, while picking flowers from a tree, died and were reborn in a state of woe. He, having seen their rebirth in a state of woe and having understood that the end of his own life was approaching and that he too would at death be reborn in that very state of woe, was frightened. Then he went to the Buddha with his five hundred remaining nymphs and said this to the Lord :

> The heart is always in a state of fear,
> And is always full of anguish drear,
> Concerning things that have now taken place,
> And things which shortly I shall have to face.
> If there's a place that's free from ev'ry fear,
> That fear-free place wilt thou to me make clear ? *

The Blessed One replied to him as follows :—

> Besides the wakening factors of the truth,
> Besides the virtues of the holy state,
> Besides restraint and relinquishment full,
> I see nothing that can bless living beings.**

At the end of the instruction, Subrahmā and his five hundred nymphs were established in the first stage of sainthood, and he, it is said, returned to his paradise, having made firm the heavenly fortunate state of life that was his before.

It should be understood that this way developed in this manner is conducive to the destruction of grief of those like Sakka.

ÑĀYASSA ADHIGAMĀYA = " For reaching the right path." The Real Eightfold Path is called the right path. Verily, this preliminary, mundane Way of the Arousing of Mindfulness made to become (grown or cultivated) is conducive to the realisation of the Supramundane Way.

NIBBĀNASSA SACCHIKIRIYĀYA = " For the attainment of Nibbāna." It is said as follows : For the attainment, the ocular experience by oneself, of the deathless which has got the name " Nibbāna " by reason of the absence in it of the lust [vāna, literally, sewing, weaving, from the root vā, to weave] called craving [taṇhā].

Truly, craving [taṇhā] sews together [saṁsibbati] or weaves [vināti] aggregate with aggregate, effect with cause, and suffering with beings. In Nibbāna there is no "vāna". Or in the man who has attained to Nibbāna there is no "vāna."

OCULAR EXPERIENCE BY ONESELF : *sensing without aid from the outside.*

This way made to become, verily, effects the attainment of Nibbāna, gradually.

Although by the phrase : "For the purification of beings," the things meant by the other phrases which follow it are attained, the significance of those other phrases that follow the first is not obvious except to a person familiar with the usage of the Dispensation [Sāsana yutti kovido].

Since the Blessed one does not at first make people conversant with the usage of the Dispensation and after that teach the Doctrine to them, and as he by various discourses sets forth various meanings, he explained the things which "the only way" effects, with the words "For the overcoming of sorrow and lamentation," and so forth.

Or it may be said that the Master explained the things accomplished by "the only way," in this manner, in order to show that every thing which leads to the purification of beings by the "only way" is dependent on the overcoming of sorrow and lamentation; that this overcoming is dependent on the destruction of suffering and grief; and that the destruction of suffering and grief is dependent on the reaching of the right path which is in turn dependent on the attainment of Nibbāna. It is a declaration of the method of deliverance, by "the only way."

Further, this is an expression of praise of "the only way." Just as the Blessed One by way of eight characteristics expressed praise in the Cha Chakka Sutta, and by way of nine characteristics, in the Ariyavaṁsa Sutta, just in the same way he expressed praise of this "only way," through the seven characteristics contained in the words "For the purification of beings", and so forth. Why did he utter talk of praise of this kind? For the purpose of bringing out the interest of these bhikkhus. The Blessed One thought : "Having heard the utterance of praise, these bhikkhus will believe that this way casts out the four onrushings [cattāro upaddave harati], namely, sorrow produced by distress of heart [hadaya santāpabhūtaṁ sokaṁ], lamentation characterised by confused talk [vācā vippalābhūtaṁ paridevaṁ], suffering produced by disagreeable bodily feeling [kāyikaṁ asātabhūtaṁ dukkhaṁ], and grief produced by disagreeable thought [cetasikaṁ asātabhūtaṁ domanassaṁ], and that it brings the three extraordinary spiritual attainments of purity, knowledge, and Nibbāna [visuddhiṁ ñāṇaṁ Nibbānanti tayo visese āvahati], and will be convinced that this instruction should be studied [imaṁ dhammadesanaṁ uggahetabbaṁ], mastered [pariyāpuṇitabbaṁ], borne in mind [dhāretabbaṁ], and memorized [vācetabbaṁ], and that this way should be made to become [imañca maggaṁ bhāvetabbaṁ]."

CATTĀRO SATIPAṬṬHĀNĀ = "The Four Arousings of Mindfulness." Four in relation to classes of objects of mindfulness.

Why did the Buddha teach just Four Arousings of Mindfulness and neither more nor less? By way of what was suitable for those capable of being trained.

In regard to the pair of the dull-witted and the keen-witted minds among tamable persons of the craving type and the theorizing type pursuing the path of quietude [samatha] or that of insight [vipassanā], in the practice of meditation, the following is stated : For the dull-witted man of the craving type the Arousing of Mindfulness through the contemplation of the gross physical body is the Path to Purity ; for the keen-witted of this type, the subtle subject of meditation of feeling. And for the dull-witted man of the theorizing type the Path to Purity is the Arousing of Mindfulness through a subject not too full of distinctions, namely, consciousness [citta] ; for the keen-witted of this type, the subject which teems with distinctions, namely the contemplation on things of the mind—mental objects [dhammānupassanā].

For the dull-witted man pursuing quietude the First Arousing of Mindfulness, body-contemplation, is the Path to Purity, by reason of the feasibility of getting at the mental reflex ; for the keen-witted of this type, because he does not continue to stay in the coarse, the second Arousing of Mindfulness, the contemplation on feeling, is the Path to Purity.

And for the dull-witted man pursuing the path of insight the subject of meditation without many distinctions, the contemplation on consciousness, is the Path to Purity; and for the keen-witted of this type the contemplation on mental objects which is full of distinctions.

Or it may be said that these Four Arousings of Mindfulness are taught for casting out the illusions [vipallāsa] concerning beauty, pleasure, permanence and an ego.

The body is ugly. There are people led astray by the illusion that it is a thing of beauty. In order to show such people the ugliness of the body and to make them give up their wrong idea the First Arousing of Mindfulness is taught.

Feeling is suffering. There are people subject to the illusion that it gives pleasure. In order to show such people the painfulness of feeling and to make them give up their wrong idea the Second Arousing of Mindfulness is taught.

Consciousness is impermanent. There are people who, owing to an illusion, believe that it is permanent. To show them the impermanence of consciousness and to wean them of their wrong belief the Third Arousing of Mindfulness is taught.

Mental objects are insubstantial, are soulless, and possess no entity. There are people who believe by reason of an illusion that these mental things are substantial, endowed with an abiding core, or a soul, or that they form part of a soul, an ego or some substance that abides. To convince such errant folk of the fact of the soullessness or the insubstantiality of mental things and to destroy the illusion which clouds their minds the Fourth Arousing of Mindfulness is taught.

Drawing distinctions, it is said: Body and feeling are the cause of zest [assādassa kāraṇa]. For the rejection of that zest of body, by the dull-witted [manda] man of the craving type [taṇhācarita], the seeing [dassana] of the ugly [asubha], in the body, the coarse object [oḷārika ārammaṇa], which is the basis of craving [taṇhā vatthu], is convenient. To that type of man the contemplation on corporeality, the First Arousing of Mindfulness, is the Path to Purity [Visuddhi Magga]. For the abandoning of that zest, by the keen-witted [tikha] man of the craving type, the seeing of suffering, in feeling, the subtle object [sukhuma ārammaṇa], which is the basis of craving, is convenient, and for him the contemplation on feeling, the Second Arousing of Mindfulness, is the Path to Purity.

For the dull-witted man of the theorizing type [diṭṭhi carita] it is convenient to see consciousness [citta] in the fairly simple way it is set forth in this discourse, by way of impermanence [aniccatā], and by way of such divisions as mind-with-lust [sarāgādi vasena], in order to reject the notion of permanence [nicca saññā] in regard to consciousness. Consciousness is a special condition [visesa kāraṇa] for the wrong view due to a basic belief in permanence [niccanti abhinivesa vatthutāya diṭṭhiyā]. The contemplation on consciousness, the Third Arousing of Mindfulness, is the Path to Purity of this type of man.

For the keen-witted man of the theorizing type it is convenient to see mental objects or things [dhamma], according to the manifold way set forth in this discourse, by way of perception, sense-impression and so forth [saññā phassādi vasena] and by way of the hindrances and so forth [nīvaraṇādi vasena] in order to reject the notion of a soul [atta saññā] in regard to mental things. Mental things are special conditions for the wrong view due to a basic belief in a soul [attanti abhinivesa vatthutāya diṭṭhiyā]. For this type of man the contemplation on mental objects, the Fourth Arousing of Mindfulness is the Path to Purity.

Consciousness and mental objects constitute the standout conditions of theorizing. Consciousness is such a condition because it is a decisive factor in the belief in permanence. Mental objects are such conditions because these are decisive factors in the belief in a soul.

Consciousness and mental objects are decisive factors of craving as well as of theorizing. And body and feeling are decisive factors of theorizing as well as of craving. Yet to point out that which is stronger in body and feeling, namely, craving, and that which is stronger in consciousness and mental objects, namely, theorizing, distinctions have been drawn.

BECAUSE HE DOES NOT CONTINUE TO STAY IN THE COARSE : *The keen-witted man pursuing the path of quietude lays hold of the gross subject of meditation, but he does not stay in that. He lays hold of feeling, the subtle subject of meditation, by way of the factors of absorption [jhāna] after attaining to and emerging from the absorption reached with the material body as subject.*

Since the heart of the man pursuing the path of insight takes to the contemplation of subtle consciousness and mental objects, these have been spoken of as the Path to Purity for the man, dull-witted or keen-witted, pursuing insight.

Further these Four Arousings of Mindfulness were taught not only for the purpose of casting out the four illusions, but for getting rid of the four floods, bonds, outflowings, knots, clingings, wrong courses, and the penetration of fourfold nutriment, too. This is according to the method of exegesis in the Nettippakaraṇa.

In the commentary it is said that by way of remembering and of meeting in one thing, the Arousing of Mindfulness is only one ; and that it is four-fold when regarded as a subject of meditation.

BY WAY OF REMEMBERING = *by way of the reflection of actions of skill and so forth of body, speech, and thought.*

MEETING IN ONE THING = *union in the one-natured Nibbāna.*

To a city with four gates men coming from the East with goods produced in the east enter by the east gate......men coming from the South......men coming from the West......and men coming from the North with goods produced in the north enter by the north gate. Nibbāna is like the city. The Real Supramundane Eightfold Path is like the city-gate. Body, mind, feelings and mental objects are like the four chief directions in space. Like the people coming from the East with goods produced in the east are those who enter Nibbāna by means of body-contemplation through the Real Supramundane Path produced by the power of body-contemplation practised in the fourteen ways. Like the people coming from the South......are those who enter......by means of feeling-contemplation......practised in the nine ways. Like the people coming from the West......are those who enter......by means of consciousness-contemplation......practised in the sixteen ways. Like the people coming from the North......are those who enter......by means of mental-object-contemplation......practised in the five ways.

On account of the cause or on account of the sameness of entry into the one Nibbāna, the Arousing of Mindfulness is said to be just one thing. The meeting in the one Nibbāna of the various Arousings of Mindfulness is called the meeting in the one thing on account of participation in that one Nibbāna or on account of their becoming all of a kind.

KATAME CATTĀRO = " What are the Four ? " This is a question indicating the desire to expound the teaching.

IDHA = " Here." In this Dispensation.

BHIKKHAVE = " Bhikkhus ". This is a term for addressing persons who accept the teaching.

Bhikkhu* is a term to indicate a person who earnestly endeavours to accomplish the practice of the teaching. Others, gods and men, too, certainly strive earnestly to accomplish the practice of the teaching, but because of the excellence of the bhikkhu-state by way of practice, the Master said : " Bhikkhu." For amongst those who accept the teaching of the Buddha, the bhikkhu is the highest owing to fitness for receiving manifold instruction. Further, when that highest kind of person, the bhikkhu, is reckoned, the rest too are reckoned, as in regard to a royal procession and the like, when the king is reckoned, by the reckoning of the king, the retinue is reckoned. Also the word " bhikkhu " was used by the Buddha to point out the bhikkhu-state through practice of the teaching in this way : " He who practises this practice of the Arousing of Mindfulness is called a bhikkhu." Verily, he who follows the teaching, be he a shining one [deva] or a human, is indeed called a bhikkhu. Accordingly it is said :

> " Well-dressed one may be, but if one is calm,
> Tamed, humble, pure, a man who does no harm
> To aught that lives, that one's a brahmin true.
> An ascetic and a mendicant too."*

KĀYE = " In the body." In the corporeal group. The group of big and small corporeal constituents, namely, things like hair of the head, hair of the body, nails, and teeth, in the sense of a collection [samūhaṭṭhena] similar to a herd of elephants, a concourse of chariots *according to grammatical method* [*sadda nayena*]. From here, the explanation is by way of word-analysis [*nirutti nayena*],

And as in the sense of a collection so also in the sense of the focus of what is filthy and therefore of what is disgusting is it "kāya." For the body [kāya] is the birthplace [āya] of the disgusting, the exceedingly repellent. The birthplace [āya] is the place of origin [uppattidesa]. Since these originate from that place [āyanti tato] it is the place of origin [āyo]. What originate? The repulsive things like hair of the head. Therefore, the body is the place of origin of disgusting or contemptible things [kucchitānaṁ ayoti kāyo].

KĀYĀNUPASSĪ = "Contemplating the body." Possessed of the character of body-contemplation or of observing the body.

Why is the word "body" used twice in the phrase: "Contemplating the body in the body?" For determining the object and isolating it, and for the sifting out thoroughly [vinibbhoga] of the apparently compact [ghaṇa] nature of things like continuity [santati].

Because there is no contemplating of feeling, consciousness or mental objects in the body, but just the contemplating of the body only, determination through isolation is set forth by the pointing out of the way of contemplating the body only in the property called the body.

In the body there is no contemplation of a uniform thing, apart from the big and small members of the body, or of a man, or of a woman, apart from such things like the hair of the head and the hair of the body.

There can be nothing apart from the qualities of primary and derived materiality, in a body.

Indeed the character of contemplating the collection of the major and the minor corporeal members is like the seeing of the constituents of a cart. The character of contemplating the collection of the hair of the head, the hair of the body and the like is comparable to the seeing of the component parts of a city; and the character of contemplating the collection of primary and derived materiality is comparable to the separation of the leaf-integument of a plantain-trunk or is like the opening of an empty fist. Therefore, by the pointing out of the basis called the body in the form of a collection, in many ways, the sifting out thoroughly of the apparently compact is shown.

In this body, apart from the abovementioned collection, there is seen no body, man, woman or anything else. Beings engender wrong belief, in many ways, in the bare groups of things mentioned above. Therefore the men of old said:

What he sees that is not (properly) seen ;
What is seen that he does not (properly) see ;
Not seeing (properly) he is shackled clean ;
And he, the shackled fool, cannot get free.

WHAT HE SEES = *What man or woman he sees. Why, is there no seeing of a man or a woman with the eye? There is. "I see a woman," "I see a man,"—these statements—refer to what he sees by way of ordinary perception. That perception, owing to wrong comprehension, does not get at the sense-basis* [*rūpāyatana*]—*in the highest sense philosophically—through the falsely determined condition of material form* [*viparīta gahavasena micchā parikappita rūpattā*].

Or the meaning is: the absence of perception which is called the seeing of primary and derived materiality beginning with things such as the hair of the head, owing to non-cognizability of the collective nature of an object like a man or a woman by eye-consciousness [*kesādibhūtupādāya samūhasankhātaṁ diṭṭhi na hoti acakkhuviññāṇa viññeyyattā*].

WHAT IS SEEN THAT HE DOES NOT PROPERLY SEE = *He does not see, according to reality by the eye of wisdom, the sense-basis which exists, the collection of primary and derived materiality beginning with hair of the head and the like* [*Yaṁ rūpāyatanaṁ kesādibhūtupādāya samūhasankhātaṁ diṭṭhaṁ taṁ paññā cakkhunā bhūtato na passati*].

NOT SEEING PROPERLY HE IS SHACKLED = *Not seeing this body as it actually is, with the eye of wisdom, he thinks: "This is mine, this am I, this is my self," and is bound with the fetter of defilement* [*Imaṁ attabhāvaṁ yathābhūtaṁ paññācakkhunā apassanto etaṁ mama esohamasmi eso me attāti kilesa bandhanena bajjhati*].

And here, by the passage : "For the determining of the object by isolating it, and for the sifting out thoroughly of the apparently compact nature of things like continuity," this too should be understood : This person contemplates in this body only the body ; he does not contemplate anything else. What does this mean ? In this definitely transient, suffering, soulless body, that is unlovely, he does not see permanence, pleasure, a soul, or beauty, after the manner of those animals which see water in a mirage. Body-contemplation is only the contemplation of the collection of qualities of transiency, suffering, soullessness, and unloveliness.

Because there is no contemplating of the body with reference to a self or to anything belonging to a self, owing to the contemplating even of collections of things like the hair of the head, there is the character of contemplating, in the body, the body which is a collection of things like the hair of the head.

The meaning should be understood thus too : " contemplating the body in the body " is the seeing of the body as a group of all qualities beginning with impermanence, step by step, as taught in the passage of the Paṭisambhidā which begins with: " In this body he contemplates according to impermanence and not permanence."

The bhikkhu sees, the body in the body, (1) as something impermanent ; (2) as something subject to suffering ; (3) as something that is soulless ; (4) by way of turning away from it and not by way of delighting in it ; (5) by freeing himself of passion for it ; (6) with thoughts making for cessation and not making for origination ; (7) and not by way of laying hold of it, but by way of giving it up.

VIHARATI = " Lives."

ĀTĀPĪ = " Ardent." What burns the defilement of the three planes of becoming is ardour. Ardour is a name for energy.

Although the term burning [ātāpana] is applied to the abandoning of defilements here, it is also applicable to right view, thought, speech, action, livelihood, mindfulness and concentration. As ardour [ātāpa] like glow [ātappa] is restricted by use to just energy generally, it is said, " Ardour is a name for energy." Or because of the occurrence of energy [viriya] by way of instigating the associated things, in the abandoning of opposing qualities, that itself (i.e. energy) is ardour [ātāpa]. In this place only energy [viriya] is referred to by " ātāpa." By taking the word ardent [ātāpī] the Master points out the one possessed of right energy or exertion [sammappadhāna].

SAMPAJĀNO = " Clearly comprehending." Endowed with knowledge called circumspection [sampajañña].

CLEARLY COMPREHENDING = *Discerning rightly, entirely and equally [Sammā samantato samañca pajānanto].*

RIGHTLY = *Correctly [Aviparītaṁ].*

ENTIRELY = *By knowing in all ways [Sabbākārapajānanena].*

EQUALLY = *By reason of proceeding through the conveying of higher and higher spiritual attainments [Uparūpari visesāvāhabhāvena pavattiyā].*

SATIMĀ = " Mindful." Endowed with mindfulness that lays hold of the body as a subject of meditation, because this yogāvacara (the man conversant with contemplative activity) contemplates with wisdom after laying hold of the object with mindfulness. Verily there is nothing called contemplation without mindfulness. Therefore the Master said : " Mindfulness is necessary in all circumstances, o bhikkhus, I declare."*

NECESSARY IN ALL CIRCUMSTANCES = *Everywhere in the states of becoming, in every sluggish and unbalanced state of mind, it is desirable. Or that by the help of which the other proper Factors of Enlightenment [Bojjhanga] are possible of being developed is "necessary in all circumstances." Here, contemplation takes place by means of wisdom that is assisted by mindfulness.*

To point out the things by the influence of which the meditation of the yogi prospers is the purpose of the words, "Ardent, clearly comprehending, and mindful."

To the non-ardent state of mind there is the obstacle of mental lassitude.

The state of mind that is not clearly comprehending commits blunders of judgment in the business of choosing the right means and in avoiding the wrong.

The state of mind which is inattentive—the mental state of absence of mindfulness—is incapable of laying hold of the right means and of rejecting the wrong means.

When the yogin is not ardent, not clearly comprehending, and not mindful, he does not succeed in accomplishing his object.

MENTAL LASSITUDE = *Inward stagnation. Indolence is the meaning.*

RIGHT MEANS = *Things like the purification of virtue [sīla visodhana].*

After the pointing out of the things that make up the condition connected with the Arousing of Mindfulness through body-contemplation, there is the pointing out of the things that make up the condition which should be abandoned in this practice with the words, "having overcome, in this world, covetousness and grief" = VINEYYA LOKE ABHIJJHĀDOMANASSAM

AROUSING OF MINDFULNESS. *Here bare mindfulness is meant. Therefore, the commentator speaks of* "THE THINGS THAT MAKE UP THE CONDITION CONNECTED WITH THE AROUSING OF MINDFULNESS." *These things are energy and so forth associated necessarily with mindfulness. Condition [Anga] = Reason [Kāraṇa].*

MINDFULNESS *denotes concentration, too, here on account of the inclusion of mindfulness in the aggregate of concentration [samādhikkhandha].*

Or since the exposition is on mindfulness, and as neither the abandoning of defilements nor the attainment of Nibbāna is wrought by mindfulness alone, and as mindfulness does not also occur separately, the pointing out of THE THINGS THAT MAKE UP THE CONDITION CONNECTED WITH THE AROUSING OF MINDFULNESS *is like the pointing out of the condition connected with absorption [jhāna]. Condition [Anga] is a synonym for constituent [avayava]. Initial application, sustained application, interest, joy and one-pointedness of mind are together with absorption as energy and the other qualities are with mindfulness.*

" Having overcome " refers to the discipline of knocking out an evil quality by its opposite good (that is by dealing with each category of evil separately) or through the overcoming of evil part by part [tadangavinaya] and through the disciplining or the overcoming of the passions by suppression in absorption [vikkhambhana vinaya].

Preliminary practice connected with the mundane path of mindfulness is pointed out by the commentator here.

" In this world." In just this body. Here the body [kāya] is the world [loka], in the sense of a thing crumbling.

As covetousness and grief are abandoned in feeling, consciousness, and mental objects, too, the Vibhanga says : " Even the five aggregates of clinging are the world."

Covetousness stands for sensual desire, and grief, for anger. As sensual desire and anger are the principal hindrances the abandoning of the hindrances is stated by the overcoming of covetousness and grief.

With covetousness are abandoned the satisfaction rooted in bodily happiness, delight in the body, and the falling into erroneous opinion which takes as real the unreal beauty, pleasure, permanence and substantiality of the body. With the overcoming of grief are abandoned the discontent rooted in bodily misery, the non-delight in the culture of body-contemplation, and the desire to turn away from facing the real ugliness, suffering, impermanence and insubstantiality of the body.

By the instruction dealing with the overcoming of covetousness and grief yogic power and yogic skill are shown.

Yogic power is the power of meditation. Yogic skill is dexterity in yoking oneself to meditation.

Freedom from satisfaction and discontent in regard to bodily happiness and misery, the forbearing from delighting in the body, the bearing-up of non-delight in the course of body-contemplation, the state of being not captivated by the unreal, and the state of not running away from the real—these—when practised produce yogic power ; and the ability to practise these is yogic skill.

There is another method of interpretation of the passage : (A bhikkhu) lives contemplating the body in the body, ardent, and so forth. " Contemplating " refers to the subject of meditation. " Lives " : lives protecting the subject of meditation which here is the body.

In the passage beginning with "Ardent," Right Exertion [Sammappadhāna] is stated by energy [ātāpa]; the subject of meditation proper in all circumstances [sabbatthika kammaṭṭhāna] or the means of protecting the subject of meditation [kammaṭṭhāna pariharaṇa upāya] is stated by mindfulness and clear comprehension [sati sampajañña]; or the quietude that is obtained [paṭiladdha samatha] by way of the contemplation on the body [kāyānupassanā] is stated by mindfulness; insight [vipassanā] by clear comprehension, and the fruit of inner culture [bhāvanā phala] through the overcoming of covetousness and grief [abhijjhā domanassa vinaya].

The subject of meditation useful in all circumstances is stated by referring to (the laying hold on) mindfulness and clear comprehension because through the force of these two qualities there is the protection of the subject of meditation and suitability of attention for its unbroken practice.

Further, of these two qualities, mindfulness and clear comprehension, the following is stated in the scholium to the Aṭṭhasālinī, Mūla Ṭīkā, "To all who have yoked themselves to the practice of any subject of meditation, to all yogins, these two are things helpful, at all times, for the removal of obstruction and the increase of inner culture."

VEDANĀSU VEDANĀNUPASSĪ......CITTE CITTĀNUPASSĪ......DHAMMESU DHAMMĀNUPASSĪ VIHARATI = "He lives contemplating feelings in the feelings......the consciousness in consciousness......mental objects in mental objects." Here the repetition of "feelings", "consciousness," and "mental objects" should be understood according to the reasons given for the repetition of the word "body" in body-contemplation.

"Feelings" = The three feelings: pleasurable, painful and the neither pleasurable nor painful. These are only mundane.

The word "feelings" is repeated to limit (or unambiguously determine) the object by isolating it [amissato vavatthānaṁ], for the analysis of the apparently compact [ghaṇa vinibbhoga] and for such other purposes, in order to prevent any straying from the contemplation on feelings to some other object. Erratic contemplation takes place because of the connection of the other non-material aggregates with feeling, and because of the dependence of non-material things like feeling on material form in the five-constituent-existence [pañca vokāra bhava] or the sensuous plane of becoming [kāma bhava].

By the repetition of the word, the limiting of the object by isolating it is shown through the pointing out of only a doer of feeling-contemplation in the property called feeling as there is no contemplating of the body or consciousness or mental objects in feeling but only the contemplating of feeling.

As, in this matter of feeling, when a pleasurable feeling occurs, there is no occurrence of the other two, and when a painful feeling or a neither pleasurable nor painful feeling occurs, there is no occurrence of the remaining ones, shown is the analysis (sifting out or penetration or dissection) of the apparently compact, the absence of permanence (or stability), by the pointing out of different feelings, after penetrating them severally and not having spoken of the state of feeling in a general way.

Through the noticing of feelings as lasting just for the measure of a moment in time the seeing of impermanence is made clear. Through the same cognizance, suffering and soullessness too are seen.

FOR THE ANALYSIS OF THE APPARENTLY COMPACT AND FOR SUCH OTHER PURPOSES. *By the words, "And for such other purposes," the following should be understood: "This yogāvacara (the Buddha's disciple who is endeavouring for spiritual insight) contemplates just feelings and not any other thing, because he is not one who contemplates by way of the lovely (the good or the desirable), after the manner of a fool who sees a gem in a bubble of water which has not the quality of a gem. He does not see in this foolish way even in the stable instant when he experiences a pleasant feeling. Much more so does he not stray away into fanciful thinking in regard to the two remaining feelings of pain and indifference. On the other hand, he contemplates along the real way of impermanence, soullessness, and the unlovely, by way of momentary dissolution, lack of power to control (sway or rule), and the trickling of the dirt of defilement, and, distinctively, contemplates suffering, as the pain of vicissitude and of the formations or the constituents of life.*

Consciousness is only mundane; and mundane, too, are mental objects. This statement will be made evident in the analytically expository portion [niddesavāra].

In the way mentioned above should the repetition of words in the contemplation of consciousness and mental objects be explained, too.

ONLY MUNDANE *as connected with the examining of mundane objects of thought in the light of impermanence, suffering and soullessness [sammasana cārassa adhippetattā].*

To be sure, in whatsoever way feeling is to be exclusively contemplated, here, the contemplating in that very way is the meaning of the words: "Contemplating feelings in the feelings." [Kevalaṁ panidha yathā vedanā anupassitabbā tathā anupassanto vedanāsu vedanānupassīti veditabbo]. In the contemplation of consciousness and mental objects too this is the method.

"How should feeling be contemplated upon?" it is asked, further. Pleasurable feeling because it is the stuff of suffering, as suffering. Painful feeling because it is the condition of bringing out trouble and so forth, as a thorn. And the neither pleasurable nor painful feeling, because of non-mastery or dependence and so forth, as transiency.

By the passage beginning with the words " TO BE SURE, IN WHATSOEVER WAY," *the commentator points to the limit of the object (excluding thereby discursive thinking that strays from the reality).*

Accordingly, the Master said :

> Who sees pleasure as suffering,
> Who sees pain as a thorn,
> Who sees as a thing that is fleeting,
> The neutral peace that's shorn
> Of pleasure and pain ; that bhikkhu will,
> Rightly, know ; and live, become still.*

WHO SEES PLEASURE AS SUFFERING = *Who sees feelings by way of the suffering natural to change, with the eye of wisdom.*

WHO SEES PAIN AS A THORN = *Who sees painful feeling as damage causing, piercing in, and as a thing hard to drive out.*

THE NEUTRAL PEACE = *The feeling of indifference is peaceful, owing to the absence of grossness as in states of pain and pleasure and by way of a restful nature.*

Who sees feelings with the thought that they are impermanent, by reason of their becoming non-existent after having come to be, owing to their being characterised by the qualities of arising and passing away, owing to their temporariness, and owing to their being in a state of constant negation, is he who sees the neutral peace of the neither pleasurable nor painful feelings as fleeting, and is indeed the bhikkhu who will rightly know and live, become still.

RIGHTLY = *Correctly.*

KNOW = *know feelings as they are.*

Further, just all feelings should be contemplated with the thought : " These are suffering, indeed."

Suffering is what it is because of the ill natural to the constituents of life [*Sankhāra dukkhatāya dukkhā*].

For this has been said by the Blessed One : " All that is felt is in suffering, I declare [Yaṁ kiñci vedayitaṁ taṁ sabbaṁ dukkhasminti vadāmi]."

ALL THAT IS IN SUFFERING = *Everything experienced is plunged, included, in suffering* [*Sabbantaṁ vedayitaṁ dukkhasmiṁ antogadhaṁ pariyāpannaṁ*], *because the ill natural to the formations, the constituents of life, cannot be conquered* [*sankhāra dukkhatā nātivattanato*].

And pleasure should also be contemplated upon as suffering. All should be explained according as the Arahat-nun Dhammadinnā spake (to her former husband Visākha, in the Cūla Vedalla Sutta of the Majjhima Nikāya): Pleasant feeling, friend Visākha, is agreeable while it lasts and is disagreeable when it changes; painful feeling is disagreeable while it lasts and agreeable when it changes; the neither pleasant nor painful feeling is agreeable when there is a knowledge of its existence and disagreeable when that knowledge is wanting.

The three feelings should be contemplated upon as pleasant and painful. When the first occurs, the second changes and the third is known, then, feeling is pleasant. When the first changes, the second occurs and the third is not known, then, feeling is painful.

The feelings should also be seen according to the seven contemplations beginning with that of impermanence, mentioned above.

The remaining division beginning with the worldly and spiritual feelings in the classification of pleasurable feeling and so forth, in feeling-contemplation, will become clear in the analytical exposition [niddesavāra].

Consciousness and mental objects, too, should be contemplated upon by way of the diversity of the divisions of object [ārammaṇa], dominance [adhipati], conascence [sahājāta], plane [bhūmi], causal action [kamma], result [vipāka], non-causative functional process [kriyā], and so forth [ādi], beginning with impermanence [aniccādīnaṁ anupassanānaṁ vasena] and by way of the division of consciousness that is with passion and so forth come down in the portion of analytical exposition [niddesavāre āgata sarāgādi bhedañca vasena].

OF THE DIVISIONS OF OBJECT......NON-CAUSATIVE FUNCTIONAL PROCESS AND SO FORTH. *Contemplation should be done by way of the division of the blue and so forth pertaining to the variety of objects visual and so forth [rūpādi arammaṇanānattassa nīlādi tabbhedassa]; by way of the division of the "low" and so forth pertaining to the diverse kinds of dominance of the will-to-do and so forth [chandādi adhipati nānattassa hīnādi tabbhedassā]; by way of the division of the spontaneous and non-spontaneous consciousness, absorption with initial application and so forth pertaining to the variety of conditions of conascence of knowledge, absorption and so forth [ñāṇa jhānādi nānattassa sasankhārikāsankhārika savitakkādi tabbhedassa]; by way of the division of lofty, middling, and so forth pertaining to the diverse planes, sensuous and so forth [kāmāvacarādi bhūminānattassa ukkaṭṭha majjhimādi tabbhedassa]; by way of the division of conduciveness to deva-plane-rebirth and so forth pertaining to the diverse kinds of moral action of skill and so forth [kusalādi kammanānattassa devagati saṁvattanīyatādi tabbhedassa]; by way of the division of the state of requital which could be perceived in this very present condition of life and so forth pertaining to the variety of dark and bright resultants of evil and good deeds [kaṇha sukka vipāka nānattassa diṭṭha dhamma vedanīyatādi tabbhedassa]; by way of the division of the three good conditions of rebirth and so forth pertaining to non-causative functional diversity of the sensuous plane and so forth [paritta bhūmakādi kriyā nānattassa tihetukādi tabbhedassa].*

Mental objects should be contemplated upon by way of own characteristic [salakkhaṇa] *of impression and the like [phusanādi];* by way of general characteristic [sāmañña lakkhaṇa] *of impermanence and the like [anicctādi];* by way of phenomenon-emptiness [suññata dhamma], *namely, by way of the void-nature called soullessness [anattatā sankhāta suññatā sabhāvassa] to explain which clearly the instruction of the portion dealing with the void in the Abhidhamma proceeded by means of the statement beginning with "At that time indeed there are phenomeṇa, there are aggregates [yaṁ vibhāvetuṁ Abhidhamme tasmiṁ kho pana samaye dhammā honti khandhā hontīti ādinā suññatāvāra desanā pavattā],* without any mention of a soul; by way of the seven contemplations of impermanence and so forth [aniccādi satta anupassanānaṁ]; and by way of the divisions of what is present and what is absent and so forth in the analytical portion [niddesavāre āgata santāsantādi bhedānañca vasena].

If, in the yogāvacara's body called the world, covetousness and grief are abandoned, in the worlds of his feelings and so forth too these are abandoned *owing to the earlier abandoning of these by the yogin* [kāmañcettha kāyasankhāte loke abhijjhā domanassaṁ pahīnaṁ vedanadi lokesu pi taṁ pahīnameva *pubbe pahīnattā*].

Still, everywhere, the abandoning of the defilements has been stated by way of the different types of persons and by way of the diversity of the thought-unit in which the development of the different subjects of the Arousing of Mindfulness takes place [nānā puggalavasena pana nānā cittakkhaṇika satipaṭṭhāna bhāvanāvasena ca sabbattha vuttaṁ]. Or it should be understood thus: It is stated in this manner in order to indicate that the abandoning of the defilements in one object implies the abandoning of the defilements in the remaining objects.

Therefore, it is not fit to speak again of the abandoning of these; for while the defilements are abandoned, they are not abandoned separately in one object after another i.e. the defilements pertaining to the body, for instance, are not first abandoned and then those belonging to the feelings and so forth, in succession, but the defilements of all objects are abandoned when the defilements are abandoned in one object.

That is due to the fact that only the defilements which can arise in the future are capable of being abandoned through the scorching out of the causes by the attainment of the Path or through measures that make the causes temporarily impotent, because of the observance of virtue and the development of absorption. Past defilements and those arising in the present are beyond the scope of abandoning.

The abandoning of the defilements of one object in the thought-unit of the Path is verily the abandoning of the defilements of all objects.

It is right to say that by the Path verily are the defilements abandoned.

The abandoning of the defilements of one person is not necessarily the abandoning of the defilements of another person [nahi ekassa pahīnaṁ tato aññassa pahīnaṁ nāma hoti]. Reference to the different types of persons is made to point this fact of possible difference of method by way of object.

THE DIVERSITY OF THE THOUGHT-UNIT. *The mundane thought-unit is meant as the preliminary path is dealt with here.*

What is abandoned temporarily by mundane meditation in the body is not suppressed in the feelings and the other objects.

Even if covetousness and grief should not occur in the feelings and the other objects, when it is suppressed in the body, it should not be stated that owing to efficient rejection by meditation opposed to covetousness and grief, there is no covetousness and grief in the other objects such as feelings and in the case of suppression by meditation, therefore, it is fit to speak of the rejection of covetousness and grief again in feeling and the other objects.

The defilements abandoned in one object are abandoned in the remaining objects too [ekattha pahīnaṁ sesesu pi pahīnaṁ hoti]. This statement refers to the supramundane meditation of Mindfulness-arousing. In the case of mundane meditation the rejection is stated everywhere with reference to bare non-occurrence of the defilements [lokiya bhāvanāya sabbattha appavatti mattaṁ sandhāya vuttaṁ].

In regard to the four objects of contemplation through the Arousing of Mindfulness, it is said in the Vibhanga thus: Even the Five Aggregates are the world [Pañca pi Khandhā lokoti hi Vibhange catūsu pi ṭhānesu vuttanti].

THE CONTEMPLATION OF THE BODY

THE SECTION ON BREATHING

Now the Blessed One desirous of bringing about diverse kinds of attainments of distinction in beings by the Discourse on the Arousing of Mindfulness began to teach the analytically explanatory portion [niddesavāra] with the words: "And how, o bhikkhus."

He did that after dividing into four the one mindfulness that is right [ekameva sammāsatiṁ] by way of the contemplation on the body, on feelings, on consciousness and mental objects.

The Blessed One's exposition of the Arousing of Mindfulness is similar to the action of a worker in mat and basket weaving who wishing to make coarse and fine mats, boxes, cases and the like should make those goods after getting a mammoth bamboo, splitting it into four, and reducing each of the parts to strips.

IDHA BHIKKHAVE BHIKKHU = "Here, o bhikkhus, a bhikkhu."

"Here". In this Dispensation of the Buddha which provides the basis for the person producing body-contemplation in all modes. By the word "here" dispensations other than the Buddha's are excluded as they do not teach body-contemplation in the complete way it is taught in the Buddhadhamma. For this is said: "Here is the recluse; untenanted by recluses are the other, opposing ways of thought."

THE PERSON PRODUCING BODY-CONTEMPLATION IN ALL MODES. *As sects outside the Buddha's Dispensation also produce a part of this contemplation, by these words, the Buddha-sāvaka's complete knowledge or all-round grasp of this contemplation, when it is practised by him, is told.*

ARAÑÑAGATO VĀ......SUÑÑĀGĀRAGATO VĀ = "Gone to the forest......or to an empty place." By this there is the making clear of the getting of an abode appropriate to the yogāvacara for the culture of mindfulness.

The mind of the yogāvacara which for a long time (before he became a recluse) had dwelt on visual and other objects does not like to enter the road of meditation and just like a wild young bull yoked to a cart runs off the road.

A neat-herd wishing to tame a wild calf nourished entirely on the milk of a wild cow ties that calf, after leading it away from the cow, to a stout post firmly sunk in the ground, at a spot set apart for it. That calf, having jumped hither and thither, and finding it impossible to run away from there, will crouch down or lie down at that very post. Even so must the bhikkhu who is desirous of taming the wild mind nourished long on the tasty drink of visible and other objects tie that mind to the post of the object of mindfulness-arousing with the rope of remembrance, after leading the mind from visible and other objects and ushering it into a forest, to the foot of a tree or into an empty place. The mind of the bhikkhu will also jump hither and thither. Not obtaining the objects it had long grown used to, and finding it impossible to break the rope of remembrance and run away, it will finally sit or lie down at that very object by way of partial and full absorption. Therefore, the men of old said :

> As one who wants to break a wild young calf
> Would tether it to stout stake firmly, here,
> In that same way the yogi should tie fast
> To meditation's object his own mind.

In this way this abode becomes appropriate to the yogāvacara. Therefore, it is said, " This (namely, the passage beginning with the words, ' Gone to the forest......') is the making clear of an abode appropriate to the yogāvacara for the culture of mindfulness."

Because the subject of meditation of mindfulness on in and out breathing is not easy to accomplish without leaving the neighbourhood of a village, owing to sound, which is a thorn to absorption, and because in a place not become a township it is easy for the yogāvacara to lay hold of this subject of meditation, the Blessed One pointing out the abode suitable for that spoke the words, " Gone to the forest," and so forth.

The Buddha is like a master of the science of building sites [vatthu vijjācariya] *because of the pointing out by him of the suitable abode for yogis* [*yogīnaṁ anurūpa nivāsaṭṭhānupadissanato*].

As a master in the science of selecting building sites, after seeing a stretch of ground good for building a town, and after considering it well from all sides, advises : " Build the town here, " and when the building of the town is happily completed receives high honour from the royal family, so the Buddha having well considered from all points the abode suitable for the yogāvacara advises : " Here, should the subject of meditation be yoked on to. " When saintship is gradually reached by the yogin, by the expression of the yogin's gratitude and admiration with the words : " Certainly, the Blessed One is the Supremely Awakened One," the Master receives great honour.

This bhikkhu, indeed, is comparable to a leopard *because like the leopard he lives alone, in the forest, and accomplishes his aim, by overcoming those contrary to him, namely, the passions.*

Just as a great king of leopards concealed in the forest in grass-bush, jungle-bush or hill-thicket, seizes wild buffaloes, elks, pigs and other beasts, this bhikkhu yoking himself to the subject of meditation gains the Four Real Paths and Fruits [Cattāro Magge ceva Ariya Phalāni gaṇhāti], one after another, in succession ; and therefore the men of old said :

As leopard in ambush lies and captures beasts,
So does this son of the Awakened One,
The striving man, the man of vision keen,
Having into the forest gone seize therein
Fruition that verily is supreme.

And so the Blessed One pointing out the forest-abode, the fit place for speedy exertion in the practice of meditation, said : " Gone to the forest " and so forth.

NISĪDATI PALLANKAṀ ĀBHUJITVĀ UJUṀ KĀYAṀ PAṆIDHĀYA PARIMUKHAṀ SATIṀ UPAṬṬHAPETVĀ SO SATOVA ASSASATI SATO PASSASATI = " Sits down, bends in his legs crosswise on his lap, keeps his body erect, and arouses mindfulness in the object of meditation, namely, the breath which is in front of him. Mindful he breathes in and mindful he breathes out."

" Bends in his legs crosswise on his lap." Three things pertaining to the sitting posture of the yogin are pointed out by that : Firmness of the posture ; easefulness of breathing due to the posture ; and the expediency of the posture for laying hold of the subject of meditation.

One sits in this posture having locked in the legs. It is the entirely thigh-bound sitting posture and is known as the lotus and the immovable posture too.

" Keeps his body erect." Keeps the vertebrae in such a position that every segment of the backbone is said to be placed upright, and end to end throughout. The body waist upwards is held straight.

"Arouses mindfulness in front." Fixes the attention by directing it towards the breath which is in front.

" Mindful he breathes in and mindful he breathes out." Breathes in and out without abandoning mindfulness.

DĪGHAṀ VĀ ASSASANTO DĪGHAṀ ASSASĀMĪTI PAJĀNĀTI DĪGHAṀ VĀ PASSASANTO DĪGHAṀ PASSASĀMĪTI PAJĀNĀTI : = "He, thinking, 'I breathe in long,' understands when he is breathing in long ; or thinking, 'I breathe out long,' he understands when he is breathing out long."

"When breathing in long, how does he understand, 'I breathe in long,'? When breathing out long, how does he understand, 'I breathe out long'? He breathes in a long breath during a long stretch of time, he breathes out a long breath during a long stretch of time, and he breathes in and he breathes out long breaths, each during a long stretch of time. As he breathes in and breathes out long breaths, each during a long stretch of time, desire [chanda] arises in him. With desire he breathes in a long breath finer than the last during a long stretch of time ; with desire he breathes out a long breath finer than the last during a long stretch of time ; and with desire he breathes in and he breathes out long breaths finer than the last, each during a long stretch of time. As with desire he breathes in and he breathes out long breaths finer than the last, each during a long stretch of time, joy [pīti] arises in him. With joy he breathes in a long breath finer than the last during a long stretch of time ; with joy he breathes out a long breath finer than the last during a long stretch of time ; and with joy he breathes in and he breathes out long breaths finer than the last, each during a long stretch of time. As with joy he breathes in and he breathes out long breaths finer than the last, each during a long stretch of time, the mind turns away from the long in-and-out-breathings, and equanimity [upekkhā] stands firm."

"SABBAKĀYAPAṬISAṀVEDI ASSASISSĀMI......PASSASISSĀMĪTI SIKKHATI = "Experiencing the whole body I shall breathe in......breathe out, thinking thus, he trains himself." He trains himself with the following idea : I shall breathe in making known, making clear, to myself the beginning, middle and end of the whole body of breathings in ; I shall breathe out making known, making clear, to myself the beginning middle and end of the whole body of breathings out. And he breathes in and breathes out with consciousness associated with knowledge making known, making clear, to himself the breaths."

"To one bhikkhu, indeed, in the tenuous diffused body of in-breathing or body of out-breathing only the beginning becomes clear ; not the middle or the end. He is able to lay hold of only the beginning. In the middle and at the end he is troubled. To another the middle becomes clear and not the beginning or the end. To a third only the end becomes clear. The beginning and the middle do not become clear and he is able only to lay hold of the breath at the end. He is troubled at the beginning and at the middle. To a fourth even all the three stages become clear and he is able to lay hold of all ; he is troubled nowhere. For pointing out that this subject of meditation should be developed after the manner of the fourth one, the Master said : Experienceing......he trains himself.

" Since in the earlier way of the practice of this meditation there should be nothing else done but just breathing in and breathing out it is said : He thinking, I breathe in......understands......and since thereafter there should be endeavour for bringing about knowledge and so forth, it is said, Experiencing the whole body I shall breathe in."

" PASSAMBHAYAṀ KĀYASANKHĀRAṀ ASSASISSĀMĪTI......PASSASISSĀMĪTI SIKKHATI = " Calming the activity of the body I shall breathe in......breathe out, thinking, thus, he trains himself." He thinks : I shall breathe in and I shall breathe out, quieting, making smooth, making tranquil and peaceful the activity of the in-and-out-breathing body. And in that way, he trains himself."

" In this connection coarseness, fineness, and calm should be understood thus : Without contêmplative effort, the body and the mind of this bhikkhu are distressed, coarse. When the body and the mind are coarse, the in-and-out-breathings too are coarse and proceed uncalmly ; the nasal aperture becomes inadequate and he has to breathe through the mouth too. But when the body and the mind are under control then the body and the mind become placid, restful. When these are restful, the breathings proceed so fine that the bhikkhu doubts whether or not the breathings are going on."

" The breathing of a man who runs down from a hill, puts down a heavy burden from his head, and stands is coarse ; his nasal aperture becomes inadequate and he breathes through the mouth, too. But when he rids himself of his fatigue, takes a bath, and a drink of water and puts a wet cloth over his heart and is sitting in the shade, his breathing becomes fine and he is at a loss to know whether it exists or not. Comparable to that man is the bhikkhu whose breaths become so fine after the taking up of the practice of contemplation that he finds it difficult to say whether he is breathing or not. What is the reason for this? Without taking up the practice of meditation he does not perceive, concentrate on, reflect on or think over the question of calming the gross activity of the breathing body, the breaths, but with the practice of meditation he does.

Therefore, the activity of the breath-body becomes finer in the time in which meditation is practised than in the time in which there is no practice. So the men of old said :

In the agitated mind and body the breath is of the coarsest [kind
In the unexcited body, fully, subtle does it wind."

" How does he train himself with the thought : Calming the activity of the body, I shall breathe in......breathe out ? What are the activities of the body ? Those things of the body of breaths, those things bound up with that body, are the activities of the body. Causing the body-activities to become composed, to become smooth and calm, he trains himself......He trains himself thinking thus : Calming the body-activity by way of (quieting) the bodily activities of bending forwards, sidewards, all over, and backwards, and (by way of the quieting of) the moving, quivering, vibrating, and quaking of the body, I shall breathe in......I shall breathe out. I shall breathe in and I shall breathe out, calming the activity of the body, by way of whatsoever peaceful and fine body-activities of non-bending of the body forwards, sidewards, all over and backwards, of non-moving, non-quivering, non-vibrating, and non-quaking of the body.*

Indeed, to that yogin training in respiration-mindfulness according to the method taught thus : " He, thinking ' I breathe in long,' understands when he is breathing in long...... Calming the activity of the body......I breathe out, thinking thus, he trains himself " [Dīghaṁ vā assasanto dīghaṁ assasāmīti pajānāti......passambhayaṁ kāyasankhāraṁ passasissāmīti sikkhati], the four absorptions [cattāri jhānāni] arise in the respiration sign [assāsapassāsa nimitte uppajjanti].

In the respiration sign = In the reflex image [paṭibhāga nimitta].

Having emerged from the absorption, he lays hold of either the respiration body or the factors of absorption.

There the yogāvacara-worker in respiration [assāsapassāsa kammika] examines the body (rūpa) thinking thus : Supported by what is respiration ? Supported by the basis [vatthunissita]. The basis is the coarse body [karaja kāya]. The coarse body is composed of the Four Great Primaries and the corporeality derived from these [cattāri mahābhūtāni upādarūpañca].

The worker in respiration examines the respirations while devoting himself to the development of insight through the means of corporeality.

The basis, namely, the coarse body, is where the mind and mental characteristics occur.

Thereupon, he, the worker in respiration, cognizes the mind (nāma) in the pentad of mental concomitants beginning with sense-impression.

The five beginning with sense-impression are sense-impression, feeling, perception, volition and consciousness. They are taken here as representative of mind.

The worker in respiration examines the mind and the body, sees the Dependent Origination of ignorance and so forth, and concluding that this mind and this body are bare conditions and things produced from conditions and that besides these there is neither a living being nor a person becomes to that extent a person who transcends doubt.

BESIDES THESE PHENOMENA THERE IS NEITHER A LIVING BEING NOR A PERSON *refers to vision that is purified* [*añño satto vā puggalo natthīti visuddhi diṭṭhi*].

Mind-and-body is a bare impersonal process. It is not unrelated to a cause and also not related to a discordant cause (which is fictive) like GOD, but is connected with (the really perceivable fact of) a cause like IGNORANCE [*Tayidaṁ dhammamattaṁ na ahetukaṁ nāpi issariyādi visamahetukaṁ atha kho avijjādīhi eva sahetukaṁ*].

A PERSON WHO HAS TRANSCENDED DOUBT *regarding the past, the future and the present (of his own existence and so forth as for instance taught in the Sabbāsava Sutta of the Majjhima Nikāya).*

And the yogi who has transcended doubt while growing insight applies the three characteristics of impermanence, suffering and soullessness to the mind and body together with the conditions and gradually reaches sainthood [sappacaya nāma rūpe tilakkhaṇaṁ āropetvā vipassanaṁ vaḍḍhento anukkamena arahattaṁ pāpuṇāti].

APPLIES THE THREE CHARACTERISTICS *in order to grasp the qualities of the aggregates according to the method taught in the Anatta Lakkhaṇa Sutta of the Saṁyutta Nikāya beginning with the words:* "WHATSOEVER FORM."

The worker in absorption, namely, he who contemplates upon the factors of absorption, also, thinks thus: Supported by what are these factors of absorption? By the basis. The basis is the coarse body. The factors of absorption are here representative of the mind. The coarse body is the body. Having determined thus, he, searching for the reason of the mind and the body, sees it in Conditions' Mode beginning with ignorance, concludes that this mind and the body comprise just conditions and things produced by conditions and that besides these there is neither a living being nor a person, and becomes to that extent a person who transcends doubt.

And the yogi who transcends doubt thus, while growing insight, applies the three characteristics of impermanence, suffering and soullessness to the mind and the body together with conditions and gradually reaches sainthood.

ITI AJJHATTAṀ VĀ KĀYE KĀYĀNUPASSĪ VIHARATI = " Thus he lives contemplating the body in the body internally." This bhikkhu dwells in contemplation of the body in his own respiration body.

By way of the practice of quietude [samatha bhāvanā] however there is no arising of the sign of full absorption [appanā nimittuppatti] in another's respiration-body.

BAHIDDHĀ VĀ KĀYE KĀYĀNUPASSĪ VIHARATI = " Or he lives contemplating the body in the body externally." Or this bhikkhu dwells in contemplation of the body in another's respiration-body.

OR......IN ANOTHER'S RESPIRATION-BODY. *This portion deals with reflection for the growth of insight and has no reference to the growth of full absorption of quietude...*

AJJHATTA BAHIDDHĀ VĀ KĀYE KĀYĀNUPASSĪ VIHARATI = " Or he lives contemplating the body in the body internally and externally." At one time in his own and at another in another's respiration-body he dwells in contemplation of the body. By this there is reference to the time when the yogi's mind moves repeatedly back and forth (internally and externally by way of object) without laying aside the familiar subject of meditation [Kālena attano kālena parassa assāsapassāsakāye etenassa paguṇakammaṭṭhānaṁ aṭṭhapetvā sañcaraṇa kālo kathito].

WITHOUT LAYING ASIDE *at intervals or from time to time or occasionally [antarantarā na ṭhapetvā].*

THE TIME WHEN THE......MIND MOVES REPEATEDLY BACK AND FORTH. *Or the time when the meditation proceeds incessantly, in the internal and external phenomena [Ajjhatta bahiddhā dhammesu pi nirantaraṁ vā bhāvanāya pavattana kālo].*

Both cannot occur at once [Eka kāle pana idaṁ ubhayaṁ na labbhati].

This pair of things stated in combination as internal and external cannot be found in the form of an object at one time, simultaneously. It is not possible to objectify (these two) together is the meaning. [Ajjhattaṁ bahiddhāti ca vuttaṁ idaṁ dhammadvayaghaṭitaṁ, ekasmiṁ kāle, ekato ārammaṇabhāvena na labbhati. Ekajjhaṁ ālambituṁ na sakkāti attho].

SAMUDAYA DHAMMĀNUPASSĪ VĀ KĀYASMIṀ VIHARATI = " He lives contemplating origination-things in the body." Just as the air moves back and forth depending on the smith's bellows' skin, the bellows' spout, and appropriate effort, so, depending on the coarse body, nasal aperture and the mind of the bhikkhu, the respiration-body moves back and forth. The things beginning with the (coarse) body are origination [Kāyādayo dhammā samudayo]. The person who sees thus is he who lives contemplating origination-things in the body.

VAYA DHAMMĀNUPASSĪ VĀ KĀYASMIṀ VIHARATI = " Or he lives contemplating dissolution-things in the body." In whatever way, the air does not proceed when the bellows' skin is taken off, the bellows' spout is broken, and the appropriate exertion is absent, even in that same way, when the body breaks up, the nasal aperture is destroyed, and the mind has ceased to function, the respiration-body does not go on. Thus through the ending of the coarse body, the nasal aperture and the mind there comes to be the ending of the respirations [kāyādi nirodhā assāsapassāsa nirodho]. The person who sees in this way is he who lives contemplating dissolution-things in the body.

SAMUDAYA VAYA DHAMMĀNUPASSĪ VĀ KĀYASMIṀ VIHARATI = " Or he lives contemplating origination-and-dissolution-things in the body." He lives contemplating origination at one time and dissolution at another [Kālena samudayaṁ kālena vayaṁ anupassanto].

ORIGINATION [*Samudaya*] *is that from which suffering arises.*

CONTEMPLATING ORIGINATION-THINGS. *Possessing the character of contemplation connected with the coarse body, the nasal aperture and the mind, the cause of the respirations* [*assāsapassāsānaṁ uppatti hetu karaja kāyādi tassa anupassanasīlo*].

As the contemplation on origination-and-dissolution-things, too, is split up as regards the scope of the object, it is not possible to objectify both origination and dissolution at the same time.

ATTHI KĀYOTI VĀ PANASSA SATI PACCUPAṬṬHITĀ HOTI = " Or, indeed, his mindfulness is established, with the thought : 'The body exists.' " Mindfulness is established for the yogin through careful scrutiny. He thinks : There is the body, but there is no being, no person, no woman, no man, no soul, nothing pertaining to a soul, no " I ", nothing that is mine, no one, and nothing belonging to anyone [Kāyoti ca atthi, na satto, na puggalo, na itthi, na puriso, na attā, na attaniyaṁ nāhaṁ, na mama, na koci, na kassacīti evaṁ assa sati paccupaṭṭhitā hoti].

YĀVADEVA = "To the extent necessary." It denote purpose.

This is said : The mindfulness established is not for another purpose. What is the purpose for which it is established ?

ÑĀṆAMATTĀYA PATISSATIMATTĀYA = "For just knowledge and remembrance." That is just for the sake of a wider and wider, or further and further measure of knowledge, and of mindfulness [aparāparaṁ uttaruttari ñāṇapamāṇatthāya ceva satipamānatthāya]. For the increase of mindfulness and clear comprehension is the meaning.

For the purpose of reaching the knowledge of body-contemplation to the highest extent [Kāyānupassanā ñāṇaṁ param pamāṇaṁ pāpanatthāya] is the meaning of: To the extent necessary for just knowledge [Yāvadeva ñāṇamattāya].

ANISSITO CA VIHARATI = "And he lives independent." He lives emancipated from dependence on craving and wrong views.

With these words is stated the direct opposition of this meditation to the laying hold on craving and wrong views.

NA CA KIÑCI LOKE UPĀDIYATI = "And clings to naught in the world." In regard to no visible shape......or consciousness, does he think : this is my soul ; or this belongs to my soul.

EVAMPI = "Thus also".

With this expression ("Thus also") the Blessed One wound up the instruction on the section on breathing.

In this section on breathing, the mindfulness which examines the respirations is the Truth of Suffering. The pre-craving which brings about that mindfulness is the Truth of Origination. The non-occurrence of both is the Truth of Cessation. The Real Path which understands suffering, abandons origination, and objectifies cessation is the Truth of the Way. Thus having endeavoured by way of the Four Truths, a person arrives at peace. This is the portal to emancipation of the bhikkhu devoted to meditation on breathing.

THE SECTION ON THE MODES OF DEPORTMENT

The Buddha, after dealing in the aforesaid manner with body-contemplation in the form of respiration-meditation, in detail, said : "And further," in order to deal exhaustively with body-contemplation, here, according to the meditation on the modes of deportment [iriyāpatha].

GACCHANTO VĀ GACCHĀMĪTI PAJĀNĀTI = "When he is going (a bhikkhu) understands: 'I am going'." In this matter of going, readily do dogs, jackals and the like, know when they move on that they are moving. But this instruction on the modes of deportment was not given concerning similar awareness, because awareness of that sort belonging to animals does not shed the belief in a living being, does not knock out the percept of a soul and neither becomes a subject of meditation nor the development of the Arousing of Mindfulness.

GOING. *This term is applicable both to the awareness of the fact of moving on and to the knowledge of the (true) characteristic qualities of moving on. The terms sitting, standing and lying down, too, are applicable in the general sense of awareness and in the particular sense of knowledge of the (true) characteristic qualities. Here (in this discourse) the particular and not the general sense of awareness is to be taken.*

From the sort of mere awareness denoted by reference to canines and the like proceeds the idea of a soul, the perverted perception, with the belief that there is a doer and an experiencer. One who does not uproot or remove that wrong perception owing to non-opposition to that perception and to absence of contemplative practice cannot be called one who makes become anything like a subject of meditation.

But the knowledge of this yogāvacara sheds the belief in a living being, knocks out the idea of a soul, and is both a subject of meditation and the development of the Arousing of Mindfulness.

Indeed, who goes, whose going is it, on what account is this going? These words refer to the knowledge of the (act of) going (the mode of deportment) of the meditating bhikkhu.

In the elucidation of these questions the following is said: Who goes? No living being or person whatsoever. Whose going is it? Not the going of any living being or person. On account of what does the going take place? On account of the diffusion of the process of oscillation born of mental activity. Because of that this yogi knows thus: If there arises the thought, "I shall go," that thought produces the process of oscillation; the process of oscillation produces expression (the bodily movement which indicates going and so forth). The moving on of the whole body through the diffusion of the process of oscillation is called going. The same is the method of exposition as regards the other postures: standing and so forth. There, too, the yogi knows thus: If there arises the thought: "I shall stand," that thought produces the process of oscillation. The process of oscillation produces bodily expression. The raising upright of the whole body from below owing to the diffusion of the process of oscillation is called standing. If there arises the thought "I shall sit," that thought produces the process of oscillation. The process of oscillation produces bodily expression. The bending of the lower part of the body and the raising upright of the upper part of the body owing to the diffusion of the process of oscillation is called sitting. If there arises the thought, "I shall lie down," that thought produces the process of oscillation. The process of oscillation produces bodily expression. The straightening or the spreading of the whole body horizontally or across, owing to the diffusion of the process of oscillation, is called lying down.

There, WHO GOES? *is a doer-question of the action of going, without first separating efficient cause and action [Tattha ko gacchatīti sādhanaṁ kriyañca avinibbhuttaṁ katvā gamana kriyā kattu pucchā]. That is for indicating just the bare phenomenon of going, through the condition of denying the-doer-state-endowed-with-a-soul [Sā kattu bhāva visiṭṭha atta paṭikkhepattā dhammamattasseva gamana dassanato]. (Or in other words the question "Who goes?" anticipates a negative answer, for according to the Abhidhamma there is no doer or goer but just a process dependent on conditions. There is merely a going. No one goes.)*

With the words, WHOSE GOING IS IT? *the commentator says the same thing in another way after separating efficient cause and action for making clear the absence of a doer-connection [Kassa gamananti tamevatthaṁ pariyāyantarena vadati sādhanaṁ kriyañca akattu sambandhi bhāva vibhāvanato].*

ON WHAT ACCOUNT IS IT? *This is a question seeking for the real reason of the action of going from which the idea of a goer is rejected. [Kiṁ kāraṇāti pana paṭikkhitta kattukāya gamana kriyāya aviparīta kāraṇa pucchā].*

*Going is here shown to be one of the particular modes of bare phenomenal movement due to appropriate cause-and-condition, without attributing it to a fallacious reason such as the one formulated thus: The soul comes into contact with the mind, the mind with the sense-organs and the sense-organs with the object (thus there is perception). [Idañhi gamanaṁ nāma attā manasā saṁyujjati mano indriyehi indriyāni atthehīti evamādi micchā kāraṇa vinimutta anurūpa paccaya hetuko dhammānaṁ pavatti ākāra viseso].**

NO LIVING BEING OR PERSON *because of the proving of the going of only a bare phenomenon and because of the absence of anyone besides that phenomenon. Now to show proof of the going of a bare phenomenon the words beginning with* ON ACCOUNT OF THE DIFFUSION OF THE PROCESS OF OSCILLATION BORN OF MENTAL ACTIVITY *were spoken by the commentator [Dhammamattasseva gamanasiddhito tabbinimuttassa ca kassaci abhāvato idāni dhammamattasseva gamana siddhiṁ dassetuṁ citta kriyā vāyo dhātu vipphārenāti ādi vuttaṁ].*

There mental activity and the diffusion and agitation in the process of oscillation which is mental activity = diffusion of the process of mental activity [Tattha citta kriyā ca vipphāro vipphandanañcāti citta kriyā vāyo dhātu vipphāro]. The commentator, by mentioning mental activity, eschews the diffusion of the process of oscillation connected with inanimate things, and by the mention of the diffusion of the process of oscillation eschews the class of mental activity producing volitional verbal-expression. By the terms mental activity and the process of oscillation, the commentator makes clear bodily expression [Tena ettha ca citta kriyāggahāṇena anindriyabaddha vāyo dhātu vipphāraṁ nivatteti; vāyodhātu vipphāraggahāṇena cetanā vacīviññatti bhedaṁ citta kriyaṁ nivatteti. Ubhayena pana kāya viññattiṁ vibhāveti].

PRODUCES THE PROCESS OF OSCILLATION. *Brings about the group of materiality with the quality of oscillation in excess.*

This group of materiality is that of the pure octad consisting of the Four Great Primaries [Mahābhūta] symbolized by earth, water, fire and air, and the four derived from these: colour, smell, taste and nutritive essence. [paṭhavī āpo tejo vāyo vaṇṇa gandha rasa ojā].

EXCESS *is to be taken here by way of capability (adequacy or competency) and not by way of measure (size or amount).*

THE PROCESS OF OSCILLATION PRODUCES EXPRESSION. *This was said concerning the process of oscillation arisen from the thought of going. This process is a condition to the supporting with energy, the bearing up, and the movement of the conascent body of materiality.*

EXPRESSION *is that change which takes place together with the intention.*

OSCILLATION *is mentioned by way of a predominant condition [adhika bhāva] and not by way of production through oscillation alone. Otherwise the state of derived materiality pertaining to expression would not be a fact [aññathā viññattiyā upādāya rūpa bhāvo durūpapādo siyā].*

He who knows (that by the diffusion of this process of oscillation born of mental activity take place going, standing, sitting and lying down) pursues the line of thinking (called investigation) in the following manner: "A living being goes," "A living being stands," (according to the false belief of those unacquainted with the reality of the matter or according to conventional speech) but truly there is no living being going or standing. This talk of a living being going or standing is similar to speech in the following way: "A cart goes." "A cart stands." In fact there is no going cart and no standing cart. When with bulls (tied to a cart) a skilful driver is driving, one conventionally speaking says: "A cart goes" or "A cart stands." In the sense of a thing not able to go of itself the body is like the cart.

Mind-born oscillations are like the bulls. Mind is like the driver. When the thought, " I go," or the thought " I stand," arises, the process of oscillation producing expression comes to existence. By the diffusion of the process of oscillation born of mental activity, going and the other modes of deportment take place and then there are these forms of conventional speech : " A living being goes," " A living being stands." " I go." " I stand." Therefore the commentator said :

> Just as a ship goes on by winds' impelled,
> Just as a shaft goes by the bowstring's force,
> So goes this body in its forward course
> Full driven by the vibrant thrust of air.
> As to the puppet's back the dodge-thread's tied
> So to the body-doll the mind is joined
> And pulled by that the body moves, stands, sits.
> Where is the living being that can stand,
> Or walk, by force of its own inner strength,
> Without conditions that give it support ?

Accordingly this yogi who considers by way of causes and conditions, the states of going, standing and so forth knows well that he is going, when he is in the state of going, that he is standing when he stands, that he is sitting when he sits, and that he is lying down when he lies down, as it is told in the passage in the discourse beginning with the words : " When he is going, a bhikkhu understands : ' I am going. ' "

YATHĀ YATHĀ VĀ PANASSA KĀYO PAṆIHITO HOTI TATHĀ TATHĀ NAṀ PAJĀNĀTI = " Or just as his body is disposed so he understands it."

ITI AJJHATTAṀ VĀ = " Thus internally." In this way the bhikkhu lives contemplating the body in the body, examining his own four modes of deportment.

BAHIDDHĀ VĀ = " Or externally." Or examining the four modes of deportment of another.

AJJHATTA BAHIDDHĀ VĀ = " Or internally and externally." Or examining at one time his own four modes of deportment and at another time another's four modes of deportment, he lives.

SAMUDAYA DHAMMĀNUPASSĪ = " Contemplating origination-things." Also dissolution-things are included here. Origination and dissolution should be dwelt upon by way of the fivefold method beginning with the words : " He, thinking, 'the origination of materiality comes to be through the origination of ignorance,' in the sense of the origin of conditions, sees the arising of the aggregate of materiality."

In the same way he sees the arising of the aggregate of materiality through the origination of craving, karma, and food, in the sense of the origin of conditions, and also while seeing the sign of birth [nibbatti lakkhana passanto pi]. He sees the passing away of the aggregate while thinking that the dissolution of materiality comes to be through the dissolution of ignorance, in the sense of the dissolution of conditions, and through the dissolution of craving, karma and food, in the same way, and while seeing the sign of vicissitude [vipariṇāmalakkhaṇa].

For the arising of the materiality-aggregate ignorance, craving, karma, and food are the principal reasons. But these are not all. As it is said that one sees the arising of the materiality-aggregate when beholding also the rebirth-sign or the bare origination state called the integration-succession [upacaya santati] of the various material forms [rūpa] becoming manifest in the conscious flux [saviññānaka santāna], owing to ignorance, craving karma, and nutriment, and from consciousness [citta] and the process of caloricity [utu], the knowledge of arising is fivefold.

Similarly the knowledge of passing away or ceasing is fivefold. The sign of vicissitude or change is the bare state of dissolution [bhanga sabhāva] called impermanency [aniccatā].

ATTHI KĀYOTI VĀ PANASSA SATI PACCUPAṬṬHITĀ HOTI = "Or, indeed, his mindfulness is established with the thought: 'The body exists'." The exposition of this is to be done in the manner already stated in the preceding section.

Here, the mindfulness which examines the four modes of deportment is the Truth of Suffering. The pre-craving which brings about that mindfulness is the Truth of Origination. The non-occurrence of either is the Truth of Cessation. The Real Path which understands suffering, abandons origination, and objectifies cessation is the Truth of the Way.

The yogi having endeavoured thus by way of the Four Truths arrives at peace.

This is the portal to emancipation up to saintship of the bhikkhu occupied with the four modes of deportment.

THE SECTION ON THE FOUR KINDS OF CLEAR COMPREHENSION

1. Clear comprehension in going forwards and backwards

After explaining body-contemplation in the form of the meditation on the four modes of deportment, the Master said, " And further," to explain body-contemplation by way of the four kinds of clear comprehension [catu sampajañña].

One who is clearly comprehending [sampajāno] is one who knows according to every way, intensively, or (item by item) in a detailed way [samantato pakārehi pakaṭṭhaṁ vā savisesaṁ jānāti]. Clear comprehension [sampajaññaṁ] is the state of that one. It is likewise the knowledge of that one [tassa bhāvo sampajaññaṁ. Tathā pavatta ñāṇaṁ].

ABHIKKANTE PAṬIKKANTE = " In going forwards (and) in going backwards." Here, the meaning is as follows :— Going forwards is called going. Going backwards is called turning back. Both these are to be found in all the four modes of deportment.

Going, here, is going after turning back (returning) and going after not turning back (going straight). Turning back is the bare fact of turning back. This dyad is only mutually supported action [Gamanañcettha nivattetvā anivattetvā ca gamanaṁ. Nivattanaṁ pana nivatti mattameva. Aññamaññamupādāna kriyā mattañcetaṁ dvayayaṁ].

First, in going, carrying the body to a position in front—*bringing the body along*—is called going forwards. Turning back—*returning thence*—is called turning back.

And in standing, one just standing and bending the body to a position in front does what is called going forwards, and one bending away behind—*drawing back*—does what is called going backwards. In sitting down, one sitting and moving on—*creeping on, sliding on*—to the front portion *comprising the frame and so forth* of the seat *i.e. chair, stool or similar thing* does going forwards ; and one moving away—*sliding back*—to the parts comprising the frame and so forth at the back of the chair or stool does what is called turning back. In lying down too the explanation is to done according to the method stated above.

SAMPAJĀNAKĀRĪ = " Practising clear comprehension." Doing without fail all actions with clear comprehension [Sampajaññena sabba kicca kārī]. Or the doing of only clear comprehension [Sampajaññasseva vā kārī].

Clear comprehension [Sampajānanaṁ] = comprehending clearly [sampajānaṁ]. Both words mean the same thing; their difference is only one of affix. DOING WITHOUT FAIL ALL ACTIONS WITH CLEAR COMPREHENSION *is the character of doing what ought to be done by oneself, with clear comprehension [attanā kattabba kiccassa karaṇa sīla].* THE DOING OF ONLY CLEAR COMPREHENSION *is the character of practising clear comprehension [sampajānassa karaṇa sīla].*

For the yogi practises only clear comprehension and is nowhere bereft of clear comprehension, in going forwards and going backwards.

There are these four kinds of clear comprehension : clear comprehension of purpose [sātthaka sampajañña], of suitability [sappāya s.], of resort [gocara s.], and of non-delusion [asammoha s].

The discerning of things rightly, entirely and equally is clear comprehension. Nothing else. This way of explanation is different from the commentary's. As it produces non-delusion in going forwards and backwards, the action, of clear comprehension is practice of clear comprehension. Who has that practice of clear comprehension is (one) practising clear comprehension.

What takes place together with the aim called growth according to the Norm is purpose. The clear comprehension of purpose in going forwards and backwards is clear comprehension of purpose. The clear comprehension of what is suitable, fit, to oneself is clear comprehension of suitability. The clear comprehension of the (mental) resort which is called the subject of meditation that is unrelinquished, in going backwards and forwards on the alms-resort and elsewhere, is the clear comprehension of resort. Clear comprehension of non-delusion is non-delusion that is clearly comprehending called non-stupefaction.

Among these four kinds of clear comprehension, the clear comprehension of purpose is the comprehension of (a worthy) purpose after considering what is worthy and not worthy, with the thought, " Is there any use to one by this going or is there not ?" One does this not having gone immediately, just by the influence of the thought, at the very moment the thought of going forwards is born.

In this context purpose is growth according to the Norm, by way of visiting a relic shrine, Tree of Enlightenment (Bodhi Tree), the Order, the elders, and a place where the dead are cast (a cemetery) for seeing the unlovely (a corpse, a skeleton and the like).

By visiting a relic shrine, a Bodhi Tree, or the Order, for producing spiritual interest, and by meditating on the waning of that interest one could reach sainthood ; by visiting elders and by getting established in their instruction one could reach sainthood; and by visiting a place where the dead are cast, by seeing a corpse there and by producing the first absorption [paṭhamajjhāna] in that unlovely object, one could reach sainthood. So the visiting of these is purposeful.

SAINTHOOD. *This is mentioned by way of the highest kind of exposition. Since the generating of quietude and insight too is growth according to the Norm for a bhikkhu.*

Some [keci] however say: Increase by way of material gain, too, is (a worthy) purpose, since material gain is helpful for the holy life.

SOME = *Dwellers at the Abhayagiri Vihāra at Anurādhapura.*

MATERIAL GAIN = *Material requisities like robes.*

Clear comprehension of suitability is the comprehension of the suitable after considering what is suitable and not.

For instance, the visiting of a relic shrine could be quite (worthily) purposeful. But when a great offering is made to a relic shrine, a multitude of people in a ten or twelve yojana area gather, and men and women according to their position go about adorned like painted figures. And if in that crowd greed could arise for the bhikkhu in an attractive object, resentment in a non-attractive one, and delusion through prejudice; if he could commit the offence of sexual intercourse; or if harm could come to the holy life of purity; then, a place like that relic shrine would not be suitable. When there could be no such harm it would be suitable.

PREJUDICE [*Asamapekkhana*] *is the name given to the grasping of an object without wise reflection by way of worldly ignorant complacency* [*gehasita aññāṇupekkhā vasena arammaṇassa ayoniso gahanaṁ*].

COMMIT THE OFFENCE OF SEXUAL INTERCOURSE *by way of bodily contact with a woman.*

HARM COME TO LIFE *through trampling down by an elephant and so forth.*

(HARM COME TO) PURITY *through seeing those of the opposite sex and so forth.*

The visiting of the Order is a purpose of worth. Still when there is all-night preaching in a big pandal in the inner village and there are crowds and one could possibly come to hurt and harm in the way mentioned earlier, that place of preaching is not suitable to go to. When there is no hurt or harm possible one may go there as it would then be suitable. In visiting elders who are surrounded by a large following suitability and non-suitability should also be determined in the way stated above.

To visit a place where the dead are cast for beholding a corpse is fit, and to explain the meaning of this the following story has been told :

It is said that a young bhikkhu went with a novice to get wood for tooth-cleaners. The novice getting out of the road proceeded in front to a place in search of wood and saw a corpse. Meditating on it he produced the first absorption and making the factors of the absorption a basis for developing insight realised the first three fruitions of saintship, while examining the conformations [sankhāre sammasanto], and stood having laid hold of the subject of meditation for realising the path of full saintship.

The young bhikkhu not seeing the novice called out to him. The novice thought thus : From the day I took up the homeless life I have endeavoured to let me never be called twice by a bhikkhu, so, I will produce the further distinction (of full sainthood) another day, and replied to the bhikkhu with the words: "What's the matter reverend sir ? " "Come," said the bhikkhu and the novice returned. The novice told the bhikkhu as follows : "Go first by this way ; then stand facing north, at the place I stood, for a while and look." The young bhikkhu followed the novice's instructions and attained just the distinction reached by the novice. Thus the same corpse became profitable to two people. For the male the female corpse is not suitable, and vice versa. Only a corpse of one's own sex is suitable. Comprehension of what is suitable in this way is called the clear comprehension of suitability.

Further, the going on the alms round of that one who has thus comprehended purpose and suitability after learning and taking up just that resort—among the thirty-eight subjects of meditation—called the subject of meditation after his own heart is clear comprehension of resort.

SUBJECT OF MEDITATION [*Kammaṭṭhāna*] *refers to the object of concentration by way of the locality of occurrence of the contemplative action that is being stated.*

RESORT [*Gocara*]. *Literally, pasturing ground. This word is applied to the wandering for alms of a bhikkhu and to the subject of meditation in the sense of the locus (sphere, range or scope) of contemplative action.*

For making manifest this clear comprehension of resort the following set of four should be understood : In the Dispensation of the Buddha a certain bhikkhu on the journey out for alms takes along with him in the mind the subject of meditation, but on the journey back from the work of alms-gathering he does not bring it along with him, having become unmindful of it. Another does not take it along with him on the outward journey, but returns from the alms-tour with the subject of meditation in his mind. Still another neither takes it along with him on the outward journey nor returns with it on the journey home. And, lastly, there is the fourth kind of bhikkhu who both takes the subject of meditation along with him on the journey out for alms and brings it back with him on the journey home.

Among these four kinds, there is a certain bhikkhu who lives thus :—By day he cleanses his mind of things that becloud—*the hindrances* [*nīvaraṇa*]—through meditation on the ambulatory and in the sitting posture. By night, likewise, on the ambulatory and in the sitting posture, through meditation, in the first watch, and in the last watch, he cleanses his mind of things that becloud, after sleeping in the middle watch.

Quite early in the day having done the duties connected with the terraces of the relic-shrine and the Bodhi-tree—sweeping and so forth—he sprinkles the Bodhi-tree with water, places water for drinking and washing and attends to the Khandhaka duties beginning with the duties connected with the teacher and the preceptor. Thereafter, having looked to the needs of his body—*that is, after bestowing that attention on the body which consists of washing the face and so forth*—he enters his dwelling and practises the subject of meditation *begun that day* [*tadahe mūla bhūtaṁ kammaṭṭhānaṁ*], at several sittings [dve tayo pallanke usumaṁ gāhāpento = during two or three sittings while the body happens to be put into a state of warming up]. *There* TWO OR THREE SITTINGS = *two or three sitting turns* [*dve tayo nisajjavāre*]. WARMING UP *is said concerning the matter of causing warmth to be taken up twice or thrice* [*dve tīṇi uṇhāpanāni sandhāya vuttaṁ*]. *The word* SITTING [*pallanka*] *means sitting by way of the thigh-bound or-locked posture* [*ūrubaddha āsana*]. *It is the posture called the lion-pose* [*sīhāsana*] *and the firm pose* [*thirāsana*]. *It is the sitting down of one with the left foot crossed on to the right thigh and the right foot on to the left thigh, by way of interlocking, through the bending of the thighs.* (One sits in meditation not for a long time at a stretch. There are short intervals of relaxation through brief changes of posture when the body gets warm or uncomfortable in the crosslegged sitting pose).

When it is time to wander for alms, he having got up from the sitting meditation-pose, and taken his bowl and robe with just the thought of meditation uppermost in mind [kammaṭṭhāna sīseneva] leaves his dwelling, attending only to the thought of meditation [kammaṭṭhānaṁ manasikarontova].

WITH JUST THE THOUGHT OF MEDITATION UPPERMOST IN MIND = *just with his subject of meditation in the forefront of the mind* [*kammaṭṭhāna mukheneva*], *keeping to the thought of meditation* [*kammaṭṭhānaṁ avijahanto*].

If, when going to his alms collecting place, the bhikkhu's thought of meditation is contemplation on the Buddha's qualities [buddhānussati kaṁmaṭṭhānaṁ], he, on arriving at the relic-shrine, enters the shrine's precincts, without having put aside his thought of meditation on the Buddha. But should his thought of meditation be something other than the Buddha-subject, he having stood at the foot of the stairway leading to the shrine-terrace, put by his thought of meditation as if it were goods hand-carried, and acquired the joy begotten of the Buddha-subject of meditation, goes up the stairway.

If the relic-shrine is a big one, it should be worshipped at four places, when the bhikkhu has gone round it three times to the right.

If it is a small shrine, it should be worshipped by the meditator in eight places when he has gone round it three times to the right just as in the case of the big shrine.

By a bhikkhu who, having worshipped a relic-shrine, has reached a Bodhi-tree shrine even the Bodhi-tree should be worshipped. And he should worship the Bodhi-tree showing meek demeanour as though he were in the very presence of the Buddha, the Bhagavā.

In this way, that monk, having worshipped relic-shrine and Bodhi-tree shrine, goes to the place where he had put by his first subject of meditation, namely, to the bottom of the stairway. There, having taken up the subject of meditation he had put by earlier, and robed himself (with the upper robe and the shoulder-cloak held together and worn as one, that is, with the upper robe falling within the shoulder-cloak at all edges), near the village with the thought of meditation uppermost in mind, he enters the village for alms.

Then, people, after seeing the bhikkhu, say : " Our venerable one is come," and having gone forward to meet the bhikkhu, taken his bowl, conducted him to the sitting-hall (hall where meals are served to the bhikkhus in a village) or to a house and made him take a seat, offer gruel to him. Thereafter, they wash and anoint his feet, and till rice is ready sit in front of him and ask him questions or become desirous of listening to a talk on the Norm from him. Even if the people do not ask him to speak to them on the Norm, the commentators say that a talk on the Norm should be given to the people in order to help them. The bhikkhu should expound the Norm *for the purpose of assisting the folk with the grace of the Norm, thinking, "If I do not expound the Norm to them, who will?"*

There is no Norm-talk separate from the thought of meditation. *This is said to strengthen the dictum of the commentators mentioned above.*

Therefore, after expounding the Norm even with the thought of meditation uppermost in mind, after partaking of the food, with just the thought of meditation uppermost in mind he leaves the village followed by the people who in spite of his requesting them to stop accompany him. There, after turning back those who followed him, he takes the road to his dwelling-place.

AFTER EXPOUNDING THE NORM EVEN WITH THE THOUGHT OF MEDITATION UPPERMOST IN MIND = *After expounding the Norm just in accordance with the character of the thought of meditation that is being attended to by oneself, by way of sticking to that thought. The method of exegesis is the same in regard to the next expression concerning food.* AFTER GIVING THANKS. *Here too the governing expression is:* EVEN WITH THE THOUGHT OF MEDITATION UPPERMOST IN MIND. THERE = *Just at the place of departure from the village. The point at which the bhikkhu actually gets out of the village.*

Then, novices and young bhikkhus who had taken their meal outside the village, having left the village earlier than this bhikkhu, see this bhikkhu coming. And they, after going forward to meet him, take his bowl and robe.

It is said that bhikkhus of old did this duty without looking at the face of the returning bhikkhu and thinking: (this is) our preceptor (or) our teacher. In ancient times, they did this duty according to the arriving-limit (the arriving division, section, or company). As the elder bhikkhu came the younger ones performed this duty not looking to see who the elder was.

Those novices and young bhikkhus question the elder thus: "Reverend Sir, who are these people to you? Are they relatives on the maternal side? Are they relatives on the paternal side?" "Having seen what do you query?" "There affection and respect for you." "Friends, what even parents find it hard to do these people do for us. Our very robes and bowls are just due to them. Owing to these people we know no fear on occasions of fear and know no lack of food on occasions of famine. There are no people so helpful to us as these folk." Speaking well of these people, thus, he goes. This bhikkhu is spoken of as a person who carries forth (takes along with him) the subject of meditation when he leaves his dwelling but does not return with the thought of meditation.

If to a bhikkhu who performs the duties detailed above, betimes, (there arises an intense feeling of discomfort owing to hunger), if his kamma-produced caloricity becomes very strong [pajjalati lit. flames up] and lays hold of the derived, assimilated material of the body owing to the absence of undigested food in the stomach, if sweat exudes from his body and if he is unable to concentrate on his subject of meditation, he takes his bowl and robe quite early in the morning, worships the relic shrine speedily, and enters the village to get gruel just when the village herds go out of their pens for pasturing. After he gets the gruel he goes to a sitting-hall and drinks it.

Then, with the swallowing of just two or three mouthfuls, the kamma-produced caloricity letting go the material of the body i.e. *the inner lining of the stomach* [*udara paṭalaṁ*] lays hold of the property of the food taken in.

And that bhikkhu, having got to the assuagement of the distress of the caloric-process like a man bathed with a hundred pots of cool water, having partaken of the (rest of the) gruel with the thought of meditation uppermost in mind, washed bowl and mouth, attended to the subject of meditation till the later forenoon meal, wandered for alms in the remaining places—*in the places where he got no gruel and so where he could still go for alms*—and taken the meal with just the thought of meditation uppermost in mind, returns, having taken up just that subject of meditation which is thenceforward present in his mind. This person is called the one who does not carry forth but returns with the thought of meditation.

KAMMA-PRODUCED CALORICITY [*kammaja tejo*] *is an expression referring to the function of that part of the alimentary tract where the bile helps digestion and from which vital heat spreads—the grahaṇī according to Āyurveda. It is stated that the commentator said* KAMMA-PRODUCED CALORICITY *concerning " the seizer " the name of the alimentary function explained above* [*gahaṇiṁ sandhāyāha*].

BECOMES VERY STRONG *means : generates a condition of heat.*

SUBJECT OF MEDITATION DOES NOT GET ON TO THE ROAD OF CONTEMPLATIVE THOUGHT *owing to the disappearance of concentration of the wearied body through hunger-fatigue.*

When in the stomach, indeed, property like cooked rice (called the underived, the unassimilated or that which is not due to pre-clinging) is absent, kamma-produced caloricity gets hold of the inner lining of the stomach. That causes the utterance of words like the following : " I am hungry ; give me food."

When food is taken, kamma-produced caloricity having let go the inner lining of the stomach gets hold of the food-property. Then the living being becomes calm. Therefore in the commentaries kamma-produced caloricity is spoken of as (a malignant spirit, a devourer of the living, frequenting pools, fording-places and the like and known by the shadow it casts on the water) a shadow-demon.

And bhikkhus, like this one, who, after drinking gruel and exerting themselves in the development of insight, reached the state of Saintship in the Buddha's Dispensation are past all numbering (so many have they been). In the Island of the Lion Race, alone [sīhala dīpe yeva], there is not a seat of sitting-hall in the various villages which is not a place where a bhikkhu, having sat and drunk gruel, attained Saintship [tesu tesu gāmesu asansālāya na taṁ āsanaṁ atthi yattha yaguṁ pivitvā arahattaṁ patta bhikkhu natthi].

" And bhikkhus, like this one," and so forth. With these words the commentator points out the state of benefit of the bhikkhu attending to the thought of meditation, even, in the way aforesaid.

But a bhikkhu who is a loose liver [pamāda vihārī lit. liver in negligence, carelessness or indolence], who is a slacker [nikkhitta dhuro lit. one who has thrown away the yoke—or the burden of right exertion—and so is an irresponsible person], having broken all observances [sabba vattāni bhinditvā] whilst living spiritually frozen through the fivefold bondage of mind [pañca vidha ceto vinibandha baddha citto viharanto], having entered the village for alms without having even shown a sign of the fact that there is a thing called a subject of meditation (or contemplation), and having walked about and eaten his meal in unbefitting company, comes out of the village an empty fellow. This bhikkhu is called a person who neither carries forth nor returns with the thought of meditation.

Who is spoken of with the words : " This one carries forth and carries back " must be known just through the means of the observance of carrying forth and carrying back (the subject of meditation from the beginning to the end of the journey to and from the village).

JUST THROUGH THE MEANS OF THE OBSERVANCE OF CARRYING FORTH AND CARRYING BACK *means : By way of whatsoever going for and returning from alms-gathering only with the thought of meditation.*

Men of good family, desirous of self-improvement, having become homeless ones in the Dispensation of the Buddha, when living in a group of ten, twenty, fifty or a hundred make a covenant of observance, with these words: "Friends, ye renounced not because ye were troubled by creditors, not because of fear of punishment from the king, and not because of difficulties of subsistence produced by famine and the like, but because ye were desirous of release here. Therefore, restrain ye the defilement that is born when going (forwards or backwards) just in the process of going ; restrain ye the defilement that is born when standing just in the process of standing ; restrain ye the defilement that is born when sitting just in the process of sitting ; and restrain ye the defilement that is born when lying down just in the process of lying down."

When after the making of such a covenant of observance they go to a village for alms, if there are stones, by the road, at distances of half-an-usabha, one usabha and one gavuta, these bhikkhus proceed attending to the subject of meditation with awareness of those stones. If in the course of going (for alms) a defilement of the mind arises in one, just in the course of going one restrains or suppresses it. If one fails to do so one stops. Then he who comes behind one stops too. And one thinks : "This bhikkhu, here, knows the unclean thought that has arisen in you ; unbecoming is that to you." Thus having reproved oneself, and developed penetrative insight one steps into the Real Ground (so ayaṁ bhikkhu tuyhaṁ uppanna vitakkaṁ jānāti ananucchavikaṁ te etanti paticodetvā vipassanaṁ vaḍḍhetvā tattheva ariya bhūmiṁ okkamati).

If one is not able to do that, one sits down and he who comes behind sits down too, it is said ; that just is the method. Should one be not able to enter into the Real Ground, then, one having stopped the defilement, goes, attending to only the subject of meditation. One does not raise the foot with mind bereft of the subject of meditation but should one do so, one, having turned, gets back again even to the earlier step.

Desirous of self-improvement (*attā kāmāti*) = (*Those bhikkhus*) *wishing for personal good and well-being* [*attano hita sukhamicchantā*]—*those wishing for* (*delighting in, intent on*) *the Norm is the true meaning* [*dhammacchandavantoti attho*]—*by reason of the fact that the Norm is verily* GOOD *and* WELL-BEING [*dhammo hi hitaṁ sukhañca tannimittakaṁ*]. *Or to the wise the Norm is the self owing to the absence of difference* (*of the Norm*) *from the self, and* (*because the Norm is contained in the self*) *owing to the* (*Norm's*) *state of being included in the living being* [*atha vā viññūnaṁ attato nibbisesattā atta bhāva pariyāpannattā ca dhammo attā nāma*]. *They* (*the bhikkhus who have genuinely renounced, in the Dispensation of the Buddha*) *desire, wish for, that* [*taṁ kāmenti icchanti*].*

Newly (*or recently*) — *at the time this sub-commentary was written—however the reading : desirous of attainment, by way of* (*moral*) *good, is seen* [*adhunā pana attha kāmāti hitavācakena attha saddena pāṭho dissati*]. *The true meaning of that is :* (*those*) *wishing for good that is connected with the Norm or* (*those*) *wishing for the Norm that is good* [*dhamma saññuttaṁ hitamicchantā hita bhūtaṁ vā dhammamicchantāti*].

UNBECOMING IS THAT *means : unbecoming is another's knowing of one's own defilement* [*parassa jānanaṁ*].

This also should be understood as included even by ANOTHER'S KNOWING : *He (the monk who is trying to overcome the adventitious defilement) makes systematic attention strong on account of (his awareness of) the hungry condition of those coming behind [pacchato āgacchantānaṁ chinna bhatta bhāva bhayenāpi yoniso manasikāraṁ paribrūhetīti idampi parassa jānaneneva sangahitanti daṭṭhabbaṁ].*

EVEN TO THE EARLIER STEP *means : just to the first footprint made with mind separate from the thought of meditation [purima pāde yevāti paṭhamaṁ kammaṭṭhāna vippayutta cittena uddharita pāda valañje yeva].*

Like the elder Mahā Phussa, the verandah-dweller. *With the stories beginning, here, the commentator lays low the misgiving about this observance, for instance, expressed thus : Just impossible that what is pointed out was, indeed, in this way, practised before [aṭṭhāne yevetaṁ kathitaṁ khvāyaṁ evaṁ paṭipaṇṇa pubboti āsankaṁ nivatteti].*

It is said that this elder dwelt for nineteen years fulfilling the observance of "carrying forth and carrying back." Ploughman, sowers, threshers of grain and other people having seen the elder go in this manner, said : "This elder goes having halted again and again. Why does he do so? Has he got confused about the way or has he forgotten aught?"

The elder by just doing the recluse's duty, with mind yoked to the thought of meditation, without giving heed to the talk of the people, attained Saintship within twenty years.

On the very day he became a Saint, a deva who was living at the end of the elder's walking path stood emitting a radiance that came from the fingers of the deva. The Four Regents of the Earth, Sakka the deva-king and Brahmā Sahampati came to serve the elder. Mahā Tissa the forest-dweller, also an elder, saw that radiance and inquired of the arahat the next day : "Last night, there was a radiance about your reverence ; what was that?"

Diverting the talk, the arahat said : "Radiance is that of light, of gem and the like." But on being pressed repeatedly with the words : "You are concealing," he acknowledged, saying, "Yes" and informed Tissa of his attainment.

Like the elder Mahā Nāga of the Black Creeper Pavilion. He, it is said, when fulfilling the observance of carrying forth and back the subject of meditation, resolved upon keeping to only the postures of standing and of walking for seven years, with the thought : "I will honour the Blessed One's great struggle." And after fulfilling for sixteen years again the observance of carrying forth and carrying back the subject of meditation, he attained Saintship.

This is said of him : He (when going out for alms to the village) raises his foot only with mind yoked to the subject of meditation. If he raises with mind not yoked thus, he turns back again. After standing at such a distance from the village as would raise (in the mind of one looking from the village) the doubt : "Is it indeed a cow or a recluse ?" and robing himself, he fills his mouth with a draught of water from the water-carrier slung over the shoulder and hanging under the armpit, having washed his bowl with water from the same source. For what reason does he fill his mouth so ? He does it thinking : "Let there be no distraction of the mind even by the uttering of the words : 'May you live long !' to people come to worship me or give me alms." But when he is asked the question, "Reverend Sir, which stage of the half-month is today ?" concerning the date, or when he is questioned about the number of monks, he answers, after swallowing the water. If there is no questioning about the day and so forth, he having spat out the water, at the village gate, at the time of leaving, goes.

Like the fifty bhikkhus who entered upon the rainy season residence, at the Monastery of the Galamba Landing Place.

On the full-moon day of July (Āsāḷha), they made this convenant of observance :—"Without attaining Saintship we shall not converse with one another."

These bhikkhus used to enter the village for alms filling the mouth with a draught of water, and when questioned about the date and so forth they acted just according to the method mentioned above.

In that village people, having seen the spots on which mouthfuls of water had been spirted forth by the returning bhikkhus, said : "Today one came; today, two." And those people thought : "What indeed is the reason that these bhikkhus neither talk with us nor with each other ? If they do not speak with each other, surely, they are persons who have had a dispute amongst themselves," and saying : "Come, we must make them forgive one another," went—in a body—to the monastery. There, they saw that no two bhikkhus were in the same place. Then a wise man in that crowd said : "Good people, a place which quarrelsome folk occupy is not like this. The relic-shrine and the Bodhi-shrine terraces are well swept. The brooms are well arranged. And water for drinking and water for washing are well set." Then those people just turned back. And the bhikkhus of that monastery ättained Saintship within three months and performed a pure Pavāraṇa ceremony.

DIVERTING THE TALK = *Turning away the talk because of unostentatiousness due to Realisation [adhigamappichatāya].* KEEPING TO ONLY THE POSTURES OF STANDING AND SITTING : *This is said by way of the postures proper to be resolved upon for adherence. One restricts oneself to these postures not however by way of refusing to practise the proper-to-be-practised and necessary posture of sitting at meal-time and on such other occasions; for, by the word, only, it should be understood that one stops the remaining forms of sitting, namely, every sitting-posture not absolutely necessary to practise, and the posture of lying down.*

I WILL HONOUR THE BLESSED ONE'S GREAT STRUGGLE. *According to my strength, I will do worship to the six-year-asceticism of extreme torture undertaken by the world's Redeemer for our sakes, since even the honouring of the Master, through conduct, is the more praiseworthy kind of worship. Not so praiseworthy is the worship (of him) with material things.*

PURE PAVARAṆA = *The Pavāraṇa through the state of destruction of the outflowings—Saintship [khiṇāsava bhāvena pavāraṇaṁ].*

Thus like the elder Mahā Nāga dweller in the Black Creeper Pavilion and like the bhikkhus who went into rainy season at the Galamba Ford Monastery, the bhikkhu (who does the observance of carrying forth and carrying back the subject of meditation) raises his foot only with mind yoked to the thought of meditation. Having reached the neighbourhood of the village, filled the mouth with a draught of water, and looked at the streets, he enters the street where there are no quarrelsome drunkards, gamesters and such folk or where there are no restive elephants, horses and the like.

There, wandering for alms, he does not go speedily like one in a great hurry since there is no ascetic practice of begging food, speedily. He goes, rather, having become motionless, like a water cart on uneven ground. Entering into each house in order, spending such time as is suitable for concluding whether there is or not the tendency to offer alms (on the part of the occupants of each house), he receives alms, and comes to the inner village, outer village or even to the monastery. There he seats himself in a place pleasant and good (proper), attends to the thought of meditation with the setting up of the perception of loathsomeness in food, and reflects by way of the similes of axle-greasing, applying ointment to ulcer and feeding on own child's flesh, and eats the food fully followed with awareness of the eight attributes, (and) not for sport, intoxication, adornment or the filling up of those places of his body that have a deficiency of flesh.

And he, having eaten, washes. Then he rests for a while the body that is tired with the business of eating. He attends to just the thought of meditation, in the time after eating as in the time before eating, and in the last watch of the night as in the first watch.

This person is called one who carries forth and carries back the subject of meditation.

The person who fulfils this observance of one who carries forth and carries back, called the carrying (of the thought of meditation) forth when going out for alms and the bringing back (of the thought of meditation) when returning from the alms-round, reaches Saintship even in the period of youth (i.e. early age or the first stage of life), if he is possessed of the sufficing condition, the wherewithal to accomplish the destruction of ignorance and its defilements.

If he fails to reach Saintship, in early age, then he reaches it in middle age ; if he fails in middle age, then at the time of death ; if he fails at the time of death, then, after becoming a deva ; if he fails as a deva, then, at a time when no Buddha has appeared on earth, he is born as a man and realises the truth as a Buddha who is not able to communicate the truth to others; and if he fails to realise the truth in that way, then, immediately on meeting a Fully Enlightened Buddha he becomes a person who intuits quickly like the elder Bāhiya Dārucīriya, or a greatly wise one like the elder Sāriputta, or one of great psychic power like the elder Moggallāna the Great, or an exponent of ascetic practice like the elder Kassapa the Great, or one endowed with clairvoyant power like the elder Anuruddha, or an expert in discipline like the elder Upāli, or an expounder of the Norm like the elder Punna Mantāṇiputta, or a forest dweller like the elder Revata, or one of great learning like the elder Ānanda, or one desirous of training like the elder Rāhula, the Buddha's son.

Among these four that form the set, he who carries forth and carries back the subject of meditation reaches the crest of the clear comprehension of resort.

Further, non-confusion in going forwards and so forth is the clear comprehension of non-delusion. That should be understood in the following way :—In this Dispensation, a monk, without confusing himself, like a blinded worldling who, while going forwards or backwards, becomes muddle-headed, and believes thus : "The soul (or self) goes forward" or "The act of going forwards is produced by the soul," or "I go forwards" or "The act of going forwards is produced by me," and the like, thinks : "When there is the arising in one of the thought 'I am going forwards,' just with that thought, appears the process of oscillation originating from mind which brings to birth bodily expression (or intimation). Thus by way of the diffusion of the process of oscillation due to mental activity, this skeleton called the body goes forward."

In raising up the foot **A** [pāduddharaṇe] two processes [dhātuyo] : extension [paṭhavī] and cohesion [āpo], are low, weak [omattā honti dubbalā], and the other two processes : caloricity [tejo] and oscillation [vāyo] are high, powerful [adhimattā honti balavatiyo] ; so, too, in stretching out the foot **B** [atiharaṇe] and in shifting away the foot **C** [vītiharaṇe]. But in dropping down the raised foot **D** [vossajjane], and likewise in keeping the foot on the ground **E** [sannikkhepane] and in pressing the foot against the ground **F** [sannirumbhane] the first two processes are high and powerful and the second, low and weak. There, the material and mental phenomena in **A** do not occur in **B** ; those in **B** do not occur in **C** ; those in **C** do not occur in **D**; those in **D** do not occur in **E**; those in **E** do not occur in **F**. These phenomena after coming into existence in the form of several sections, links, and parts, break quickly just in those places, crackling like sesamum seeds thrown into a heated pan. In this matter, who is the one that goes forward, or whose going forwards is there? In the highest sense (paramatthato), what takes place is the going, the standing, the sitting down and the lying down of the processes. With material form in the several divisions (groups or parts),

One conscious state arises
And quite another ceases.
In sequence, like a river's flow,
These states (of mind and matter) go.
[Aññaṁ uppajjate cittaṁ aññaṁ cittaṁ nirujjhati
Avīcimanusambandho nadī soto va vattati].

Low [*Omattā*] = *Negligible* [*Avamattā*], *poor in regard to standard* [*lāmakappamāṇā*].

Since the process of caloricity with (its cognate process) oscillation coming (as a servant or follower) behind it [*vāyo dhātuyā anugatā tejo dhātu*] *is the condition for upraising* [*uddharaṇassa paccayo*], *caloricity and oscillation are in preponderance, by reason of capability, in the action of upraising. Caloricity is specially conducive to the action of upraising and so in upraising oscillation is subordinate to caloricity. The processes of extension and cohesion are low in the action of upraising owing to their incapacity to raise up.*

Since the process of oscillation with (its cognate process) caloricity coming (as a servant or follower) behind it [*tejo dhātuyā anugatā vāyo dhātu*] *is the condition for stretching out and shifting away* [*atiharaṇa vītiharaṇānaṁ paccayo*], *oscillation and caloricity are in preponderance by reason of capability, in stretching out and shifting away. Oscillation is naturally active and because in the actions of stretching out and shifting away its movement is excessive, caloricity is subordinate to oscillation in these actions. The other two processes are low in stretching out and shifting away because of the incapacity of these processes to stretch out and to shift away.*

RAISING UP *is the lifting of a foot from a place already stepped on to.*

STRETCHING OUT *is the carrying of a foot to the front from the place on which one is standing.*

SHIFTING AWAY *is the carrying of a foot sidewards (by moving it laterally) for the purpose of avoiding stake and the like, or for avoiding contact with the other foot already set on the ground.*

Or STRETCHING OUT *is the carrying of a foot (near) to the place where the other foot is set and* SHIFTING AWAY *is the carrying of a foot further to a point beyond the place on which the other foot is.*

Since the process of cohesion with (its cognate process) extension coming (as a servant or follower) behind it [paṭhavī dhātuyā anugatā āpo dhātu] is the condition for dropping down [vossajjane paccayo], cohesion and extension are in preponderance by reason of capability in the action of dropping down. The nature of cohesion is most gravid and so in the laying down of an upraised foot extension is subordinate to cohesion. Because of their incapacity to drop down what is upraised the processes of caloricity and oscillation are called low in this connection.

Since the process of extension with (its cognate process) cohesion coming (as a servant or follower) behind it [āpo dhātuyā anugatā paṭhavī dhātu] is the condition for the keeping (of a foot) on the ground, extension and cohesion are in preponderance by reason of capability, in the keeping (of a a foot) on the ground. In keeping the foot on the ground too, as in the state of something fixed, cohesion is subordinate to extension owing to the excessive functioning of the latter process.

Cohesion is subordinate to extension also by way of the contactual action of the process of extension in pressing the foot against the ground.

And here DROPPING DOWN *is lowering by way of relinquishment or laying down. The setting down, thence, of the foot, on the ground and so forth is* KEEPING THE FOOT ON THE GROUND. *After keeping the foot on the ground, the coming to a complete standstill of the action of going, by way of contacting is* PRESSING THE FOOT AGAINST THE GROUND.

THERE = *In this going forward or among the six aforesaid divisions known as raising up, stretching out, shifting away, dropping down, keeping down, and pressing against.*

IN RAISING UP = *In the moment of upraising.* MATERIAL AND MENTAL PHENOMENA = *The material phenomena proceeding in the form of upraising (or through the mode of upraising), and the mental phenomena originating that materiality* DO NOT OCCUR IN STRETCHING OUT *by reason of their existing only for a moment. Throughout, this is the method of exegesis in this passage.*

JUST IN THESE PLACES = *Wherever, in the divisions beginning with upraising, phenomena come to be, just in those very places, they perish. To be sure, owing to swift change there is no going over of phenomena to another place.*

SECTIONS = *Divisions.* LINKS = *Joints.* PARTS = *Portions. And all here is stated concerning the abovementioned divisions of the action of going which take place in the form of a differentiated serial process.*

More fleet than the group of devas running before the Sun's chariot—the group of devas in the shape of horses with keen-edged razors attached to their heads and hoofs, engaged in and taken to going, plunging forwards, some above and some below, but never knocking against each other, though moving close together—is the moment of existence of material phenomena.

As the break-up of sesamum seeds that are roasted takes place almost at once with the sound of crackling, the destruction of conditioned phenomena takes place almost at once with phenomena's arising. For similar to the crackling sound, the sign of the breaking up of the sesamum seeds, is ARISING, *the sign (indicatory) of the (eventual) breaking up of conditioned phenomena, owing to the destruction (inevitably and) assuredly of phenomena that have arisen.*

WHO IS THE ONE THAT GOES FORWARD? *Just no one.* [*Ko eko abhikkamati nābhikkamati yeva*].

Could it be said: WHOSE GOING FORWARD IS THERE? *No. why? In the highest sense, what takes place is the going, the standing, the sitting down, and the lying down of the processes.*

The passage just mentioned is for dispelling the false idea of a self that goes forward which a confused blinded worldling is apt to possess or the passage is stated by way of objection and refutation.

WITH MATERIAL FORM IN THE SEVERAL DIVISIONS [*tasmiṁ tasmiṁ koṭṭhāse rūpena saddhiṁ*] *means: with material form in the aforesaid sixfold division.*

The conscious state or the thought-unit that comes into existence when any material form comes into existence runs a course of its own and does not get into close contact with the material form in question, nor does it get into repeated contact or relation with that material form. Therefore it is said: one conscious state arises with material form and quite another ceases when that material form ceases. By reason of the absence of close or repeated contact [*apaccāmaṭṭhattā*] *of mind with matter this happens. Tension, oscillation or vibration of mind is quicker than that of matter, seventeen times.*

The words: WITH MATERIAL FORM *in relation to the first sentence of the stanza mean: with whatsoever material form arising simultaneously with a conscious state* [*yena kenaci sahuppajjanakena rūpena*]. *And the same words in relation to the second sentence of the stanza refer to the material form already arisen and existing at the starting point of the seventeenth thought-unit that occurs after the ceasing-phase of the thought-unit with which the aforesaid material form arose and which material form arisen already has a total duration from its arising to ceasing of seventeen consecutive thought-units and is possessed of the nature of ceasing together with the cessation of the seventeenth thought-unit mentioned above, namely, of the seventeenth thought-unit in its phase of dissolution or ceasing* [*dutiya pada sambandhe pana rūpenāti idaṁ yaṁ tato nirujjhamāna cittato upari sattarasama cittassa uppādakkhaṇe uppannaṁ tadeva tassa nirujjhamāna cittassa nirodhena saddhiṁ nirujjhanakaṁ sattarasa cittakkhaṇāyukaṁ rūpaṁ sandhāya vuttaṁ*].

Material and mental phenomena would perhaps be taken as things of equal duration, if the matter were put in a different way to this. Should these two kinds of phenomena be wrongly considered as things of equal duration then there would be contradiction with such commentarial sayings as: " Material form is slow-changing, is tardy as regards ceasing," and with such textual sayings as: " I do not see a single thing so swiftly changing, o bhikkhus, as this mind" [*Aññathā rūparūpadhammā samāṇāyukā siyuṁ yadi ca siyuṁ atha rūpaṁ garu pariṇāmaṁ dandha nirodhanti ādi atthakathā vacanehi nāhaṁ bhikkhave eka dhammampi samanupassāmi evaṁ lahu parivattaṁ yathāyidaṁ bhikkhave cittanti evamādi pāḷi vacanehi ca virodho siyā*].

Since the nature of mind and mental characteristics [*citta cetasikā*] *is to cognize or to have objects, mind and mental characteristics arise cognizing* [*vibhāventā*] *according to their strength* [*yathā balaṁ*] *the thing become a condition to mind and mental characteristics, in the form of an object or the thing become an object-condition to mind and mental characteristics* [*attano ārammaṇa paccayabhūtamattaṁ*]. *And immediately after the accomplishment or the effectuating of that which comprises the nature or quality of mind and mental characteristics, and that quality is just the process of cognizing, there occurs the ceasing of mind and mental characteristics* [*tesaṁ sabhāva nipphatti anantaraṁ nirodho*].

Material phenomena, however, do not take objects, have no objects [*anārammaṇā*] ; *they do no cognizing. Material phenomena have to be cognized* [*pakāsetabbā*]. *Cognizibility's fulfilment* [*pakāsetabba bhāva nipphatti*] *occurs with sixteen thought-units* [*solasahi cittehi hoti*]. *Hence the reduction of material phenomena to seventeen thought-units, together with the one thought-unit of the past, is acknowledged, by the commentator, it is said.* [*Tasmā eka cittakkhaṇatītena saha sattarasa cittakkhaṇāyukatā rūpadhammānaṁ icchitāti*].

The swift changeability of mind or consciousness [*viññāṇassa lahuparivattitā*] *takes place through the mere combination of the other three mental aggregates with variform consciousness (the protean mind) and through the mere combination of objects with the same consciousness that is replete with variegation* [*lahuparivattana viññāṇa visesassa sangati matta paccayatāya tiṇṇaṁ khandhānaṁ visaya sangatimattatāya ca*].

The state of slow change of material form [*rūpassa garu parivattitā*] *occurs owing to the condition of sluggishness of the primaries, namely, of the processes of extension, cohesion, caloricity and oscillation symbolised by earth, water, fire and air, respectively* [*dandha mahā bhūta paccayatāya*].

Only the Tathāgata, he who has arrived at the Truth by traversing the Ancient Road of the Buddhas, has knowledge of the different processes according to reality [*yathā bhūtaṁ nānā dhātu ñaṇaṁ kho pana tathāgatasseva*]. *And by means of that knowledge of the Tathāgata, the condition of pre-nascence as just a material phenomenon is stated. Likewise, by that knowledge of the Tathāgata, the condition of post-nascence, too, is stated. Because of the statement of the pre-nascent and post-nascent conditions (the idea of) the identity of moment of occurrence of mental and material phenomena is just not fit. Therefore it was said by the commentator, the elder Ānanda thus: Just according to the method stated should the meaning be understood here* [*tena ca pure jāta paccayo rūpa dhammova vutto pacchā jāta paccayo ca tathevāti rūpārūpa dhammānaṁ samānakkhaṇatā na yujjateva tasmā vuttanayenevettha attho veditabboti ācariyena vuttaṁ*].

This matter was stated in this way because it is easy to understand the simultaneity of cessation of mind and bodily or vocal expression [*tadetaṁ cittānuparivattiyā viññattiyā eka nirodha bhāvassa suviññeyyattā evaṁ vuttaṁ*].*

The meaning should be understood thus: Quite another conscious state (i.e. thought-unit) ceases with the ceasing of the material form arisen at the starting point of the seventeenth thought-unit which is earlier to the material form together with expression that is physical, in short, seventeen thought-units arise and pass away during the life-time of all material form except those connected with expression [*Tato sāviññattikena puretaraṁ sattarasama cittassa uppādakkhaṇe uppannena rūpena saddhiṁ aññaṁ cittaṁ nirujjhatīti attho veditabbo*].

The passage should be constructed thus: One conscious state ceases and quite another arises i.e. the conscious states at the arising and the ceasing of material phenomena are different [*Aññaṁ cittaṁ nirujjhati aññaṁ uppajjate cittanti yojetabbaṁ*]. *Indeed one is the word explanation; another is the explanation of the sense* [*Añño hi saddakkamo añño atthakkamo*]. *While the conscious state arisen earlier is ceasing it ceases in just the form of proximity-condition and so forth to another conscious state arising after it* [*Yaṁ hi purimuppannaṁ cittaṁ taṁ nirujjhantaṁ aññassa pacchā uppajjamānassa anantarādi paccaya bhāveneva nirujjhati*]. *Even another conscious state which has just obtained a condition thus arises* [*Tathā laddha paccayameva aññampi uppajjate cittaṁ*]. *And here (mind is) in a different state by reason of the difference of occasion* [*Avatthā visesato cettha aññathā*].

2. Clear comprehension in looking straight on and in looking away from the front

ALOKITE = " In looking straight on. " VILOKITE = " In looking away from the front." Here, looking straight on [ālokitaṁ] = seeing in the direction in front of oneself [purato pekkhanaṁ]. Looking away from the front [Vilokitaṁ] = Looking out in all other directions [Anudisā pekkhanaṁ].

And other kinds of seeing, by way of turning the eyes in the direction above, in the direction beneath and in the direction behind are called .looking upwards, looking downwards and looking backwards. Here those are not taken. But just these two—looking straight on and looking away from the front—are taken, by way of what is befitting. Or, by this method, it is said, all those are also taken.

BY WAY OF WHAT IS FITTING = *In the form of that which is suitable to a recluse.*

Since looking downwards could happen in such actions as sweeping and plastering the floor with clay and cow-dung, looking upwards in removing cob-webs and other similar actions, and looking backwards in such actions as the avoiding of danger coming from behind, it is said, that the commentator uttered the passage beginning with the words: OR, BY THIS METHOD. *By that the commentator points out that the statement is also one of the kind that implies what is not expressed—an elliptical statement.*

Here, the comprehending of purpose (in looking straight on), without having just looked by the force of the thought, when the thought "I shall look straight on " arises, is clear comprehension of purpose. That should be understood by making the venerable elder Nanda the example of a person who perceives through experience by the body [kāya sakkhi].* The following is stated in this connection : " Should looking straight on in the eastern direction become a thing that must be done, by Nanda, he looks straight on in the eastern direction, having reflected with all his mind thus : 'May no covetous, grief-producing, mean, unskilful, mental phenomena flow upon (overcome) me while I am looking in the eastern direction.' There, he becomes mindful, thus. " Further, purposefulness and suitability, here, too, should be understood just according to the manner in which they are explained in connection with the worshipping of a relic shrine and so forth.

When the venerable elder Nanda was working for insight he slid into an unfavourable state of mind beginning with boredom in regard to the holy life and on becoming aware of that state of mind of his, he stirred himself, saying, " I will restrain myself well." Then having become energetic and very conscientious regarding guardedness at the doors of the controlling faculties of sense, he reached the state of one of great perfection in self-restraint, through the fulfilment of all duties. By reason of that perfection the Master placed him in the position of pre-eminence in regard to controlling faculty restraint, with the words : "This one, namely, Nanda, O bhikkhus, is the chief among my disciples endowed with controlling faculty restraint."

Because clear comprehension of resort is just the keeping to the course of meditation, **looking straight on** and **looking away from the front** should be done just according to each person's meditation (on the aggregates, processes and bases or on a contemplation-device and so forth) with the thought of meditation uppermost in mind.

Within, it is said, there certainly is no self or soul which looks straight on or looks away from the front. Still, at the arising of the thought " I shall look straight on," and with that thought, the process of oscillation [vāyo dhātu] originating from mind [citta samuṭṭhāna] bringing into being bodily expression [viññatti] arises. Thus owing to the diffusion of the process of oscillation born of mental activity [citta kiriya vāyodhātu vipphāra], the lower eyelid goes down and the upper eyelid goes up. Surely there is no one who opens with a contrivance.

Thereupon, eye-consciousness arises fulfilling the function of sight [tato cakkhu viññāṇaṁ dassana kiccaṁ sādhentaṁ uppajjati], it is said. Clear comprehension of this kind here is indeed called the clear comprehension of non-delusion [evam sampajānanaṁ panettha asammoha sampajaññaṁ nāma]. Further, clear comprehension of non-delusion should be also understood, here, through accurate knowledge of the root (mūla pariññā), through the casual state (āgantuka bhāva) and through the temporary state [tāvakālika bhāva]. First (is the consideration) by way of the accurate knowledge of the root :—

> There is (first) the mental state of the life-continuum,
> And (then) there are adverting, seeing, receiving,
> Considering, determining, and impulsion
> Which is seventh (in cognition's course).
>
> Bhavaṅgāvajjanañceva dassanaṁ sampaṭicchanaṁ
> santīraṇaṁ votthapanaṁ javanaṁ bhavati sattamaṁ.

There, in the course of cognition, the life-continuum goes on fulfilling the function of a (main) factor of the rebirth-process [tattha bhavaṅgaṁ upapatti bhavassa aṅga kiccaṁ sādhayamānaṁ pavattati] ; after the turning round of the life-continuum, barely active mind process, fulfilling the function of adverting or attending to an object at the sense-door of the eye, goes on [taṁ āvaṭṭetvā kiriya mano dhātu āvajjana kiccaṁ sādhayamānā]; from the cessation of that, fulfilling the function of seeing, eye-consciousness goes on [tannirodhā cakkhu viññāṇaṁ dassana kiccaṁ sādhayamānā]; from the cessation of that, resultant mind process, fulfilling the function of receiving, goes on [tannirodhā vipāka mano dhātu sampaṭicchana kiccaṁ sādhayamānā]; from the cessation of that, resultant mind consciousness process, fulfilling the function of considering, goes on [tannirodhā vipāka mano viññāṇa dhātu santīraṇa kiccaṁ sādhayamānā]; from the cessation of that, barely active mind consciousness process, fulfilling the function of determining, goes on [tannirodhā kiriya mano viññāṇa dhātu votthapana kiccaṁ sādhayamānā]; from the cessation of that, impulsion impels seven times [tannirodhā sattakkhattuṁ javanaṁ javati].

Now, among the mental states of the life-continuum and so forth or even in the mental state of the first impulsion, there is no **looking straight on** or **looking away from the front**, by way of lust, hatred or ignorance by him who sees in any direction. Also there is no such stained vision by him in the mental state of the second impulsion, the third, the fourth, the fifth, sixth or even in the seventh impulsion. But when like soldiers in a battlefield, the mental states, after breaking-up gradually are fallen, one atop of another, there takes place **looking straight on** or **looking away from the front**, by way of lust, hate and ignorance, accompanied by the discriminatory thought: "This is a woman," or " This is a man," much in the same way the fallen are distinguished after a battle; for in the frenzy of fighting there is no room for recognition of the individuals engaged in the fray.*

Thus here in the first instance, clear comprehension of non-delusion should be understood, by way of the accurate knowledge of the root.

The passage beginning with the words: WITHIN, IT IS SAID, THERE CERTAINLY IS NO SELF OR SOUL *is stated to explain that* LOOKING STRAIGHT ON *or* LOOKING AWAY FROM THE FRONT *is, to be sure, just a variety of occurrence of even bare phenomena and that therefore clear comprehension of non-delusion is the knowing of that fact as it really is [yasmā pana ālokitādi nāma dhamma mattasseva pavatti viseso tasmā tassa yathāvato jānanaṁ asammoha sampajaññanti dassetuṁ abbhantareti ādi vuttaṁ].*

Accurate knowledge of the root [mūla pariññā] = comprehension of the fundamental reason of impulsion at the mind-door [mano dvārika javanassa mūla kāraṇa parijānanaṁ].

Through the casual state [*āgantuka bhāva*] *: through the state of one come as a stranger* [*abbhāgata bhāva*]. *Through the temporary state* [*tāvakālika bhāva*] *: through the state of proceeding only at a certain moment* (*taṁ khaṇa matta pavattakassa bhāva*].

FULFILLING THE FUNCTION OF A (MAIN) FACTOR OF THE REBIRTH-PROCESS *means: accomplishing the principal work of a link; what is stated by that is this: having become substance. The life-continuum is, indeed, the principal factor and the principal substance because of similarity to the relinking mind. Therefore, it is called the principal factor and substance or it is called so owing to its fulfilling of the function of a ground or reason by way of the causal condition of unbroken procedure* [*paṭṭhāna bhūtam aṅga kiccaṁ nipphādentaṁ sarīraṁ hutvāti vuttaṁ hoti, bhavaṅgaṁ hi paṭisandhi sadisattā paṭṭhānaṁ aṅgaṁ paṭṭhānañca sarīranti vuccati, avicchedappavatti hetu bhāvena vā kāraṇa kiccaṁ sādhayamānanti attho*].

The expression: AFTER THE TURNING ROUND OF THAT *has been stated by way of general reference to the life-continuum, threefold as regards procedure: past thought-unit of the life-continuum, movement of the life-continuum and stoppage of the life continuum. At this place* TURNING ROUND *refers just to the stoppage of the life-continuum* [*Tam āvaṭṭetvāti bhavaṅga sāmañña vasena vuttaṁ pavattākāra visesa vasena pana atītādinā tibbidhaṁ tattha ca bhavaṅgupacchedasseva āvaṭṭanaṁ*].

FROM THE CESSATION OF THAT (TANNIRODHĀ) = *Owing to the dissolution of that* [*Tassa nirujjhanato*]—*expression of reason by way of proximity-condition* [*anantara paccaya vasena hetu vacanaṁ*].

EVEN IN THE FIRST IMPULSION *and so forth ending with* THE SEVENTH IMPULSION. *This passage has been stated concerning the absence (in a definite way) of lust, hate and ignorance with the thought:* THIS IS A WOMAN *or* THIS IS A MAN, *in the course of cognition at the five doors of sense. In this matter, indeed, owing to the existence of mental states, by way of adverting and the rest up to determining, without radical reflection, on account of reflecting unwisely prior to adverting-determining, impulsion that is with a bare semblance of greed arises in regard to a liked object such as a female form, and impulsion that is with a bare semblance of hate arises in regard to an object not liked. There is however no occurrence of lust, hate and ignorance in an extreme way, with strong moral consequences in the course of sense-door cognition. Only in the course of mind-door cognition lust, hate and ignorance occur absolutely, that is, with strong moral consequences. But impulsion of the course of sense-door cognition is the root of lust, hate and ignorance of the mind-door course of cognition. Or even all beginning with the mental state of the life-continuum can be taken as the root of mind-door impulsion. Thus accurate knowledge of the root has been stated by way of the root-reason of mind-door impulsion. The casual state and the temporary state (are) indeed (stated) on account of the newness of just impulsion of the course of cognition at the five doors of sense and on account of the brevity of the same impulsion* [*paṭhama javanepi*

.........pe.........sattama javanepīti idaṁ pañca dvārika vīthiyaṁ ayaṁ itthī ayaṁ purisoti rajjana dussana muyhanānamabhāvaṁ sandhāya vuttaṁ tattha hi āvajjana votthabbanānaṁ puretaraṁ pavattāyoniso manasikāra vasena ayoniso āvajjana votthabbanākārena pavattanto iṭṭhe itthī rūpādimhi lobha sahagata mattaṁ javanaṁ uppajjati aniṭṭhe ca dosa saha gata mattaṁ na pana ekanta rajjana dussanādi hoti tassa pana mano dvārikassa rajjana dussanādino pañca dvārika javanaṁ mūlaṁ yathā vuttaṁ vā sabbampi bhavaṅgādi evaṁ mano dvārikassa javanassa mūla kāraṇa vasena mūla pariññā vuttā. Āgantuka tāvakālikatā pana pañca dvārika javanasseva apubba bhāva vasena ittaratā vasena ca].

AFTER BREAKING UP GRADUALLY ARE FALLEN, ONE ATOP OF ANOTHER, *on account of the turning round—changing, moving—early and late or before and after or below and above, in the form of the arising of the mental state of the life-continuum* [*heṭṭhā ca upari ca parivattamāna vasena aparāparaṁ bhavaṅguppatti vasena*].

Likewise indeed (*is indicated*) *the falling after breaking down of the* (*other*) *mental states on account of the arising of the mental state of the life-continuum* [*Tathā bhavaṅguppāda vasena hi tesaṁ bhijjitvā patanaṁ*].

By this indeed the commentator shows, by way of the gradual arising of the earlier and the later mental state of the life-continuum, the arising of the impulsion of the mind-door course of cognition which is different to the impulsion of the course of cognition at the five doors of sense [*Iminā pana heṭṭhimassa uparimassa ca bhavaṅgassa aparāparuppatti vasena pañca dvārika javanato visadisassa mano dvārika javanassa uppādaṁ dasseti*].

Because of the proceeding of lust and the like by just the way of mind-door impulsion, the commentator said even thus : THERE TAKES PLACE LOOKING STRAIGHT ON OR LOOKING AWAY FROM THE FRONT, BY WAY OF LUST HATRED AND IGNORANCE.

On an object falling within reach of consciousness at the eye-door, impulsion arises right at the very end when from the movement of the life-continuum onwards, the states of adverting, seeing, receiving, considering and determining, having arisen, have ceased.

That impulsion is like a visitor, at the eyedoor which is comparable to a house belonging to the states of adverting and the rest mentioned above born there before the arising of impulsion.

As it is not fit for a visitor who has arrived at a strange house for the purpose of getting some assistance from the owners of the house to do any kind of ordering when the owners themselves are silent, so it is unfit for impulsion to be involved in lust, hate and ignorance, at the eyedoor house of adverting and the other states of mind, when those states of mind are themselves not lusting, hating or bound up with ignorance. Clear comprehension of non-delusion should thus be known by way of the casual state.

Verily, at the eyedoor, the mental states that close with the state of determining arise and break up together with associated phenomena, at just those places on which they arise. They do not see each other. Therefore the mental states that close with determining are brief and temporary. There, as in a house of the dead, where there is one more to die just at that very instant, it is not proper for that one who is to die to be given to delight in dancing and singing and the like, even so, at a sense-door, when the states of adverting and the rest with associated phenomena have died just where they arose, it is not fit for the remaining impulsion that is to die shortly to take delight in anything by way of lust and the like. Clear comprehension of non-delusion should be understood thus by way of the temporary state.

LIKE A VISITOR = *Like someone come specially, a stranger* [*Agantuka puriso viya*].

Visitors are of two kinds, by way of a guest, that is, a person who comes and goes, a person who does not stay permanently in a place, and by way of someone who comes specially to a place, a stranger. In this connection one who is an acquaintance, or one who is known is a guest. One who is not an acquaintance and is unknown is a stranger. According to the context here a stranger is meant.

Since to these mental states there is just that duration limited to the process of rise-and-fall of mental phenomena, these states of mind are called temporary.

And further this clear comprehension of non-delusion should be understood, by way of the reflection on the aggregates, bases, processes and conditions.

To be sure, here, eye and visible object are materiality-aggregate ; seeing is consciousness-aggregate ; feeling that is associated with seeing is feeling-aggregate ; perceiving is perception-aggregate and those beginning with sense-impression are formation-aggregate. Thus looking-straight-on-and-looking-away-from-the front is seen in the combination of these five aggregates. There, who singly, looks straight on ? Who looks away from the front ?

SEEING = *Eye-consciousness* [*Cakkhuviññāṇaṁ*]. *By reason of knowing the acts of looking straight on and of looking away from the front in that way only as " eye-consciousness ", adverting and the rest are left out, as bare seeing only is in " eye-consciousness."* [*tassa vaseneva ālokana vilokana paññāyananto āvajjanādīnamagahaṇaṁ*].

Separate from that fivefold aggregate who, singly, looks straight on ? Who, singly, looks away from the front ? None, singly, only by oneself, indeed, looks straight on and none, singly, only by oneself, looks away from the front—this reply is intended to be given to the questions.

In the same way, eye is eye-base ; visible object is materiality-base ; seeing is mind-base ; feeling and so forth, the associated things, are thing-base. Thus looking-straight-on-and-looking-away-from-the-front is seen in the combination of these four bases. There, who, singly, looks straight on ? Who looks away from the front. Likewise, eye is eye-process ; visible object is materiality-process ; seeing is eye-consciousness-process ; and the things beginning with feeling associated with eye-consciousness are mind-process. Thus looking-straight-on-and-looking-away-from-the-front is seen in the combination of these four processes. There who, singly, looks straight on ? Who looks away from the front ? Exactly, in the manner already stated, eye is support-condition ; visible object is object-condition ; adverting is condition of proximity, contiguity, decisive-support, absence and disappearance ; light is condition of decisive-support and those beginning with feeling are conascence-condition. Thus looking straight-on-and-looking-away-from-the-front is seen in the combination of these conditions. There, who, singly, looks straight on ? Who looks away from the front ?

With the words : LIGHT IS THE CONDITION OF DECISIVE-SUPPORT, *the conditionality of seeing is stated through the Suttanta method, through the way of illustrated discourse, discursively, indirectly.*

Conascence-condition too belongs to just seeing. This is (given as) only an example owing to the obtaining also of conditions of mutuality, association, presence, non-disappearance and so forth.

Here, in this way, by reflection on the aggregates, bases, processes, and conditions, too, clear comprehension of non-delusion should be understood.

3. Clear comprehension in the bending and the stretching of limbs.

SAMMIÑJITE PASĀRITE = "In bending and in stretching." In the bending and the stretching of the joints.

The consideration of purpose and lack of purpose in regard to any contemplated act of bending or stretching, and the taking up of that which is purposeful, after not bending and stretching according to merely the mind's inclination, is clear comprehension of purpose.

In this matter, a person who experiences pain every moment due to standing long with bent or stretched hands or feet does not get concentration of mind (mental onepointedness), his subject of meditation entirely falls away, and he does not obtain distinction (absorption and so forth). But he who bends or stretches hands, and feet for the proper length of time does not experience pain, gets concentration of mind, develops his subject of meditation and attains distinction. Thus the comprehension of purpose and non-purpose should be known.

Clear comprehension of suitability is the comprehension of the suitable after considering the suitable and the non-suitable even in a matter that is purposeful. In this connection, the following is the method of explanation : It is said that in the terrace of the Great Relic Shrine, while young bhikkhus were rehearsing the doctrine, young bhikkhunis standing at the back of the bhikkhus were listening to the rehearsal. Then a young bhikkhu came into bodily contact with a bhikkhuni while stretching out his hand, and, by just that fact, became a layman. Another bhikkhu in stretching his foot stretched it into fire and his foot got burnt to the bone. Another stretched his foot on an ant-hill and was bitten in the foot by a poisonous snake. Another bhikkhu stretched out his hand till it rested on the pole of a robe-tent ; a ribbon-snake on the pole bit the hand of that bhikkhu.

Therefore the stretching of one's limbs should be done in a suitable and not an unsuitable place. This should be understood here as clear comprehension of suitability.

Just by the showing of the tribulation of non-comprehension of that, the felicity of comprehension is made clear ; thus here, the illustration of these should be understood.

IN THE TERRACE OF THE GREAT RELIC SHRINE = *In the terrace of the great relic shrine known by the name of Hemamālī, at Anurādhapura, in Lankā, built by the king Duṭṭhagāmiṇi.*

BY JUST THAT FACT, BECAME A LAYMAN = *By reason of coming into bodily contact with a female, that bhikkhu having become filled with longing for sense-delights turned to the lower life of the world.*

ON THE POLE OF A ROBE-TENT = *On a pole fixed to th roof of a tent covered with robes.*

It is said by the commentator that bhikkhus having made a robe-tent were in that tent rehearsing the doctrine even on the terrace of the Great Relic Shrine.

It is said by the commentators, the elders Ānanda and Dhammapāla, that the ribbon-snake is a snake-species found in Lion Island.

Clear comprehension of resort should indeed be illustrated by the story of the senior bhikkhu called Great Elder.

It is said that Great Elder seated in his day-quarters bent his arm quickly whilst talking to his resident pupils and then after putting back his arm to the position in which it first was, bent it again slowly. The resident pupils questioned him thus : " Reverend Sir, why, after bending the arm quickly, did you, having placed it in the position in which it first was, bend it slowly ? " " Friends, until now, I did not bend arm with mind separate from the subject of meditation ever since I began to attend to the subject of meditation. Therefore, having put back the arm in the place it was first in, I bent." " Good ! , Reverend Sir. A bhikkhu should be one who acts thus. " Here, too, it should be understood that the non-abandoning of the subject of meditation is clear comprehension of resort.

SUBJECT OF MEDITATION = *The subject of meditation of the elements (modes or processes) that is according to the method about to be stated with the words " Within there is no soul " and so forth.*

Within there is no soul that bends or stretches. By the diffusion of the process of oscillation born of mental activity, bending and stretching occur. Indeed, here, it should be understood that the knowing in this way is clear comprehension of non-delusion.

4. Clear comprehension in wearing shoulder-cloak and so forth

SANGHĀṬI PATTA CĪVARA DHĀRAṆE = " In wearing the shoulder-cloak the other (two) robes and the bowl."

In this connection, purpose is what accrues materially to one, on the almsround, and what is stated by the Blessed One according to the method beginning with the words, " for keeping out cold, for keeping out heat. "

Suitable to one who is naturally warm-bodied is fine clothing, and that is suitable to one who is weak, too. To the susceptible to cold is suitable thick clothing made of two pieces of cloth laid one over the other and stitched together (called also a double cloth). Non-suitable to these is clothing contrary to the kind mentioned above.

A worn-out robe is verily not suitable as that robe will even be hindrance-causing when one patches and sews or darns it.

Likewise, hindrance-causing are robes of silk, fine hemp and similar material that stimulate cupidity. For to the lone-dweller in the forest such robes are productive of loss of clothing and of life.

With the words, TO THE LONE-DWELLER IN THE FOREST SUCH ROBES ARE PRODUCTIVE OF LOSS OF CLOTHING, *the commentator mentioned in part what constitutes the loss of* (*or destruction of*) *the life of purity and it is stated so because clothing is property free to be taken or used by or accessible to thieves and the like.*

The robe acquired by wrong means of livelihood and the robe which decreases the good and increases the bad in the one who wears it, are irreversibly not suitable.

Just by that statement (*of irreversibility*) *the commentator shows that the non-suitable mentioned earlier is not non-suitable absolutely, because of the possibility of the non-suitable mentioned earlier becoming suitable to someone, somewhen, owing to this or that reason. This pair* (*of robes mentioned*) *here is however absolutely non-suitable, on account of the absence of suitability to anyone, anywhen.*

Here, from the foregoing, clear comprehension of the suitable and the non-suitable should be understood ; as the holding fast to the line of meditative thought, *by way of the non-abandoning of the line of contemplation which the commentator is going to state* [*vakkhamāna kammaṭṭhānassa avijahana vasena*], clear comprehension of resort should be understood.

Within there is nothing called a soul that robes itself. According to the method of exposition adopted already, only, by the diffusion of the process of oscillation born of mental activity does the act of robing take place. The robe has no power to think and the body too has not that power. The robe is not aware of the fact that it is draping the body, and the body too of itself does not think : 'I am being draped round with the robe." Mere processes clothe a process-heap, in the same way that a modelled figure is covered with a piece of cloth. Therefore, there is neither room for elation on getting a fine robe nor for depression on getting one that is not fine.

WITHIN. *In one's own mental flux* [*Abbhantareti attano santāne*].

BODY TOO. *Body too is only an ego-concept* [*Kāyopīti atta paññatti matto kāyopi*].

I = *Karma produced body* [*Ahanti kamma bhūto kāyo*].

PROCESSES = *External processes called robes* [*cīvara sankhātā bāhirā dhātuyo*].

PROCESS-HEAP = *The internal process-collection called the body* [*Dhātu samūhanti kāya sankhātaṁ ajjhattikaṁ dhātu samūhaṁ*].

Some honour an ant-hill where a cobra de capello lives, a tree-shrine, and so forth, with garlands, perfumes, incense, cloth, and similar things. Others maltreat these objects. Ant-hill, tree-shrine and the like are, however, neither elated by the good nor depressed by the bad treatment. Just in the same way there should be no elation on receiving a good robe or depression on getting a bad one. Clear comprehension of non-delusion should be understood, in this connection, as the proceeding of reflective thought, in this way.

And in using the bowl clear comprehension of purpose should be understood, by way of the benefit obtainable through the action of one who takes the bowl unhurriedly and thinks : "Going out to beg with this I shall get alms."

With the seeing of the purpose, the obtaining of food, should the bowl be taken by one. In this way indeed does clear comprehension of purpose come to be.

To one with a lean body which is weak a heavy bowl is not suitable. And not suitable is a damaged bowl that is tied with thread and stopped in four or five places and hard to wash properly. A bowl that is hard to wash well, certainly, is not fit. There will be inconvenience caused to him who washes that kind of bowl.

A BOWL THAT IS HARD TO WASH WELL : *This was said concerning a bowl difficult to wash properly, naturally, though it may be without mends.*

A bright bowl which shines like a gem and therefore is capable of stimulating the cupidity of others is not suitable for the same reasons given in regard to robes of silk, fine hemp and so forth.

Just irreversibly unsuitable are the bowl acquired by wrong means of livelihood and the bowl by which good decreases and evils increase. Through this explanation, clear comprehension of suitability in this connection should be understood.

And by the fact even of the holding fast to the subject of meditation should clear comprehension of resort be understood.

Within there is nothing called a self that is taking the bowl. As stated already, by the diffusion of the process of oscillation born of mental activity, there is the taking of the bowl. In this matter of taking the bowl, the bowl cannot think. Hands too cannot think. The bowl does not cognize that it is taken by the hands. Hands do not cognize that the bowl is taken by them. Just processes take a process-heap. It is comparable to the taking of a red-hot vessel with a pair of tongs. By way of the proceeding of reflective thought in this way, clear comprehension of non-delusion should be understood in bowl-taking.

And further, it is like this : When kindly people see, in a refuge for the helpless, unfortunate persons, with hands and feet cut off, and with blood, pus, and many maggots in the open wounds, and give to the unfortunate persons bandages and medicine in containers, some of the miserable sufferers in the refuge may get thick bandages and containers not shapely ; others may get thin bandages and shapely containers. None of the sufferers will feel elated or depressed about the kind of bandages and containers they receive. That is because they merely want cloth to cover their wounds and containers for keeping medicine. Now, the bhikkhu who regards the robe as a bandage, the bowl as a medicine-container, and alms-food as medicine in the bowl, through clear comprehension of non-delusion should be taken as a person endowed with the highest clear comprehension.

A PERSON ENDOWED WITH THE HIGHEST CLEAR COMPREHENSION *should be known by way of the discernment of fineness of the characteristic activity of one possessed of the highest clear comprehension and by way of the highest state of the previous practisers of clear comprehension.*

5. Clear comprehension in the partaking of food and drink.

Purpose there is the eightfold purpose referred to with the words, " Not for sport " and so forth in the formula of reflection on the four requisites of a bhikkhu. As that should clear comprehension of purpose be known.

Non-suitable to one is the food by which to that one there is discomfort, whatever the food may be in quality or taste : coarse or fine or bitter or sweet or anything else. Suitable is food that does not cause discomfort.

Just irreversibly non-suitable are these : the food acquired by wrong means of livelihood and the food by which good decreases and evils increase in one who partakes of it. Food which is got by right means and food which does not cause decrease of good and increase of evil in the one taking it are suitable.

In this matter of the partaking of food, clear comprehension of suitability should be understood according to the explanation given above, and the clear comprehension of resort should be understood by way of the non-abandoning of the subject of meditation.

Within there is no eater called a self. As stated already, by the diffusion of the process of oscillation born of mental activity, only, there is the receiving of food in the bowl ; by the diffusion of the process of oscillation born of mental activity, only, there is the descent of the hand into the bowl ; and by the diffusion of the process of oscillation born of mental activity, only, the making of the food into suitable lumps, the raising of the lumps from the bowl, and the opening of the mouth take place. No one opens the jaws with a key. No one opens the jaws with a contrivance. Just, by the diffusion of the process of oscillation born of mental activity, take place the putting of a lump of food in the mouth, the pestle-action of the upper row of teeth, the mortar-work of the lower row of teeth, and the tongue's activity comparable to that of the hand collecting together material that is being crushed. Thus that lump of food in the mouth is mixed together with the thin saliva at the end of the tongue and the thick saliva at the root of the tongue. That food in the mortar of the lower teeth, turned by the tongue moistened by the saliva, and ground fine by the pestle of the upper teeth is not put into the stomach by anyone with a ladle or a spoon. Just by the process of oscillation it goes in. There is no one within who having made a straw mat is bearing each lump that goes in. Each lump stands by reason of the process of oscillation. There is no one who having put up an oven and lit a fire is cooking each lump standing there. By only the process of caloricity the lump of food matures. There is no one who expels each digested lump with a stick or pole. Just the process of oscillation expels the digested food.

It is oscillation [vayodhātu] that does the taking onward, the moving away from side to side ; and it is oscillation that bears, turns round, pulverizes, causes the removal of liquidity, and expels.

Extension [Paṭhavīdhātu] also does bearing up, turning round, pulverizing and the removal of liquidity.

Cohesion [Āpodhātu] moistens and preserves wetness.

Caloricity [Tejodhātu] ripens or digests the food that goes in.

Space [Ākāsadhātu] becomes the way for the entering of the food.

Consciousness [Viññāṇadhātu] as a consequence of right kind of action knows in any particular situation.

According to reflection of this sort, should the clear comprehension of non-delusion be understood here.

TAKING ONWARD = *moving on up to the mouth.*

MOVING AWAY FROM SIDE TO SIDE : *taking forwards from there to the belly.*

Again, TAKING ONWARD = *carrying beyond the mouth-aperture.*

MOVING AWAY FROM SIDE TO SIDE = *taking what is going belly-wards, side-wise.*

BEARS = *causes to stand in the stomach.*

TURNS ROUND = *causes to turn back and forth.*

PULVERIZES = *causes the complete powdering as if by a pestle.*

EXPELS = *causes the depositing outside the belly.*

In regard to the functions of the process of extension, too, the explanation is similar to that which has been already stated.

Indeed, these—bearing, turning, pulverizing, drying—the process of oscillation is able to do, only, together with the process of extension. Not singly by itself. Therefore, these—bearing, turning, pulverizing, the removal of liquidity or drying—,too, are stated by way of the functions of the process of extension.

MOISTENS = *makes humid.*

PRESERVES WETNESS : *Just as there is no very great drying by the process of oscillation and so forth, so the process of cohesion preserves wetness by not wetting quite.*

THE WAY = *the way for entering, turning round, expelling (actually the openings or vacuities which provide the range for such functions).*

PROCESS OF CONSCIOUSNESS = *mind-consciousness process, the knowledge in regard to seeking food, swallowing and the like.*

IN ANY PARTICULAR SITUATION = *in any function of seeking, swallowing or other similar act.*

RIGHT KIND OF ACTION. *The act which even completes a function and becomes a condition for any particular kind of knowledge. That act causes fulfilment of even the knowledge of the scope of that function, by reason of that knowledge not coming to be without the act.*

KNOWS. *Perceives, understands, by way of seeking, by way of full experience of swallowing, by way of the digested, the undigested and so forth.*

It should be understood that as knowledge is always preceded by the adverting or the turning of the mind to a thing, knowledge too is included here.

Further, the clear comprehension of non-delusion should be understood through reflection on the unpleasantness connected with food, in the following ten ways : By way of the need to go to get it (1), to seek it (2), the process of eating it (3), by way of the receptacle (in the form of secretion of bile, and so forth) (4), by way of the belly (5), by way of food that is indigested (6), by way of food that is digested (7), by way of the consequences of eating (8), by way of the trickling or oozing of food from the body's openings in the form of excretions (9), and by way of the pollution due to food (10).

The detailed exposition of the contemplation on the unpleasantness connected with food is given in the Path of Purity (and its scholium, The Casket of the Highest Thing, Paramattha Mañjūsā).

BY WAY OF THE NEED TO GO FOR IT (FOOD) : *By way of going towards the alms-village in the sense of wandering for alms. The return journey is also included.*

BY WAY OF THE NEED TO SEEK IT : *By way of wandering for alms in the alms-village. Entry into a retiring hall and the like get included in this, naturally.*

BY WAY OF THE PROCESS OF EATING IT : *By way of taking in the contemptible food comparable to dog's vomit in a dog's food trough, rid of colour and odour just when the tongue turns the food which has been reduced to a pulp by the pestles of the teeth.*

BY WAY OF THE RECEPTACLE (IN THE FORM OF EXCRETION OF BILE, PHLEGM, PUS AND BLOOD): *Through the food thus taken in becoming the condition for prime contemptibility, by way of the fourfold receptacle placed on the top of the stomach.*

What stands, exists, there, in the upper part of the stomach is the staying place, the receptacle.

BY WAY OF THE FOOD THAT IS INDIGESTED : *By way of non-preparation of the food in the stomach and the intestines for absorption by the body, through the process of karma-produced caloricity called "the seizer" a supposed organ of the body which functions in digestion, according to Āyurvedic teaching of ancient India.*

BY WAY OF FOOD THAT IS DIGESTED : *Digested through just the karma-produced process of caloricity abovementioned.*

BY WAY OF THE CONSEQUENCES OF EATING : *By way of effect. By way of the business called the bringing about of carcase-products like hair, and diseases like skin eruptions through the digested and indigested food. This is stated by the commentator as the fruit of food.*

BY WAY OF THE TRICKLING OR OOZING OF FOOD FROM THE BODY'S OPENINGS IN THE FORM OF EXCRETIONS : *By way of the flowing out from eye, ear and several other openings, here and there. For it is said by the Ancients :*

Hard eats, soft eats, food and drink superfine,
Get in at one door and get out by nine.

BY WAY OF THE POLLUTION DUE TO FOOD : *By way of the smearing throughout, when eating, of the hands, lips, and other members of that kind, and, after eating, of the nine openings or doors of the body.*

6. Clear comprehension of cleansing the body.

UCCĀRA PASSĀVAKAMME = "In defecating and in urinating" means : When the time is come, *when the time is proper,* if one does not defecate or urinate, then, one's body perspires, one's eyes reel, one's mind is not collected, and illnesses *in the form of sharp pain, fistula, and so forth* arise for one. But to one who defecates and urinates at the proper time none of these discomforts, disadvantages, troubles and illnesses arise. This is the sense in which this matter should be understood, and in this sense should clear comprehension of purpose in defecation and urination be taken.

By defecating or urinating in an improper place, one commits disciplinary offences, one goes on getting a bad name, and one endangers one's life. *Fields occupied or frequented by humans and places occupied or frequented by devas, and deva-sanctuaries, are improper. Angry men and spirits cause even death to those who defecate or urinate in such places. By using such places for cleansing the waste of the body bhikkhus and bhikkhunis become guilty of the disciplinary offences of minor wrong-doing (dukkaṭā) or of acts expiable by confession (pācittiyā) according to the circumstances.*

But to one evacuating the bowels or the bladder in a place suitable for such evacuation those offences or troubles just mentioned above have no reference. And by way of that fitness of place clear comprehension of suitability should be understood.

By the non-abandoning of the subject of meditation, clear comprehension of resort should be understood.

Within there is no doer of the act of defecation or urination. Only by the diffusion of the process of oscillation born of mental activity defecation and urination occur. Just as in a matured boil, by the bursting of the boil, pus and blood come out without any kind of wishing to come out and just as from an overfull water-pot water comes out without any desire for coming out, so, too, the faeces and urine accumulated in the abdomen and the bladder are pressed out by the force of the process of oscillation. Certainly this faeces-and-urine coming out thus is neither that bhikkhu's own nor another's. It is just bodily excretion. When from a water-vessel or calabash a person throws out the old water, the water thrown out is neither his nor others'. It simply forms part of a process of cleansing. In the form of reflection proceeding in this way clear comprehension of non-delusion should be understood here.

7. Clear comprehension of walking and so forth.

Now we come to the explanation of the instruction dealing with clear comprehension "in walking, in standing in a place, in sitting in some position, in sleeping, in waking, in speaking and in keeping silence" = GATE ṬHITE NISINNE SUTTE JĀGARITE BHĀSITE TUṆHĪBHĀVE.

By the words: "When he is going, a bhikkhu understands: 'I am going,'" and so forth postures of long duration are indicated. And by the words, "in going forwards and backwards.........in bending and in stretching," postures of middling duration; and by the words, "in walking, in standing.........in sleeping," postures of short, brief duration. Therefore in these three parts of the instruction the practising of clear comprehension should be known even by the triple method stated here.

POSTURES OF LONG DURATION [*Addhāna iriyāpathā*] *: postures kept up long or postures existing in a process of going far or of one wayfaring long.*

POSTURES OF MIDDLING DURATION [*Majjhimā*] *: postures proceeding neither too long in time nor involving too long wayfaring, namely, those connected with wandering for alms and so forth.*

POSTURES OF SHORT DURATION [*Cuṇṇikā iriyāpathā*] *: postures become diminutive, by reason of brief duration and proceeding by way of going about and so forth in the monastery or elsewhere.*

The Elder Tipiṭaka Mahā Sīva, indeed said: Who, after walking or exercising long in the ambulatory, stands and reflects: "The bodily and mental things which existed during the time of exercise on the ambulatory ended just there on the ambulatory", is called a doer of clear comprehension in walking.

Who, after standing for a long time in study or answering a question or minding a subject of meditation, sits and reflects: "The bodily and mental things which existed during the time of standing ended just at the time of standing," is called a doer of clear comprehension in standing.

Who, after sitting for a long time in study or other similar work, lies down and reflects : " The bodily and mental things which existed when sitting ended just at the time of sitting," is called a doer of clear comprehension in sitting.

Who, after lying down falls asleep, and, then, after getting up from his sleep, reflects : " The bodily and mental things which existed during the time of sleep ended just during sleep," is called a doer of clear comprehension in sleeping and waking.

By reason of proximity of the word " waking ", here the action of lying down is only sleep in the sense of the descent of the mind into the state of the life-continuum. It is not merely the stretching out of the back.

The non-occurrence of processes which make action or are made of action is sleep ; the occurrence, waking.

Action is doing, function of body and so forth (i.e. bodily expression or verbal expression, kāyaviññatti vā vacīviññatti). The processes which make action produce the function of bodily expression or the function of verbal expression. Or action is the double function of adverting. The things made of or produced from that action or double function are processes made of action. For by way of adverting, when there is the stoppage of the life-continuum, courses of cognition arise. [*Karaṇaṁ kriyā kāyādikiccaṁ. Taṁ nibbatentīti kriyāmayāni. Athavā āvajjanadvayakiccaṁ kriyā ; tāya pakatāni, nibbattāni vā kriyāmayāni. Avajjanavasenahi bhavaṅgupacchede sati vīthicittāni uppajjanti*].

Processes are things which go on, move changing, by arising gradually in different ways. Somewhere there is the reading " of mental states " " of action-making mental states, kriyāmaya cittānaṁ." It should be understood that is not a reading of the Ancients as it is against the commentary and scholium to the Abhidhamma and other books. [*Aparāparuppattiyā nānappakārato vattanti parivattantīti pavattāni. Katthaci pana cittānanti pāṭho. So Abhidhammaṭṭhakathādīhi taṭṭīkāhi ca viruddhattā na Porāṇa pāṭhoti veditabbo*].

Impulsion of either course of cognition (mind-door or five-door course of cognition) is a process made of action. Therefore it is said in the scholium to the Abhidhamma, "On account of the condition of processes making action of body and so forth and by reason of the condition of originating action of adverting, impulsion of either course of cognition, or just of every process of the six doors gets known as a process which makes or is made of action." [*Javanaṁ sabbampi vā chaddvārika vīthi cittaṁ kriyāmaya pavattāni. Tenāha Abhidhammaṭīkāyaṁ kāyādi kriyāmayattā avajjanakriyā samuṭṭhitattā ca javanaṁ sabbampi vā chaddvarapavattaṁ kriyāmaya-pavattaṁ nāmāti*].*

NON-OCCURRENCE : *Non-arising (of the processes which make action or are made of action) at the time of falling asleep is called sleep. Thus the thing should be understood. Otherwise sleep could be called the proceeding of even all states of door-free consciousness (namely, every instance of the supervention of the life-continuum), before and after the six-door states of consciousness ; so, it should be understood that the supervention of the life-continuum at a time other than that of falling asleep is included in waking. [Appavattanti niddokkamana kāle anuppajjanaṁ suttaṁ nāmāti attho gahetabbo. Itarathā chaddvārika cittānaṁ pure carānucaravasena uppajjantānaṁ sabbesampi dvāravimutta cittānaṁ pavattaṁ suttaṁ nama siyā, evañca katvā niddokkamana kālato aññasmiṁ kāle uppajjantānaṁ dvāravimutta cittānampi pavattaṁ jāgarite sangayhatīti veditabbaṁ].*

He who whilst speaking thinks : " This sound arises dependent on the lips, teeth, tongue, palate, and the act of the mind that accords to that sound," speaks, mindful and clearly comprehending.

He who for a long time having studied or expounded the Teaching or recited the words of his subject of meditation, or cleared a question, later, on becoming silent, thinks : " The bodily and mental things which arose during the time of speaking ended just then," is called a doer of clear comprehension in speaking.

He who, after remaining silent long considering the Teaching or his subject of meditation, thinks that the bodily and mental things that existed in the time of silence ended just then, that the occurrence of derived material qualities is speech, and that the non-occurrence of these is silence is called a doer of clear comprehension in keeping silence.

This dominance of non-delusion stated by the Elder Mahā Sīva is intended here in this Discourse on the Arousing of Mindfulness. But in the Discourse on the Fruit of the Homeless Life (Sāmaññaphala Sutta) even the entire four-fold clear comprehension is found. Therefore in a special way, here, only by way of clear comprehension of non-delusion should be understood the state of doing clear comprehension.

The occurrence of the sound-base is speech ; its non-occurrence is silence [saddāyatanassa pavattanaṁ bhāsanaṁ appavattanaṁ tuṇhī].

Since, indeed, in the exposition of the Elder Mahā Sīva the state of clear comprehension is considered by way of the vision of the ending then and there of material and mental qualities occurring in posture after posture, without a break, the state of clear comprehension should be known by way of the insight portion of the clear comprehension of non-delusion come down in the Discourse on the Arousing of Mindfulness ; not by way of the detailing of the four-fold clear comprehension. Therefore, only, in the Discourse on the Fruit of the Homeless Life (Sāmaññaphala Sutta) is that four-fold clear comprehension intended.

The dominance of non-delusion refers to the statement to which non-delusion is the dominant or principal thing. This statement of the Elder Mahā Sīva contains the reason that is found only in the Satipaṭṭhāna Sutta in this connection, namely, clear comprehension of non-delusion, by way of the insight portion or turn; and not the detailing of four-fold clear comprehension as given in the Sāmaññaphala Sutta.

In all statements the meaning of the term "clear comprehension" should be understood by way of only clear comprehension that is endowed with mindfulness. Indeed in the Book of Classifications (Vibhangappakaraṇe) these, are put just in this way: "One goes forward, mindful and clearly comprehending; one goes backwards, mindful and clearly comprehending."*

By the words ONLY CLEAR COMPREHENSION THAT IS ENDOWED WITH MINDFULNESS *both the importance of clear comprehension by way of function and that of mindfulness are taken. Indeed it is not the pointing out of merely the condition of mindfulness with clear comprehension; for it is said, "nowhere does knowledge exist without mindfulness."*

Now in order to reinforce that thing by the Classificatory Method too [Vibhanga nayenāpi tadatthaṁ samatthetuṁ] the words, "Indeed, in the Book of Classifications" and so forth were spoken by the commentator.

By this, indeed, one makes clear the importance even of mindfulness here as of clear comprehension. [Iminā pī hi sampajaññassa viya satiyā pettha paṭṭhānaṁ (padhānaṁ) yeva vibhāveti].

There, "THESE" *refers to the synoptical statement beginning with "In going forwards and in going backwards, he is a doer of clear comprehension." [Tattha etāni padānīti abhikkante patikkante sampajāna kārī hotīti ādīni uddesa padāni].*

The reciters of the Middle Collection [Majjhimabhāṇakā] however and the scholars of the Abhidhamma [Abhidhammikā] say thus: "A certain bhikkhu goes thinking the while of something else, considering something else (that is, not thinking of or considering his action of going, or his subject of meditation).

Another goes without causing the abandoning of the subject of meditation. In the same manner, a certain bhikkhu thinking the while of something else, considering something else, is standing, sitting, or sleeping (lying down); another sleeps (lies down) without causing the abandoning of the subject of meditation." [Eko bhikkhu gacchanto aññaṁ cintento aññaṁ vitakkento gacchati. Eko kammaṭṭhānaṁ avissajjetvā va gacchati. Tathā eko tiṭṭhanto nisidanto sayanto aññaṁ cintento aññaṁ vitakkento sayati. Eko kammaṭṭhānaṁ avissajjetvā va sayati].

*Indeed the earnest bhikkhu comprehends thus : The material and mental qualities which existed at the east end of the ambulatory passed away just there without reaching the west end of the ambulatory. The material and mental qualities which existed at the west end of the ambulatory, too, passed away just there without reaching the east end of the ambulatory. The material and mental qualities which existed at the very centre of the ambulatory passed away just there without reaching either end of the ambulatory. The material and mental qualities which existed in walking passed away without reaching the position of standing. The material and mental qualities which existed in the position of standing passed away just there without reaching the position of sitting ; of sitting, without reaching the position of sleeping. He causes the mind to enter the life-continuum, the unconscious, again and again comprehending in this way. He arises only after taking up the subject of meditation. This bhikkhu is a doer of clear comprehension in walking (going about) and so forth. In this way, however, the subject becomes unclear in sleep ; the subject of meditation should not be made unclear. Therefore the bhikkhu having exercised to the full extent of his ability on the ambulatory, stood, and sat, lies down comprehending thus : "The body is unconscious ; the bed is unconscious. The body does not know, 'I am lying down on the bed.' The bed also does not know. 'On me the body is lying down.' He, whilst just comprehending again and again thus : "The unconscious body is lying down on the unconscious bed," causes the mind to enter the life-continuum, the unconscious. He awakes only after taking up the subject of meditation. This bhikkhu is called a doer of clear comprehension in sleeping.**

ITI AJJHATTAṀ = "Thus internally." Thus the bhikkhu lives contemplating the body in the body by way of the laying hold of the fourfold comprehension, either in his own body or in another's body, or at one time in his own body, and in another's at another time. And, here too, "in contemplating origination" and so forth, the origin and the dissolution of only the materiality aggrègate should, in the exposition, be taken out. The remainder is to be understood just by the method already stated by the commentator. Here, the Truth of Suffering is the mindfulness which lays hold of the fourfold clear comprehension ; the Truth of Origination is the pre-craving which originates that mindfulness ; the non-occurrence of either is the Truth of Cessation ; the Real Path already stated is the Way-truth. Thus, the bhikkhu having striven by way of the Four Real Truths reaches peace. This is verily the means of deliverance up to saintship of one who lays hold of the fourfold clear comprehension.

THE SECTION OF REFLECTION ON REPULSIVENESS

After explaining body-contemplation by way of the fourfold clear comprehension, to explain it by way of the reflection of repulsiveness, the Master said : " And further," and so forth.

Everything that should be said in connection with the passage beginning with " On just this body " and so forth is stated in detail, taking into consideration all aspects of the matter, in the Path of Purity, the Visuddhi Magga, and its scholium, The Casket of the Highest Thing, Paramattha Mañjūsā ; a summary of that account is given here.

This reflection by way of mindfulness directed bodywards, called the reflection of repulsiveness is unknown to non-Buddhists in the form of subject of meditation development (kammaṭṭhāna bhāvanā vasena). Hence it is a thing which comes into being when a Buddha arises; not at other times. This mindfulness directed bodywards leads to the following :

Great moral-emotional upsurge (Mahā saṁvega)
The great tranquillity or security based on effort (Mahā yogakkhema)
Great mindfulness and clear comprehension (Mahā sati sampajañña)
Attainment of insight-knowledge (Ñāṇadassanapaṭilābha)
Happy living here and now (Diṭṭhadhammasukhavihāra)
Realisation of the fruition of wisdom and freedom* (Vijjāvimuttiphalasacchikiriya).

This mindfulness has been explained in the following sections : Breathing-in-and-out ; four kinds of deportment ; the fourfold clear comprehension ; the reflection on repulsiveness ; the reflection on the elements or modes of existence ; and the nine cemetery contemplations.

There are these seven kinds of skill in study to be acquired in regard to this subject of meditation by :

Repetition of the thirty-two parts of the body verbally (vacasā).

Repetition of the parts only mentally (manasā).

Determining of the hair of the head and so forth according to colour (vaṇṇato).

Determining of the parts according to shape (saṇṭhānato).

Determination of situation of the parts as above or below the navel on the upper or lower side of the body, directionally (disāto).

Determination of the place in the body occupied by a part, that is, determination spatially (okāsato).

Determination of one part by the position of another to it and by way of dissimilarity of one part to another (paricchedato).

There are these ten kinds of skill in reflecting on this subject of meditation :

Doing the meditation gradually as one climbing a stairway one step after another in due order taking one part after another serially (anupubbato).

Doing it not too quickly (nātisighato).

Doing it not too slowly (nātisaṇikato).

Doing it by warding off mental rambling (vikkhepapaṭibāhanato).

Practice by way of going beyond the concept of hair and so forth to the idea of repulsiveness (paṇṇattisamatikkamanato).

Practice by gradual elimination of the less clear parts (anupubbamuñcanato).

Practice by way of the part which is the source of ecstasy (appanāto).

Practice by way of the Three Discourses : Adhicitta,* Sītibhāva,** and Bojjhangakosalla.***

The following is the application of the simile : Like the bag with the two openings is the body made up of the four great primaries, earth, water, fire and air. The thirty-two parts beginning with hair-of-the-head are like the various grains thrown into that bag after mixing them. Like a man with seeing eyes is the yogin. Comparable to the time when after unloosing the bag the various grains become clear to one reflecting is the time when the thirty-two parts become clear to the yogin.

ITI AJJHATTAṀ = "Thus internally." The bhikkhu lives contemplating the body in his body or in another's. Sometimes he contemplates the body in his own body at other times in another's, by way of laying hold on things beginning with the hair of the head.

From here the meaning should be known just in the way already stated by the commentator. Here the mindfulness which lays hold of the thirty-two parts, is the Truth of suffering. Having interpreted, thus, the portal to emancipation should be understood.

THE SECTION OF REFLECTION ON THE MODES OF MATERIALITY

The Master having explained body-contemplation in the form of reflection on the repulsiveness of the thirty-two parts of the body, said: "And further", now, to set forth body-contemplation by way of reflection on the modes (or elements) of materiality.

The elaboration of the meaning together with the application of the simile, in this connection, is as follows:

Just as if some cow-butcher or a cow-butcher's apprentice, a man who works for his keep, having killed a cow and made it into parts were sitting at a four-cross-road, just so, a bhikkhu reflects, by way of the modes, on the body, in any one of the four postures thus: "There are in this body the modes of extension, cohesion, caloricity, and oscillation."

The cow-butcher does not get rid of the cow-percept while feeding the cow, driving it to the place of slaughter, tying it and putting it up there, killing it, and even when seeing the dead carcase of the cow; not until he cuts it up and divides it into parts does the cow-percept disappear. To that butcher sitting (with the meat before him) after cutting up the cow, however, the cow-percept disappears, and the perception of flesh comes into being. To him there is not this thought: "I am selling the cow; these people are taking away the cow." But to him, indeed, there occurs this thought: "I am selling flesh; these people, indeed, are taking away flesh."

To the bhikkhu, similarly, the being-percept or the person-percept does not disappear the while he does not reflect, by way of the modes of materiality, on this body as it is placed or disposed in whatsoever position, after sifting thoroughly the apparently compact aggregation. To him reflecting by way of the modes of materiality, however, the perception of a being disappears; the mind gets established by way of the modes of materiality. Therefore, the Blessed One declared: "A bhikkhu reflects on just this body according as it is placed or disposed, by way of the modes of materiality, thinking thus: 'There are, in this body, the mode of solidity, the mode of cohesion, the mode of caloricity, and the mode of oscillation.' O bhikkhus, in whatever manner, a clever cow-butcher or a cow-butcher's apprentice, having slaughtered a cow and divided it by way of portions should be sitting at the junction of a four-cross-road, in the same manner, a bhikkhu reflects.........

.........thinking thus : ' there are, in this body, the mode of solidity ....and the mode of oscillation." = IMAMEVA KĀYAṀ YATHĀṬHITAṀ YATHĀ PAṆIHITAṀ DHĀTUSO PACCAVEKKHATI : ATTHI IMASMIṀ KĀYE PAṬHAVĪDHĀTU ĀPODHĀTU TEJODHĀTU VĀYODHĀTŪTI. SEYYATHĀPI BHIKKHAVE DAKKHO GOGHĀTAKO VĀ GOGHĀTAKANTEVASĪ VĀ GĀVIṀ VADHITVĀ CĀTUMMAHĀPATHE BILASO PAṬIVIBHAJITVĀ NISSINNO ASSA EVAMEVA KHO BHIKKHAVE BHIKKHU IMAMEVA KĀYAṀ.........PACCAVEKKHATI ATTHI IMASMIṀ KĀYE PAṬHAVĪDHĀTU.........VĀYODHĀTŪTI.

Comparable to the cow-butcher is the yogi, to the cow-percept the percept of a being; to the four-cross-road, the fourfold posture ; and to the state of sitting with the cow's flesh in front after dividing the cow into parts, the reflection by way of the modes of materiality. Here, this is the textual explanation. Details of the reflection on the modes of materiality as a subject of meditation, however, are given in The Path of Purity.

ITI AJJHATTAṀ = "Thus internally". One dwells contemplating the body in the body thus by way of the laying hold of the four modes of materiality, in one's own or in another's body or at one time in one's own and at another time in another's body. From here on the exposition should be known just by the method already mentioned. The mindfulness which lays hold of the four modes of materiality is the Truth of Suffering. Thus the portal to deliverance should be known.

By the word PLACED *there is the elucidation of occasion by way of own (or particular) function of material things known as the body in various moments [kāya sankhātaṁ rūpadhammānaṁ tasmiṁ tasmiṁ khaṇe sakicca vasena avatthāna paridīpanaṁ].*

By the word DISPOSED *here the following meaning should be known : By way of condition, the putting down or settling owing to the arrangement of several conditions [Paccaya vasena tehi tehi paccayehi pakārato nihitaṁ].*

REFLECTS (*Paccavekkhati*) = *Considers again and again, sees analytically, part by part, separately, after sifting thoroughly with the eye of wisdom [Paṭi paṭi avekkhati ñāṇacakkhunā vinibhujjitvā visuṁ visuṁ passati].*

THE SECTION ON THE NINE CEMETERY CONTEMPLATIONS

After explaining body-contemplation in the form of the modes of materiality, the Master said, " And further," in order to explain body-contemplation through the nine cemetery contemplations.

UDDHUMĀTAṀ = " Swollen ". By reason of the swelled state of the corpse comparable to a pair of wind-filled bellows owing to the gradually uprisen bloatedness after death.

VINĪLAKAṀ = " Blue " is stated to be the colour of fully differing shades [viparibhinnavaṇṇaṁ]. Blue is that corpse which is reddish in the protuberantly fleshy parts, and whitish in the purulent parts, while, in those parts which are predominantly blue it seems to be as though covered with a blue mantle. This is the descriptive statement of the " blue " corpse.

VIPUBBAKAJĀTAṀ = " Festering " is the corpse that is full of pus flowing from the broken parts or from the nine openings of the body.

SO IMAMEVA KĀYAṀ UPASAṀHARATI AYAMPI KHO KĀYO EVAṀ DHAMMO EVAṀ BHĀVĪ ETAṀ ANATĪTOTI = " He thinks of his own body thus : ' Verily, this body of mine, too, is of the same nature as that (dead) body, is going to be like that body, and has not got past the condition of becoming like that body.

This has been stated : By the existence of these three : life [āyu], warmth [usmā], consciousness [viññāṇaṁ], this body can endure to stand, to walk, and do other things ; by the separation of these three however this body is indeed a thing like that corpse, is possessed of the nature of corruption, is going to become like that, will become swollen, blue and festering and cannot escape the state of being like that, cannot transcend the condition of swelling up, becoming blue and festering.

ITI AJJHATTAṀ = " Thus internally." Thus by laying hold of the state of swelling and so forth, in regard to one's own body or another's, or at one time in regard to one's own and at another in regard to another's, one dwells contemplating the body in the body.

KHAJJAMĀNAM = " Whilst it is being eaten" : When crows and other creatures after sitting on the belly or another part of the corpse are eating the carcase by picking the flesh of the belly, of the lips, the corners of the eye and so forth.

SAMAṀSALOHITAṀ = "Together with (some) flesh and blood": With the flesh and blood still remaining.

NIMMAṀSALOHITAṀ = "Blood-besmeared (skeleton) without flesh." When though rid of flesh the blood is still not dry.

AÑÑENA = "In a different place": In a different direction.

HATTHAṬṬHIKAṀ = "Bone of the hand": The sixty-four kinds of bones of the hand. When these are lying in different places separate from one another. In the explanation of the bone of the foot and so forth the method is the same as this.

TEROVASSIKĀNI = "More than a year old": Beyond a year in a state of exposure.

PUTĪNI = "Rotten": Just those in the open become rotten by being exposed to wind, sun and rain for over a year. Bones buried in the earth last longer.

CUÑÑAKAJĀTĀNI = "Become dust": Scattered in the form of powder.

Everywhere, according to the method already stated beginning: "He thinks of his own body thus: 'Verily, this body of mine too is of the same nature as that (dead) body, is going to be like that body, and has not got past the condition of becoming like that body.'"

ITI AJJHATTAṀ = "Thus internally": Thus through the laying hold of the corpse from the state in which it is being eaten by crows and other creatures to the state when it is dust one dwells contemplating the body in one's own body, or in another's or at one time in one's own body and at another time in another's body.

Further having stopped here one should put together the nine cemetery contemplations thus:

EKĀHAMATAṀ VĀ DVĪHIMATAṀ VĀ TĪHIMATAṀ VĀ = "A body dead one, two or three days." This is the first contemplation.

KĀKEHI KHAJJAMĀNAṀ = "Whilst it is being eaten by crows." This portion of the Discourse where the devouring of the body by various kinds of animals is stated refers to the second contemplation.

AṬṬHIKASAṀKHALIKAṀ SAMAṀSALOHITAṀ NAHĀRUSAMBANDHAṀ = "A skeleton together with (some) flesh and blood held in by the tendons." This is the third contemplation.

NIMMAṀSALOHITAMAKKHITAṀ NAHĀRUSAMBANDHAṀ = " A bloodsmeared skeleton without flesh but held in by the tendons." This is the fourth.

APAGATAMAṀSALOHITAṀ NAHĀRUSAMBANDHAṀ = " A skeleton held in by the tendons but without flesh and not besmeared with blood." This is the fifth.

AṬṬHIKĀNI APAGATASAMBANDHĀNI = " Bones gone loose, scattered in all directions." This is the sixth.

AṬṬHIKĀNI SETĀNI SANKHAVAṆṆŪPANIBHĀNI = " Bones white in colour like a conch." This is the seventh.

AṬṬHIKĀNI PUÑJAKITĀNI TEROVASSIKĀNI=" Bones more than a year old heaped together." This is the eighth.

AṬṬHIKĀNI PUTĪNI CUÑÑAKAJĀTĀNI = " Bones gone rotten and become dust." This is the ninth.

EVAṀ KHO BHIKKHAVE = " Thus, indeed, o bhikkhus." He said this bringing to an end body-contemplation after pointing out the nine cemetery contemplations. The mindfulness which lays hold of the nine cemetery contemplations is the Truth of Suffering ; the previous craving which originates that mindfulness is the Truth of Origin ; the non-occurrence of both that mindfulness and the craving is the Truth of Cessation. The Real Path that understands suffering, casts out the origin, and has cessation for its object is the Truth of the Way. Endeavouring in this way by means of the Four Truths one arrives at peace. This is for the bhikkhu who lays hold of the nine cemetery contemplations the portal of deliverance up to saintship.

Now, these are the fourteen portions which comprise body-contemplation : The section on breathing in and breathing out, on the postures, on the four kinds of clear comprehension, of reflection on repulsiveness, on the modes of materiality, and on the nine cemetery contemplations. There, only the sections on breathing in and breathing out and of the reflection on repulsiveness can become meditation-subjects of full absorption. As the cemetery contemplations are stated by way of consideration of disadvantages, dangers or evils, all the remaining twelve are only meditation-subjects of partial absorption.

THE CONTEMPLATION OF FEELING

The Blessed One having in this way set forth the Arousing of Mindfulness through the fourteenfold method of body-contemplation, now said, " And how, o bhikkhus," in order to expound the ninefold method of contemplation of feeling.

There, the meaning of " pleasant feeling," = SUKHAṀ VEDANAṀ, is as follows: The bhikkhu when experiencing a bodily or mental pleasant feeling knows, " I experience a pleasant feeling."

Certainly, while they experience a pleasant feeling, in sucking the breast and on similar occasions, even infants lying on their backs know that they experience pleasure. But this yogāvacara's knowledge is different. Knowledge of pleasure possessed by infants lying on their backs and other similar kinds of knowledge of pleasure do not cast out the belief in a being, do not root out the percept of a being, do not become a subject of meditation and do not become the cultivation of the Arousing of Mindfulness. But the knowledge of this bhikkhu casts out the belief in a being, uproots the perception of a being, is a subject of meditation and is the cultivation of the Arousing of Mindfulness. Verily, the knowledge meant here is concerned with experience that is wisely understood through inquiry.

Who feels? No being or person. Whose is the feeling? Not of a being or person. Owing to what is there the feeling? Feelings can arise with (certain) things—*forms, sounds, smells and so forth*—as objects. That bhikkhu knows, therefore, that there is a mere experiencing of feeling after the objectifying of a particular pleasurable or painful physical basis or of one of indifference. (There is no ego that experiences) *because there is no doer or agent* [*kattu*] *besides a bare process* [*dhamma*]. *The word " bare " indicates that the process is impersonal.* The words of the Discourse, "I experience (or feel)," form a conventional expression, indeed, for that process of impersonal feeling. It should be understood that the bhikkhu knows that with the objectification of a property or basis he experiences a feeling.

It is said that an Elder of Cittala Hill was sick, turning over from side to side, again and again, and groaning with great pain. To him a young bhikkhu said : " Venerable Sir, which part of your body is painful? " " A specially painful place, indeed, there is not ; as a result of taking certain things (such as forms, sounds etc.) for object there is the experiencing of painful feeling," replied the Elder. "Venerable Sir, from the time one knows that, is not bearing up befitting?" said the young bhikkhu. "I am bearing up, friend," said the Elder. "Bearing up is excellent, Venerable Sir," said the young bhikkhu. The Elder bore up. Thereafter, the aerial humour caused injury right up to the heart. His intestines protruded out and lay in a heap on the bed. The Elder pointed that out to the young bhikkhu and said: "Friend, is bearing up so far befitting?" The young bhikkhu remained silent. The Elder, having applied concentration with energy, attained saintship with Analytical Knowledge and passed away into the final peace of Nibbāna, *in the state of consciousness immediately after the course of reflection on the fruit of saintship,* thus realising the highest and passing away nearly at the same time.

Just as when experiencing a pleasant feeling, "when experiencing a painful feeling......a neither-pleasant-nor-painful spiritual feeling he understands, 'I experience a neither-pleasant-nor-painful spiritual feeling'".

Thus the Blessed One when expounding the non-corporeal subject of meditation after the corporeal subject of meditation expounds it by way of feeling. For twofold is the subject of meditation: the subject of meditation of corporeality or materiality and the subject of meditation which is non-corporeal or non-material. This twofold subject of meditation is also spoken of as the laying hold of the mental and the laying hold of the material.

While the Blessed One is expounding the material subject of meditation by way of brief or lengthy reflection he expounds the discernment of the four modes (or elements) of materiality [dhātu]. Both those ways of reflection are pointed out fully, in the Path of Purity.

While expounding, however, the mental subject of meditation generally the Master expounds it by way of the contemplation on feeling.

Threefold, indeed, is the establishing in the mental subject of meditation: by way of sense-impression, feeling and mind. How? To some yogāvacara, indeed, when the material subject of meditation is laid hold of, when there is the first impact of mind-with-mental-characteristics on the object (or the first apprehension of that object), the sense-impression that arises with the contacting of that object becomes clear. To another the feeling that arises with the experiencing of that object becomes clear. To yet another the consciousness that arises with the knowing of that object becomes clear.

When sense-impression becomes clear, not only does sense-impression arise; together with that sense-impression, arise feeling perception volition and consciousness.

When feeling becomes clear the other four too arise.

Also when consciousness becomes clear the other four arise.

The bhikkhu, on reflecting thus : " Dependent on what is this group of five things ?, " knows as follows : " Dependent on the (coarse) corporeal base [vatthu]."

That coarse body [karaja kāya] about which it is said : " And indeed this consciousness of mine is depending on, is bound up with this body," that, in its actual nature consists of the four great physical things, the four great primaries, and the physical qualities sourcing from the four great primaries. These physical qualities are called derived materiality. Here, the bhikkhu sees mind and body, thinking, " The (coarse) corporeal base aforesaid is body ; the five beginning with sense-impression are mind."

In this connection there are the five aggregates because the body is the aggregate of materiality and the mind, the four aggregates of non-material things. There is neither a fivefold aggregation separate from the mind and body nor a mind and body separate from the fivefold aggregation. The bhikkhu who tries to find out what the cause of these five aggregates is sees that these are due to ignorance, etc. Henceforth the bhikkhu lives with thorough knowledge thinking that this thing, the fivefold aggregation, is only something conditioned and includes what is produced from conditioning. It is a congeries of bare formations, indeed,—of bare processes. He applies to it, by way of the mind and body that exist together with conditions, according to the gradual succession of insight-producing knowledge, the words : " impermanent," " subject-to-suffering," and" soulless."

After getting suitable weather conditions, a person of advantage to him spiritually, food that agrees with him, or fitting doctrinal instruction, the bhikkhu desirous of realisation says, " Today, today," fixed in one posture, reaches the acme of insight and stands fast in the fruit of saintship. For the three kinds of persons aforesaid the subject of meditation up to saintship is expounded, in this way.

Here, however the Blessed One speaking of the non-material or mental subject of meditation speaks by way of feeling. While expounding by way of sense-impression or consciousness the subject of meditation does not become clear. It seems dark. But by way of feeling it becomes clear. Why ? Because of the clearness of the arising of feeling. Indeed the arising of pleasant or painful feeling is clear. When pleasant feeling arises spreading through and flowing over the whole body making one to utter the words : " Ah 'tis joy, " it is like causing one to eat fresh clarified butter cooled in very cold water a hundred times after being melted again and again, also a hundred times; it is like causing one to be massaged with an emollient oil worth a hundred pieces ; and it is like causing one to be cooled of a burning fever with a thousand pots of cold water.

When painful feeling arises spreading through and flowing over the whole body making one to bewail with the words, " Alas, what woe," it is like the applying on one of a heated ploughshare ; it is like the sprinkling upon one of molten copper ; and it is comparable to the hurling into dried grass and trees, in the forest, of bundles of wood firebrands.

Thus the arising of pleasant or painful feeling becomes clear, but the arising of the neither-pleasant-nor-painful feeling is dark, and unclear.

The neither-pleasant-nor-painful feeling becomes clear to one who grasps it methodically, thinking : " At the disappearance of pleasure and pain, by way of contrariety to the pleasant and the unpleasant, is the neutral neither-pleasant-nor-painful feeling."

To what is it comparable ? To a deerhunter following the hoofmarks of a deer which midway having gone up a flat rock is fleeing. The hunter after seeing the hoofmarks on the hither and thither side of the rock, without seeing any trace in the middle, knows by inference : " Here the animal went up, and, here, it went down ; in the middle, on the flat rock, possibly it went through this part."

Like the hoofmark at the place of going up the arising of pleasurable feeling becomes clear. Like the hoofmark at the place of descent the arising of painful feeling becomes clear. Like the grasping through inference of the part traversed over the rock by the deer is the laying hold of the neither-pleasant-nor-painful feeling methodically with the thought : At the disappearance of pleasure and pain, by way of contrariety to the pleasant and the unpleasant, is the neutral neither-pleasant-nor-painful feeling."

In this manner, the Blessed One having expounded at first the form subject of meditation, later, pointed out the formless subject of meditation, by way of feeling, having taken it out from the fivefold aggregation distinguishingly.

Not only here did he point it out thus. In the Cūla Taṇhāsankhaya, the Cūla Vedalla, the Mahā Vedalla, the

Raṭṭhapāla, Māgandiya, Dhātuvibhanga, and Āanañjasappāya of the Majjhima Nikāya ; in the Mahā Nidāna, Sakkapañha, and Mahā Satipaṭṭhāna of the Dīgha Nikāya ; in the Cūla Nidāna, Rukkhūpama, and Parivīmaṁsana Suttas of the Saṁyutta Nikāya; in the whole of the Vedanā Saṁyutta of the same Nikāya; and in many another discourse did the Master point out the formless subject of meditation, by way of feeling, having taken out feeling from the fivefold aggregation, after first expounding the form subject of meditation.

This is another method of understanding : (He) understands, " I experience a pleasant feeling " = SUKHAṀ VEDANAṀ VEDIYĀMĪTI PAJĀNĀTI. By the absence of painful feeling at the moment of pleasant feeling, he knows, while experiencing a pleasant feeling : " I am experiencing a pleasant feeling." By reason of that knowledge of the experiencing of pleasant feeling, owing to the absence now of whatsoever painful feeling that existed before and owing to the absence of this pleasant feeling, before the present time, feeling is called an impermanent, a not lasting, and a changeful thing. When he knows the pleasant feeling, in the pleasant feeling, thus, there is clear comprehension. For it is said, in the 78th Sutta of the Majjhima Nikāya, by the Blessed One : " When one experiences a pleasant feeling, Aggivessana, then one does not experience a painful feeling or a neither-pleasant-nor-painful feeling. Only the pleasant feeling does one then experience. When one experiences a painful feeling, Aggivessana, then one does not experience a pleasant or a neither-pleasant-nor-painful feeling. Only a painful feeling does one then experience. When one experiences a neither-painful-nor-pleasant feeling, then, one does not experience a pleasant or a painful feeling. Only a neither-pleasant-nor-painful feeling does one then experience. Pleasant feeling, indeed, Aggivessana is a thing that is impermanent, put-together, dependently originating, decaying, passing away, fading and ceasing. So is painful feeling and the neither-pleasant-nor-painful feeling. The learned, real disciple, Aggivessana, seeing thus, turns away from pleasant feeling even as he does from the painful, and the neither-pleasant-nor-painful feelings. Turning away, he detaches himself ; by absence of attachment, he frees himself ; freed, he knows thus : " I am freed of craving. Destroyed by me is rebirth ; lived by me is the Highest Life of the Real Way ; done by me is the work of making become the Real Way that must be made to become ; and (concerning the sixteenfold work of the development of the Real Way) there is no more work to be done by me."

Pleasant worldly feeling refers to the six joyful feelings connected with the six sense-doors, and dependent on that which is tainted by defilements.

Pleasant spiritual feeling refers to the six joyful feelings connected with the six sense-doors, and not dependent on sense-desire.

Painful worldly feeling refers to the six feelings of grief connected with the six sense-doors, and dependent on that which is tainted by defilements.

Painful spiritual feeling refers to the six feelings of grief connected with the six sense-doors, and not dependent on sense-desire.

Worldly neither-pleasant-nor-painful feeling refers to the six feelings of indifference connected with the six sense-doors, and dependent on that which is tainted by defilements.

Spiritual neither-pleasant-nor-painful feeling refers to the six feelings of indifference connected with the six sense-doors, and not dependent on sense-desire.

The division into pleasant worldly feeling and so forth is in the 137th Sutta of the Majjhima Nikāya.

AJJHATTAṀ = "Internally": The bhikkhu dwells contemplating feelings in the feelings that are his own by laying hold of the pleasant, painful or neither-pleasant-nor-painful feeling. Or he dwells contemplating feelings in the feelings of others by laying hold of the pleasant, painful or neither-pleasant-nor-painful feeling, in the way told above. Or at one time he contemplates his own feelings and at another, another's.

SAMUDAYADHAMMĀNUPASSĪ" = "Contemplating origination-things." In this contemplation of feeling, the bhikkhu dwells seeing the origination and the dissolution of the aggregate of feeling or seeing the origination of feeling at one time and the dissolution of feeling at another time, by way of ignorance, craving and so forth, in the five ways mentioned in the Section on the Modes of Deportment.*

From here on it should be understood that the exposition is just according to the method followed in the explanation of body-contemplation.

Indeed, the mindfulness that lays hold of feeling is the Truth of Suffering. Thus the portal of deliverance for the bhikkhu who lays hold of feeling should be understood.

THE CONTEMPLATION OF CONSCIOUSNESS

After explaining the ninefold Arousing of Mindfulness in regard to feeling the Master began the explanation of the contemplation of consciousness in the sixteenfold way with the words, "And, how, o bhikkhus."

In this section there is no reference to hypercosmic truth because in the sifting of things thoroughly to see their transient, pain-laden and soulless nature only the cosmic things are handled, and so there is in this matter of penetrative knowledge of things no bringing together of cosmic and hypercosmic things.

Here follows the elucidation of terms mentioned in this section :

SARĀGAṀ CITTAṀ = "The consciousness with lust." Karmically unwholesome eight conscious states of the sensuous plane of existence. These are together with greed in the sense of springing from it.

VĪTARĀGAṀ CITTAṀ = "The consciousness without lust." Karmically wholesome and karmically neutral cosmic states of consciousness.

The two spontaneous and non-spontaneous conscious states karmically unwholesome accompanied by grief, linked to resentment and springing from hate, the conscious state karmically unwholesome accompanied by neither pain nor pleasure, linked to scepsis and springing from ignorance, and the conscious state karmically unwholesome accompanied by neither pain nor pleasure, linked to flurry, springing from ignorance—these four do not associate with the consciousness with lust division or the consciousness without lust division.

SADOSAṀ CITTAṀ = "The consciousness with hate." The two conscious states karmically unwholesome accompanied by grief (mentioned above).

VĪTADOSAṀ CITTAṀ = "The consciousness without hate." Karmically wholesome and karmically neutral cosmic states of consciousness.

The other ten karmically unwholesome conscious states of the sensuous plane of existence do not associate with either the consciousness with hate division or the consciousness without hate division.

SAMOHAṀ CITTAṀ = " The consciousness with ignorance." The conscious state, karmically unwholesome, linked to scepsis (mentioned above), and the conscious state, karmically unwholesome, linked to flurry (mentioned above).

Because, indeed, ignorance arises in all karmically bad states, the other karmically bad states too should be mentioned, here. In just this division all the twelve karmically bad, unwholesome or unskilful conscious states are included.

VĪTAMOHAṀ CITTAṀ = " The consciousness without ignorance." Karmically wholesome and karmically neutral cosmic states of consciousness.

SANKHITTAṀ CITTAṀ = " The shrunken state of consciousness." The conscious state fallen into sloth and torpor. That is called the shrivelled or contracted state of mind.

VIKKHITTAṀ CITTAṀ = " The distracted state of consciousness." The conscious state accompanied by flurry. That is called the dissipated mind.

MAHAGGATAṀ CITTAṀ = " The state of consciousness become great." The conscious state of the sensuous-ethereal [rūpāvacara] plane of existence and of the purely ethereal [arūpāvacara] plane of existence.

AMAHAGGATAṀ CITTAṀ = " The state of consciousness not become great." The conscious state of the sensuous plane of existence.

SAUTTARAṀ CITTAṀ = " The state of consciousness with some other mental state superior to it." That refers to any conscious state belonging to the sensuous plane.

ANUTTARAṀ CITTAṀ = "The state of consciousness with no other mental state superior to it." That refers to any conscious state belonging to the sensuous-ethereal [rūpāvacara] or the purely ethereal [arūpāvacara] plane.

SAMĀHITAṀ CITTAṀ = " The quieted state of consciousness." It refers to the conscious state of him who has full or partial absorption.

ASAMĀHITAṀ CITTAṀ = " The state of consciousness not quieted." It refers to the conscious state without either absorption.

VIMUTTAṀ CITTAṀ = "The freed state of consciousness." That refers to the conscious state emancipated partially from defilements through systematic or radical reflection or to the conscious state emancipated through the suppression of the defilements in absorption. Both these kinds of emancipation are temporary.

AVIMUTTAṀ CITTAṀ = "The unfreed state of consciousness."

That refers to any conscious state without either kind of temporary emancipation.

In the mundane path [lokiya magga] of the beginner there is no place for the supramundane kinds of emancipation through extirpation [samuccheda], stilling [paṭippassaddha] and final escape [nissaraṇa].

ITI AJJHATTAṀ = "Thus internally." The bhikkhu lives contemplating consciousness in consciousness, by laying hold on the consciousness with lust and so forth when these states of consciousness proceed in his own flux or in another's flux or by laying hold of these conscious states at one time as they proceed in his own flux and at another time as they proceed in another's flux.

SAMUDAYAVAYADHAMMĀNUPASSĪ = "Contemplating origination-and-dissolution-things." Here, the arising of the aggregate of consciousness should be explained with the pointing out of the origination of consciousness from the origination of ignorance and so forth, in the five ways, according to the method shown in the Section on the Modes of Deportment. And the passing away of consciousness should also be explained in the same way as it is shown in the Section on the Modes of Deportment.

From here on there is nothing new in the method of explanation. The mindfulness which lays hold of consciousness is the Truth of Suffering. Thus, the portal of deliverance up to Saintship of the bhikkhu who lays hold of consciousness as a subject of meditation ought to be understood.

IN THE CONSCIOUSNESS WITH LUST, *lust occurs as a mental concomitant arising and passing away along with a conscious state and sharing with that conscious state the object and basis of consciousness. In this sense of a conscious state well-knit with lust one speaks of* THE CONSCIOUSNESS WITH LUST. *The term* CONSCIOUSNESS WITHOUT LUST *is used as a contrary of the term "consciousness with lust"; not as a contradictory. That becomes clear when we know that the work to be done in this contemplation of the mind consists of the laying hold of the things of the three planes of cosmic existence for the purpose of developing the conviction based on insight in regard to cosmic impermanence, cosmic suffering and cosmic insubstantiality. In no state of cosmic thought can it be said that the latency of lust is destroyed and so the term "consciousness without lust" indicates only a relatively lust-free conscious state.*

The grouping of conscious states, here, it is said, may be questioned. For instance, in the two states of CONSCIOUSNESS WITH HATE *is there just absence of lust because these two states are not well-knit together with lust? Could there not be in them a trace of lust functioning as a distant condition as when a man's lust for a woman produces hate towards another who stands between him and the possession or enjoyment of his object of lust? If there indeed could not be such a trace of lust in these two conscious states of hate, are these even states of consciousness without lust? When the commentator said that the four remaining karmically bad states do not associate with either the consciousness with lust or without lust, he only wanted to show them just separate from the pair known by the phrases, with lust and without lust. If so then would not one fall into partial knowledge? No. Because of their being included in the pairs (though not in the lust pair).*

CONSCIOUSNESS WITH IGNORANCE *is twofold. It is either accompanied by* SCEPSIS *or by* FLURRY.

As this consciousness in either of its forms is fit to be called a delusion by way of particularity owing to excessive aberration and special endowment with ignorance, these two forms, namely, the one LINKED TO SCEPSIS *and the one* LINKED TO FLURRY *are in an outstanding manner "with ignorance."*

By reason of the mind proceeding slackly in a shrivelled state owing to want of interest in the object and more or less with displeasure, there is THE SHRUNKEN STATE OF CONSCIOUSNESS. *This is a name applicable to the five karmically unwholesome sensuous conscious states not marked by spontaneity.*

There is the conscious state associated with flurry in the sense of flurry having become powerful in the consciousness.

"All karmically bad conscious states are indeed accompanied by flurry."

The mental state accompanied by flurry is called THE DISTRACTED MIND *because it spreads outside its object by way of diffused thinking.*

By the ability to suppress the defilements and by the abundance of fruition and by the great length or extent of the series of its particular courses of cognition there is a STATE OF CONSCIOUSNESS BECOME GREAT. *Or there is a state of consciousness become great by reason of lofty regenerative wish and so forth.*

The state of consciousness become great is the mind that has reached the ground of the sensuous-ethereal and the purely ethereal planes of existence. As there is nothing in the cosmos greater than the sensuous-ethereal and the purely ethereal the commentator explained the consciousness become great by reference to these two highest planes of existence.

THE STATE OF CONSCIOUSNESS WITH SOME OTHER MENTAL STATE SUPERIOR TO IT *refers to the consciousness that has not reached the highest possible planes of attainment in cosmic existence or the consciousness that can become more fine and* THE STATE OF CONSCIOUSNESS WITH NO OTHER MENTAL STATE SUPERIOR TO IT *is that which has got to the highest planes of cosmic existence or that which has reached the acme of fineness of cosmic states of mind.*

THE CONTEMPLATION OF MENTAL OBJECTS

THE FIVE HINDRANCES

1. Sensuality

After explaining the Arousing of Mindfulness of the sixteenfold contemplation of consciousness, the Master said : " And, how, o bhikkhus," in order to expound the fivefold contemplation of mental objects [dhamma],—things spiritual and material.

Further, the laying hold of pure corporeality or materiality was taught by the Blessed One in the instruction on body-contemplation and in the instruction on the contemplation of feeling and consciousness, the laying hold of the purely spiritual. Now in order to teach the laying hold of a mixture of the material and the spiritual, he said, " And, how, o bhikkhus," and so forth. Or in the contemplation on the body the laying hold on the aggregate of corporeality or materiality was spoken of by the Master ; in the contemplation on feeling, the laying hold on the aggregate of feeling ; in the contemplation on mind, the laying hold on the aggregate of consciousness ; and now in order to speak of even the laying hold of the aggregates of perception and formations, he said " And, how, o bhikkhus," and so forth.

There, in the Discourse, the word, SANTAṀ = " present ". It means existing by way of occurrence, practice or repeated happening. ASANTAṀ = " Not present." Not existing, by way of non-occurrence or because of rejection from the mind by way of reflection or concentration.

In connection with the hindrances it must be known that the hindrance of sensuality arises because of wrong reflection on an object that is sensuously agreeable, pleasant, favourable. Such an object is either sensuality itself or that which produces sensuality —the sensuality-object.

Wrong reflection is inexpedient reflection, reflection on the wrong track. Or it is reflection which considers the impermanent as permanent, pain as pleasure, non-soul as soul, the bad as good.

Sensuality arises when wrong reflection occurs plentifully in a sensuously good object. Therefore the Blessed One said that the condition for the arising of fresh sensuality and for the increase and expansion of existing sensuality is plentiful wrong reflection on a sensuously auspicious or promising object.

Sensuality is cast out, indeed, with right reflection on a sensuously inauspicious or unpromising object. Such an object itself or the jhāna developed through such an object is meant by the term sensuously inauspicious object.

Right reflection is expedient reflection ; reflection going on the right track. It is reflection that considers the facts of impermanence, suffering, soullessness and of impurity, according to reality.

When there is much right reflection on the sensuously inauspicious or unpromising object sensuality is knocked out. Therefore the Blessed One said that the condition for keeping out new sensuality and for casting out old sensuality is abundant right reflection on the sensuously inauspicious or unpromising object.

Further, there are six things which lead to the casting out of sensuality : Taking up the sensuously inauspicious subject of meditation ; application for the development of the jhāna on the sensuously inauspicious subject of meditation ; the guarded state of the controlling faculties of sense ; moderation in food ; the sympathy and support of good men in the endeavour ; stimulating talk that helps the accomplishment of the object in view.

Explaining these six it is said : Taking up refers to the taking up of the tenfold object sensuously inauspicious, impure, or bad ; the man who takes it up will cast out sensuality. Sensuality will also be cast out, by him who develops the jhāna on the sensuously inauspicious subject of meditation, by him who guards the controlling faculties of sense by closing the six sense doors, and by him who knows the measure of food for sustenance and of whom it is said :

> Enough it is for the comfort of the almsman
> Who has put aside all thoughts of body and life,
> Who has his thoughts yoked on to craving's wane,
> To stop eating when he could eat some four
> Or five more lumps for which there's belly-room,
> And, with drink of water, end his begged repast.*

It will also be cast out by him who keeps the company of men like the Elder Tissa, the worker in the sensuously inauspicious subject of meditation, sympathetic towards those who endeavour in accomplishing the casting out of sensuality and by talk connected with the tenfold sensuously inauspicious object. Therefore it is said by the commentator that six things are conducive to the casting out of sensuality.

The sensuality cast out by these six things becomes incapable of arising, in the future, through the attainment of the path of saintship.

Hindrances have to be cast out first in the course of proper training. With the casting out of the hindrances there is induced jhāna, the means of attaining quietude. Thus indeed is body-contemplation surely taught with quietude preceding.

Afterwards is given the higher instruction in regard to all divisions beginning with what should be understood—the aggregations and the sense-bases which ought to be understood, and the factors of enlightenment which should be developed. Therefore, here too, the development of quietude is desired so far as it is for the sake of insight.

It is said: "The instruction on the Arousing of Mindfulness has insight as the chief thing, abounds in insight."

Since there is no state of yoking together of the good and the bad moral qualities similar to the yoking of two bulls to a cart,—since the good and the bad do not exist together—from the absence of sensuality at the time of seeing one's mind through knowledge it is said: BY WAY OF OCCURRENCE. *At the moment of seeing wisely the occurrence of sensuality there is no sensuality as good and bad states of mind cannot exist together.*

EXISTING *means: When it is found in one's own mental flux.*

Sensuously inauspicious or unpromising objects are the ten inanimate things: 1. *the corpse that is swollen,* 2. *blue,* 3. *festering,* 4. *fissured,* 5. *mangled,* 6. *dismembered,* 7. *cut and dismembered,* 8. *with blood,* 9. *wormy,* 10. *become a skeleton. Details of these may be found in The Path of Purity in the exposition of the subject of meditation on the foul.*

And the perception of hair of the head and so forth, because it is called in the Girimānanda Sutta the perception of the sensuously inauspicious or impure, is taken as the sensuously inauspicious animate thing.

The jhāna on the sensuously inauspicious object occurs in an inanimate or animate sensuously inauspicious thing. And the indication of the four kinds of wrong reflection and the four kinds of right reflection in regard to the sensuously inauspicious object is for the purpose of pointing out fully the subject.

The four kinds of consideration of the impure as pure, the impermanent as permanent, suffering as pleasure, and non-soul as soul are the four kinds of wrong reflection and the four kinds of consideration of the impure as impure and so forth are the four kinds of right reflection.

The taking up of the practice of considering the repulsiveness of any of the eleven kinds of the sensuously inauspicious or the practice of contemplation on the sensuously inauspicious object is "taking up" or "upholding."

The application to the development of the thought bent on the sensuously inauspicious object which brings partial and full concentration is application for the development of the jhāna on the sensuously inauspicious subject of meditation.

Certain teachers say that as there is no opportunity for sensuality in him who knows the proper measure of food to be taken, through absence of trouble owing to that knowledge from sloth and torpor, sensuality is cast out in such a person. Just this reason is given in even the expository portion : The person who practises moderation in food brings about the perception of impurity bound up with that food, for instance, through the alteration of food by way of bodily excretions, and dwells on other similar thoughts as well as on the idea of corporeal subjection to food. Such a person casts out sensuality.

The Elder Tissa referred to in the commentary above is the Elder Mahā Tissa (of Anurādhapura), who saw the teeth of a woman and who by doing right reflection on their bony nature cast out sensuality through jhāna.

According to the Abhidhamma method of instruction, even the whole world is the hindrance of sensuality. Therefore the commentator said : THROUGH THE ATTAINMENT OF THE PATH OF SAINTSHIP [*Abhidhamma pariyāyena sabbo pi loko kamacchandanīvaraṇanti āha arahattamaggenāti*].

2. Anger

Verily, wrong reflection on an object of resentment produces anger. In this connection anger itself as well as the object which causes anger is called the resentment-object, or the sign of resentment. Wrong reflection has just the same character everywhere, and when it occurs much in the resentment-object or the resentment-sign, anger arises. Therefore the Blessed One said that intense wrong reflection on an object of resentment is the cause of fresh anger and of the increase and expansion of anger already existing.

By right reflection of the liberating thought of love, the thought of love that frees the heart, indeed, anger gets cast out. The term " love " here is applicable both to partial concentration (upacāra samādhi) and full concentration (appanā samādhi). Heart-liberating love is only full concentration. Right reflection has the same character throughout. When it occurs strong in the thought of love, anger is removed from the heart. Therefore the Master said : " There is, o bhikkhus, the liberation of the mind through love. Intense right reflection on love is the condition for keeping out new anger and for throwing out anger that is already in the heart."

And it is said that these six things help to cast anger out: Taking up the practice of the love subject of meditation; applying oneself to the development of jhāna on the thought of love; reflection on one's action as one's own property; abundance of wise consideration; sympathetic and helpful companionship of the good; and stimulating talk that assists the development of the thought of love and the overthrow of anger.

In explanation the commentator said: Anger will be put down in one who takes up the love subject of meditation by way of spreading it particularly or separately Or if one takes up the love subject of meditation by way of spreading it generally, without particularisation or directional restriction in space, then too anger will be put down, in one.

Anger vanishes also through the development of jhāna by spreading love restrictedly with differentiation in seven or twenty-eight ways or by spreading it unrestrictedly without differentiation in five or twenty ways or by spreading it directionally towards the ten points in space.

Anger vanishes in one who reflects thus too: "What will you do to him by becoming angry?" "Will you be able to destroy things like his virtue?" "Have you not been born here just by your own actions and will you not also by your own actions get reborn hereafter?" "Getting angry with another is comparable to the state of him who wishes to strike another with glowing coals, red-hot crowbar, excreta and such other damaging things after taking them up in his bare hands." "And what can another who is angry with you do to you?" "Can he destroy your virtue or any other similar thing of yours?" "He, too, has been born here as a result of his actions and will be reborn hereafter just according to his actions." "Like a present not accepted is that anger of his and like a handful of dust thrown against the wind, that anger of his alights on his own head." In this way one reflects on one's own action as one's own property and also another person's action as that person's own, and puts out anger.

To one remaining in an abundance of wise consideration after reflecting on action as one's or another's own property, anger vanishes. And it vanishes in him who is in the company of a sympathetic friend who delights in developing the jhāna of the thought of love like the Elder Assagutta and through stimulating talk on the thought of love when in any one of the four postures. Therefore is it said: Six things are conducive to the casting out of anger. The anger cast out by these six things, however, is finally destroyed by the attainment of the stage of the Anāgāmi, the Never-returner.

The thought of love [mettā] is a sublime state of mind [brahmavihāra]; it is one's own state of freedom from hatred. A detailed description of the way of developing love as a subject of meditation is given in the Path of Purity.

The following summary of hints gathered from different scholia and the Path of Purity will be helpful to a beginner:

The love thought of meditation is different from worldly attachment. It is based on wishing well to all beings. The idea of possession of the loved object is foreign to it. It is not a state of mind that encourages exclusiveness. The aim of the meditation is finally to include in the ambit of one's goodwill all beings equally, without distinction. "The liberation of the mind through love" refers only to full concentration. Without reaching full concentration there is no effective freedom from anger. The beginner who works at this subject of meditation is not to practise the thought of love at first:

On a sensuously promising object of the opposite sex, as attachment towards it might arise in the yogi's mind.

On a dead person, as the practice would be futile.
On an enemy, as anger might arise.
On an indifferent person, as the practice might prove wearisome.

On one who is very dear as the arousing of friendly thoughts without attachment towards such a one would be tiring, and as mental agitation might occur should even some slight trouble overtake that one.

TAKING UP THE PRACTICE OF THE LOVE SUBJECT OF MEDITATION *is the generating, the bringing about of the characteristic, sign or mark, of the love thought of meditation of him who through loving-kindness gathers together all beings with goodwill.*

The reflection on the thought of love itself is the sign of the love thought of meditation, because the reflection arisen first is the reason of the later reflection.

SPREADING IT PARTICULARLY: *Consecutively in the following order: to oneself, to a friend, an indifferent person, and an enemy.* SPREADING IT GENERALLY: *By breaking down all barriers, limits, and reservations which separate oneself from all others, and extending the same kind of friendly thought to all.* DIRECTIONALLY: *Extending the thought of love towards one point of the compass, for instance, the east. These three kinds of spreading of the thought of love refer to the stage of meditation of* "TAKING UP THE PRACTICE OF THE THOUGHT OF LOVE" *which covers the training from the beginning to the attainment of partial concentration (upacāra samādhi). In regard to this stage of meditation the following is stated: Spreading the thought of love after particularizing the direction by way of a monastery, a street, village and so forth is one way and spreading the thought of love towards a direction in space generally by way of the eastern direction and so forth without specifying a monastery and so forth is another way of practice.*

THE DEVELOPMENT OF THE JHĀNA ON THE THOUGHT OF LOVE *is the practice again and again of the thought of love that has got partial concentration. The development is done in three ways:* 1. *The spreading of the love thought universally. This is done by wishing that all living beings (satta), all breathing things (pāṇa) all beings born (bhūta), all persons (puggala), all who have reached a state of individuality (attabhāvapariyāpanna) be without hatred, disease, and grief, and be happy taking care of themselves (averā-, abyāpajjhā-, anighā hontu, sukhī attānaṁ pariharantu).* 2. *Spreading the thought of love by way of restricted groups of beings. This is done by wishing that all females, all males, all purified ones, all non-purified ones, all divine beings, all humans, all beings fallen to states of woe, be without hatred, disease and grief and happy taking care of themselves.* 3. *Spreading the thought of love directionally in space. This is done by restricting the thought of love towards each of the ten directions in space: the cardinal points, the intermediate points and the zenith and nadir. And it is also done by wishing that the beings in each of the directions taken up, according to the divisions and groups given above, be without hatred and so forth according to the formula already mentioned.*

3. Sloth and Torpor

Through wrong reflection on a state of boredom and the like sloth and torpor come to be. Boredom is just dissatisfaction. Lassitude is bodily laziness. Languidity of body is the bending of the body torpidly in getting up and in similar actions. Lethargy after a meal is a dizziness or slight faint which is due to eating a principal meal. It is also called the discomfort which follows such a meal. The mind's sluggishness is the dulness of the mind. An abundance of wrong reflection on boredom and similar states of mind produces sloth and torpor. Therefore the Blessed One said that much wrong reflection on boredom, lassitude, languidity of body, lethargy after a meal, and the mind's sluggishness, is a condition for the production of fresh sloth and torpor and the increase and expansion of sloth and torpor already come into being.

Through right reflection on inceptive energy and similar states of mind is brought about the overthrow of sloth and torpor. Inceptive energy is the effort first set a-foot. Exertion is more powerful than the inceptive energy because it leaves indolence behind. And because of its assailing further and further of the destructive condition, progressive endeavour is more powerful than exertion. By the exercise of right reflection intensely on this threefold strenuousness sloth and torpor are cast out. Therefore the Blessed One said that the condition for keeping out new sloth and torpor, and for casting out sloth and torpor that is old is abundant right reflection on the element of inceptive energy, of exertion and of progressive endeavour.

There are six things which lead to the casting out of sloth and torpor: The seeing of the reason of sloth and torpor in the fact of eating too much or gluttony; the changing of the postures completely; reflection on the perception of light; staying in the open; sympathetic and helpful companionship of the good; and stimulating talk that assists in dispelling sloth and torpor.

There is the following explanation of these six things: The bhikkhu who has eaten gluttonously is assailed by sloth and torpor while doing his recluse duty of meditation in his day or night quarters as by a mighty elephant pressing down on him, but that one who practises moderation in food is not troubled thus with these hindrances. In one who thus sees the characteristic of sloth and torpor in gluttony there is the casting out of sloth and torpor.

Sloth and torpor disappear in him who changes over from the posture which induces sloth and torpor to another; in him who reflects on the brightness or the light of the moon, a lamp or a torch by night, and on the light or brightness of the sun by day; in him who lives in the open; in him who associates with sympathetic and helpful companions, like the Elder Mahā Kassapa, who have dispelled sloth and torpor; and by stimulating talk connected with a strict recluse-regimen.

Therefore is it said: Six things lead to the casting out of sloth and torpor. The yogi understands thus: The sloth and torpor cast out by these six things are stopped from arising for ever in the future by the attainment of the path of saintship.

THE BHIKKHU WHO HAS EATEN GLUTTONOUSLY *after the manner of the well-known types of Brahminical gormandizers mentioned in ancient Indian books. There are five kinds of these greedy eaters:* 1. *He who eats until he has to be raised up by the hand from his seat.* 2. *He who lies rolling just where he has eaten and eats as long as he likes.* 3. *He who eats until he slips off his waist cloth.* 4. *He who fills himself with food in such a way that it seems as if a crow could peck at the food in him.* 5. *He who having filled his belly full and vomitted eats more food again, or he who eats until he vomits.*

ON THE LIGHT OR BRIGHTNESS OF THE SUN BY DAY: *The meaning should be understood thus: Sloth and torpor vanish in him, too, who at night is reflecting on the image of the perception of the brightness of the sun he got by day.*

Here it may be helpful to state the eight ways of dealing with torpor taught by the Master to the Elder Mahā Moggallāna: 1 *One should neglect to mind the thought which says that drowsiness is descending on one,* or 2 *one should reflect on the Dhamma,* or 3 *repeat or recite the Dhamma,* or 4 *pull both earlobes and rub or massage the limbs with the hands, or* 5 *getting up from the sitting position, apply water on and rub the eyes, and look into the distance, at the constellations in the starry sky, or* 6 *reflect on the thought of light, or* 7 *fix the thought on the ambulatory, aware of the ends of it with the controlling faculties of sense turned inwards and the mind kept in, or* 8 *sleep conscious of the time of waking and on awaking get up quickly thinking that one will not give oneself to the comforts of lying down, reclining and languor, when all other seven ways fail.*

4. Flurry and Worry

Wrong reflection on mental agitation brings about flurry and worry. Mental agitation is inner turbulence. Actually it is flurry and worry, only. Intense wrong reflection on that mental agitation produces flurry and worry. Therefore the Blessed One said that wrong reflection on mental agitation when plentifully done produces fresh flurry and worry and increases and expands flurry and worry already in existence.

The casting out of flurry and worry occurs through right reflection on mental tranquillity called concentration and an abundance of right reflection on mental tranquillity says the Blessed One is a condition for the keeping out of fresh flurry and worry and the dispelling of flurry and worry already in the mind.

Six things are conducive to the casting out of flurry and worry: Knowledge; questioning; understanding of disciplinary rules; association with those more experienced and older than oneself in the practice of things like virtue; sympathetic and helpful companionship; and stimulating talk that helps the rejection of flurry and worry.

In explanation it is said as follows: Flurry and worry disappear in him who learns in the spirit and in the letter one, two, three, four or five collections of Scripture. This is how one gets over flurry and worry by knowledge. Questioning means: inquiring much about what is befitting and not according to the practice of the Order. In him who does this, too, flurry and worry disappear. Then these twin evils disappear in him who has got the mastery of the Discipline due to practical application of and conversance with the nature of the Rule of the Buddha's Order. This is the understanding of the disciplinary rules. Association with those more experienced and so forth: the going to the presence of and the conversing with virtuous elders in the Order. By such visits flurry and worry disappear in one. Sympathetic and helpful companionship: association with experts of the Disciplinary Rules like the Elder Upāli the first of the great masters of the Discipline in the Order of the Buddha. In such company flurry and worry disappear. Stimulating talk in this connection refers particularly to matters of disciplinary practice by which one comes to know what is befitting and what is not. By this flurry and worry vanish in one. Therefore, is it said that six things lead to the rejection of flurry and worry, but the flurry cast out by these things finally ceases to arise in the future through the attainment of the path of Saintship, and the worry cast out by these things finally ceases to arise in the future through the attainment of the path of the Non-returner.

In their own state or actually as they are individually, FLURRY AND WORRY *are two different things. Still, as worry in the form of repentance or remorse for ill done and good undone is similar to flurry which is characterized by distraction and disquiet of mind,* MENTAL AGITATION *is called flurry and worry.*

Mental agitation does not overtake the intelligent well-read man who probes into things by way of what is written in books and by way of the significance and import of the things themselves. Therefore, it is said that by way of KNOWLEDGE *not merely of the Disciplinary Rules, but by way of knowledge of the ninefold Buddha-word, beginning with the Discourses, according to the principles of the method already stated and by the application of the proper remedies mentioned by way of* QUESTIONING *and so forth remorse and regret for ill done and good undone do not take place.*

By associating with elders who are older than oneself in the practice of the precepts of virtue and similar good things, who are restrained, aged, matured seniors, there is brought to one a measure of restraint, matured bearing, dignity and calm and flurry and worry are cast out.

GOOD COMPANIONSHIP *refers to association with those versed in the Discipline who are able to dispel worry as regards any doubt concerning what is proper and improper practice.*

5. Scepsis

Wrong reflection on things which are founded on doubt brings about the arising of scepsis. Things which are founded on doubt are known as just scepsis owing to the state of being the reason of scepsis again and again. Therefore the Blessed One said that wrong reflection on things founded on doubt is the condition for fresh scepsis and for the increase and expansion of scepsis already arisen. By right reflection on wholesome things karmically and the like there is the casting out of scepsis. Therefore, the Blessed One said that right reflection on things which are karmically wholesome and not, things blameful and blameless, things to be practised and not to be practised, things of low and high value, things dark and fair comparable to the bad and the good, done intensely, keeps out fresh scepsis and casts out scepsis that has already come into existence.

There are these six things which help to throw out scepsis: The state of being learned in the Buddha's teaching; of inquiring about the Buddha, the Teaching, and the Order of Real Saints; of understanding thoroughly the nature of the Discipline; of being decided about the truth of the Buddha, the Teaching, and the Order of the Real Saints; sympathetic and helpful companionship; and stimulating talk that helps to dispel scepsis.

The first has been explained earlier. It is the knowledge of the Scriptures generally both in the letter and the spirit. The second is obvious. The third indicates a state of mastery of the Discipline through practical application and great conversance with it at first hand. The fourth is the strong inclination towards or reliance on the Triple Gem called the faith that is capable of settling in the object of the virtues of the Buddha, the Teaching and the Order. The fifth is association with good companions like the Elder Vakkali, bent, inclined, sliding towards faith, mentally. The sixth is stimulating talk on the Triple Gem at all times possible in every state of behaviour. One can cast away scepsis by means of these six things, but the scepsis cast out by these six things does not ever arise in the future only when it is destroyed by the attainment of the first stage of the saint.

THINGS WHICH ARE FOUNDED ON DOUBT *are things which stand or proceed on doubt. Taking scepsis itself one sees that the scepsis arisen first is the particular reason by way of a common cause of the scepsis arisen afterwards.*

Surely by the knowledge of the Teaching and by inquiry all doubt is cast out.

ITI AJJHATTAṀ = "Thus internally." In this way the bhikkhu lives contemplating the mental objects, by laying hold of the five hindrances amongst the mental objects of his own mind or amongst the mental objects in another's mind or at one time amongst the mental objects of his own mind, and at another time amongst the mental objects of another's mind.

Here origination and dissolution, only refer to the origination of the five hindrances by way of wrong reflection on sensuously attractive or beautiful objects etc., and the dissolution of the five hindrances by wise reflection on the impurity of the sensuous objects etc.

Here the mindfulness which lays hold of the hindrances is the Truth of Suffering. Thus the portal of deliverance of the bhikkhu who lays hold of the hindrances should be understood.

THE AGGREGATES

Having expounded the contemplation of mental objects by way of the five hindrances, the Master said, " And, further, o bhikkhus," in order to explain the contemplation of mental objects by way of the fivefold aggregation.

PAÑCASU UPĀDĀNAKKHANDHESU = " In (the mental objects of) the five aggregates of clinging." The five aggregates of clinging are the groups that grasp life. The congeries of mental objects become the condition of clinging is the meaning. This is a brief indication of these aggregates. For the statement about the aggregates at length the talk on the aggregates in the Path of Purity should be read.

ITI RŪPAṀ = " Thus is material form." So far is there material form and no further. In this way the bhikkhu perceives material form according to nature. In regard to feeling and the things that come afterwards the same is the method of exegesis. This is the brief indication of meaning of the matters referred to here. For the lengthy explanation on these things one should read the talk on the aggregates in the Path of Purity.

ITI RŪPASSA SAMUDAYO = " Thus is the arising of material form." The arising of material form and the other aggregates should be known according to the fivefold way (mentioned in the Section on the Modes of Deportment) through the arising of ignorance and so forth.

ITI RŪPASSA ATTHANGAMO="Thus is the disappearance of material form." The disappearance of material form and the other aggregates should be known according to the fivefold way (mentioned in the Section on the Modes of Deportment) through the passing away of ignorance and so forth. One should read the talk on the aggregates in the Path of Purity for further explanation.

ITI AJJHATTAṀ = " Thus internally." In this way the bhikkhu lives contemplating mental objects by laying hold of the fivefold aggregation of clinging amongst his own mental objects or amongst the mental objects of another or at one time in his own and at another time in another's mental objects.

The origination and dissolution of the fivefold aggregate should be brought forward and connected by way of the fifty characteristics of the five groups, with the extended application of the words: "From the arising of ignorance the arising of material form comes to be."

From here on according to the method already stated by the commentator should the exposition be.

ACCORDING TO NATURE *means : according to the nature of breaking-up, according to the nature of the eye, colour and the like in regard to material form, and according to the nature of experiencing, the nature of pleasure and the like in regard to feeling. In this way all other connected things should be interpreted.*

THE SENSE-BASES

After explaining the contemplation of mental objects by way of the aggregates the Master said: "And, further, o bhikkhus," in order to explain the contemplation of mental objects by way of the sense-bases.

CHASU AJJHATTIKA BĀHIRESU ĀYATANESU = "In (the mental objects of) the six internal and the six external sense-bases." The eye, the ear, the nose, the tongue, the body and the mind are the six internal sense-bases, and material form, sound, smell, taste, tactual object, and mental object are the six external sense-bases.

CAKKHUṀ PAJĀNĀTI = "(He) understands the eye." He understands the sensory apparatus of the eye, by way of its own distinct function and salient characteristic.

RŪPE PAJĀNĀTI = "(He understands) material form (objects) that are visible." He understands material form arising from the four producers of corporeality, namely, karma consciousness, climate and nutriment [kamma citta utu āhāra], by way of their own distinctive function and salient characteristic.

YAṀ TADUBHAYAṀ PAṬICCA UPPAJATI SAṀYOJANAṀ = "The fetter that arises dependent on both (eye and forms)." He understands according to distinct function and characteristic the tenfold fetter that arises dependent on both eye and forms—the tenfold fetter of sensuality, resentment, pride, speculative theory, scepsis, belief in rites and ceremonies, the desire to go on existing, envy, avarice and ignorance.

" How does this tenfold fettering arise ? " asks one.

The fetter of sensuality arises for him who by way of sensuous enjoyment takes delight in a pleasant sense-object become visible at the eye-door. For him who is annoyed or angry at the sight of an unpleasant object, the fetter of resentment arises and the fetter of pride arises in him who thinks : No one but me is able to consider the object wisely. The fetter of speculative theory comes to be in him who takes material form to be permanent and everlasting. The fetter of scepsis arises in him who thinks in this way : Is the material form a being or a being's ? The fetter of the desire to go on existing arises in him who wishes thus : To be sure, in a favourable state of existence this material form will become easy of access. The fetter of rites and ceremonies arises in him who undertakes to perform rites and ceremonies thinking : In the future it will be possible to obtain such an object as this by taking up the observance of rites and ceremonies. The fetter of envy arises in him who contemplates grudgingly : Should no others get this material form, it would be good, indeed. The fetter of avarice arises in one who stints for another the material form belonging to one.

The fetter of ignorance arises (with all the previously mentioned fetters), with all sensuous passion and the like, by way of the relation of conascent nescience.

YATHĀ CA ANUPPANNASSA SAṀYOJANASSA UPPĀDO HOTI TAÑCA PAJĀNĀTI = " He understands how the arising of the non-arisen (tenfold) fetter comes to be." He understands that the (tenfold) fetter had not arisen earlier owing to some cause of non-occurrence.

YATHĀ CA UPPANNASSA SAṀYOJANASSA PAHĀṆAṀ HOTI TAÑCA PAJĀNĀTI = " He understands how the abandoning of the arisen (tenfold) fetter comes to be." He understands the reason for the abandoning of just the (tenfold) fetter arisen through previous non-abandoning or through occurrence.

YATHĀ CA PAHĪṆASSA SAṀYOJANASSA ĀYATIṀ ANUPPĀDO HOTI TAÑCA PAJĀNĀTI = " He understands how the non-arising in the future of the abandoned (tenfold) fetter comes to be." He understands the reason for the non-arising in the future of even the (tenfold) fetter abandoned by way of rejection of separate factors through right reflection [tadangavasena] and through absorption [vikkhambhana vasena].

Owing to what reason does the tenfold fettering cease to arise in the future finally?

The path of stream-winning or the first stage of saintship is the reason for final cessation of the five fetters of speculative theory, scepsis, rites and ceremonies, envy, and avarice. The path of once-returning or the second stage of saintship is the reason for the final cessation of sensuality and resentment of a gross kind and the residuum of these two fetters finally ceases by reason of the attainment of the path of never-returning, the third stage of saintship.The fact which makes the fetter of pride, of the desire to go on existing, and of ignorance to cease finally in the future is the path of final purification, saintship, the fourth stage of saintliness.

The same is the method of exegesis in SOTAÑCA PAJĀNĀTI SADDE CA PAJĀNĀTI = "He understands the ear and sounds." Further. in this connection, the talk on the sense-bases in full should be understood as stated by the commentator in the Path of Purity.

ITI AJJHATTAṀ = "Thus internally." The bhikkhu lives contemplating the mental objects by laying hold of the internal sense-bases in his own mental objects or in another's or by laying hold of the external sense-bases in another's mental objects or in his own or at one time in his own and at another time in another's mental objects.

Origination and dissolution should be brought forward and connected here by the extended application of the method indicated by the words: "From the origin of ignorance the origin of the eye" to the sense-bases of material form in the aggregate of materiality, to the mental sense-base in the aggregate of consciousness, and to the sense-base of the mental object in the other non-material aggregates, according to the method of exegesis already stated by the commentator. The hypercosmic things should not be taken. From here onward the exposition is according to the method already shown by the commentator.

The two groups of six sense-bases are stated by way of determining the sense-doors and the sense-objects of the arising of sixfold consciousness. Of the consciousness or mind aggregate included in a course of cognition of eye-consciousness just the eye-base is the "door" of origin, and the base of the material form is the object. So it is in the case of the others. But of the sixth sense-base the part of the mind-base called the life-continuum, the unconscious mind, is the "door" of origin [Chaṭṭhassa pana bhavangamana-sankhāto manāyatanekadeso uppatti dvāraṁ]. And in a particular or special way the mind-object-base is the object [Asādhāranañca dhammāyatanaṁ ārammanaṁ].

DEPENDENT ON BOTH : *The eye become a condition by way of decisive support and the material forms, the objects, become a condition by way of objective predominance and objective decisive support [Cakkhuṁ upanissaya paccayavasena paccayabhūtaṁ rūpe ārammaṇādhipati ārammaṇupanissaya vasena paccayabhūte ca paṭicca].*

THE FACTORS OF ENLIGHTENMENT

1. Mindfulness

After explaining the contemplation of mental objects by way of the internal and the external sense-bases, the Master said, " And further, o bhikkhus," in order to talk on the contemplation of mental objects, by way of the Factors of Enlightenment, the mental limbs of a being who is awaking *from the stupor of the passions that soil or who is penetrating the Real Truths of Suffering, its Cause, its Cessation, and the Way Leading to the Cessation of Suffering.*

Limbs are members or constituent parts of the awaking mind.

SANTAṀ = " Is present ". Existing by way of attainment.

The enlightenment factor called mindfulness is the enlightenment factor of mindfulness.

Because in these enlightenment factors, the yogāvacara effectively gets enlightened, the yogāvacara is called " Complete Enlightenment " from the time he begins strenuous contemplation on insight. *It is a name for him who stands in the practice starting from the arising of the knowledge of the rise and fall of phenomena.*

The sevenfold completeness or harmony beginning with mindfulness by which he awakes, effectively, rises from the sleep of the defilements, or penetrates the Truths, is " Complete Enlightenment." The components of that " Complete Enlightenment " or of the harmony called " Complete Enlightenment " are the factors of enlightenment.

The instruction of the Discourses is figurative and as this instruction on the Arousing of Mindfulness is set going by way of the mundane eightfold path, it is said by the commentator that the yogāvacara is " Complete Enlightenment." Otherwise he should be a Pure Disciple [ARIYA SĀVAKA]. *The yogāvacara is considered the personification of the factors of complete enlightenment by which he can reach Nibbāna.*

In the other factors of enlightenment the word-meaning should be understood in the same way.

ASANTAṀ = " Is absent ". Not existing through lack of attainment.

YATHĀ ANUPPANNASSA = "How (the arising) of the non-arisen." First, is the enlightenment factor of mindfulness. There are things which condition the enlightenment factor of mindfulness and an abundance of right reflection on them is the reason that is conducive to the arising of the non-arisen enlightenment factor of mindfulness and for the increase, the expansion and completion by culture of the arisen enlightenment factor.

Thus it comes into being: Just mindfulness comprises the things which condition the enlightenment factor of mindfulness. Right reflection has just the characteristic already mentioned, and when right reflection occurs plentifully in the things which condition the enlightenment factor of mindfulness, the enlightenment factor of mindfulness arises.

Further, four things lead to the arising of the enlightenment factor of mindfulness: Mindfulness with clear comprehension, the avoiding of persons with confused minds, association with persons who keep mindfulness ready for application, inclination towards mindfulness.

In explanation it is said: Mindfulness arises through mindfulness with clear comprehension in the seven positions beginning with that of "going forwards"; *or the mindfulness arousing the knowledge which grasps the purpose of these actions is mindfulness with clear comprehension, and as mindfulness with clear comprehension everywhere is a state which brings about the cultivation of mindfulness, mindfulness with clear comprehension is necessary for the arising of mindfulness. As the abandoning or rejection of contrary things and the practice of suitable things are necessary for the arising of fresh karmically wholesome things so the eschewing of persons bereft of mindfulness, association with persons who cultivate mindfulness, the state of being not engaged with the first kind and the state of being engaged with the second are necessary for the arising of the enlightenment factor of mindfulness.*

Mindfulness arises through the avoiding of persons who are confused in mind like crows that come cawing to food thrown; through association with persons who keep mindfulness ready for application like the Elder Tissadatta *who in the Terrace of the Wisdom-tree having got a golden ticket authorizing him to expound the Norm* [*Bodhi maṇḍe suvaṇṇa salākaṁ gahetvā*] *entered the assembly saying: "In which one of the eighteen languages shall I expound the Teaching?"* and the Elder Abhaya *who is mentioned as the Elder Dattābhaya by the commentator;* and through the state of mind tending for originating mindfulness in all postures, in all kinds of behaviour or disposition of the body. And the bhikkhu knows that the completion by culture of the enlightenment factor of mindfulness brought into being by these four ways takes place by means of the attainment of the path of saintship.

2. Investigation of Mental Objects

There are karmically good and karmically bad things......right and wrong comparable to bright and dark things and an abundance of right reflection on them is the reason conducive to the arising of the non-arisen enlightenment factor of the investigation of mental objects and for the increase, expansion and the completion of culture of that enlightenment factor when it has arisen.

Here, right reflection is the conscious state that is associated with knowledge and which arises by way of perceiving, according to actuality, the nature, function, characteristic and so forth of the several skilful (or wholesome) states of mind and the like. Because it is correct reflection it is called right (or radical) reflection.

Six things lead to the arising of this enlightenment factor: Inquiring about the aggregates and so forth; the purification of the basis (namely, the cleaning of the body, clothes and so forth); imparting evenness to the (five spiritual) controlling faculties; avoiding the ignorant; associating with the wise; reflecting on the profound difference of the hard-to-perceive processes of the aggregates, modes (or elements), sense-bases and so forth; and the inclining (sloping, bending) towards the development of the enlightenment factor of the investigation of mental objects.

Inquiring about the aggregates and so forth means: seeking the meaning of the aggregates, the modes (or elements), sense-bases controlling faculties, powers, enlightenment factors, way factors, absorption factors, the meditation for quietude, and the meditation for insight *by asking for explanation of knotty points regarding these things in the Five Nikāyas with the commentaries from teachers of the Norm.*

Purification of the basis is the cleaning of the personal basis the body and the impersonal basis: clothes and dwelling place. The flame of a lamp is unclear when its wick, oil and container are dirty; the wick splutters, flickers; but the flame of a lamp that has a clean wick, oil and container is clear and the wick does not spit; it burns smoothly. So it is with knowledge. Knowing that arises out of the mind and mental qualities which are in dirty external and internal surroundings is apt to be impure, too, but the knowledge that arises under clean conditions is apt to be pure. In this way cleanliness leads to the growth of this enlightenment factor which comprises knowledge.

Personal cleanliness is impaired by the excessive length of hair of the head, nails, hair of the body, by the excess of humours, and by the dirt of perspiration; cleanliness of impersonal or external things is impaired when robes are worn out, dirty and smelly, and when the house where one lives is dirty, soiled and untidy. So personal cleanliness should be secured by shaving, hair-cutting, nail-paring the use of pectoral emetics and of purgatives which make the body light, and by shampooing, bathing and doing other necessary things, at the proper time. In a similar way external cleanliness should be brought about by darning, washing and dyeing one's robes, and by smearing the floor of one's house with clay and the like to smoothen and clean it, and by doing other necessary things to keep the house clean and tidy.

Imparting evenness to the (five spiritual) controlling faculties is the equalising of the controlling faculties of faith, energy, mindfulness, concentration and wisdom.

Equalising is making neither more nor less effective functionally.

When faith outstrips the others through over-activity the others are thrown out of gear. Then energy finds it impossible to exert ; mindfulness, to attend to the object ; concentration, to be non-distracted ; and wisdom, to see. Therefore that over-activity of faith should be made to wane either by reflection on the phenomenal nature of the thing (faith) or by not attending to that thing when thinking of which faith becomes excessive. The story of the Thera Vakkali* is the illustration of over-active faith.

Faith outstrips the others because of the unclearness of wisdom and the laxity and so forth of energy and the others, through the excessive zeal of the function of faith, in regard to a believeable object, an object that generates trust. Energy is unable to do the work of exerting, and of supporting the associated mental characteristics and to avoid indolence.

Mindfulness is not able to do the work of attending to the object, of continuing to be at the object, after coming to it.

Concentration is not able to do the work of non-distraction, of rejecting distraction.

To see the object, according to actuality as if one were seeing a physical thing with the eye, wisdom is not able.

These four faculties are unable to do their work because of their being overwhelmed by the faculty of faith acting very strong. Only by the evenness of function can the mental things which exist together with consciousness, and are the principal things amongst conascent mental things, namely, the five spiritual controlling faculties, accomplish their work. Not otherwise.

Reflection on the phenomenal nature of the thing (*faith*). *By examining the object of faith by way of the conditioned and the produced from the conditioned and the like, by scrutiny according to actuality.*

The story of the Thera Vakkali. *This venerable person who fulfilled his duties through keen faith liked to behold the Master always. The Master admonished him saying, " What shall it profit you to see this impure body? Who sees the Norm, sees me,"* *and urged him to practise a subject of meditation. He was unable to apply himself to the practice of the subject of meditation and as he was inclined to destroy himself, he went up to a place that was a steep declivity. Then the Master showed himself by his psychic power as if he were seated before the thera and spoke these words:*

The bhikkhu who is full of joy and believes in
the Dispensation of the Buddha
can reach the peaceful happy state
of the ceasing of activities.

Gladdened by the words of the Master he set up the development of insight, but as his faith was very strong he was not able to enter into the joy of insight. The Master knowing this gave him the subject of meditation after correcting it with the imparting of evenness of the controlling faculties. The thera after putting himself in the path of practice taught by the Master, and after doing hard work in regular order, reached saintship.

If however the controlling faculty of energy becomes too powerful then neither will the faculty of faith be able to do its work of arousing faith in a settled way in its object nor will the remaining controlling faculties be able to perform their functions. Therefore, in such a case, energy should be made to lessen its activity by the development of the enlightenment factors of calm, concentration and equanimity. The story of the Thera Soṇa* is given as an illustration of overdone energy.

THE STORY OF THE THERA SOṆA. *This refers to Soṇa Thera who was of delicate constitution. After getting a subject of meditation from the Master he was living in Cool Wood, and he thought thus: "My body is delicate and it is not possible to reach happiness with comfort only. Even after being exhausted, the duty of the recluse should be done." Thereupon, he decided, while giving himself up to exertion, to keep to only the two postures of standing and walking. Owing to excessive walking blisters appeared on the soles of his feet and caused him great pain. He continued to make strong effort in spite of the pain but could not produce a state of distinction in meditation with his excessive energy.*

The Master visited Soṇa, instructed him with the simile of the lute, corrected the Thera's subject of meditation showing him the method of applying energy evenly and went to Vulture Peak. Having applied energy evenly according to the method given by the Master, and after working hard for insight, the Thera, making become inner growth, established himself in Arahatship.

Even thus should the incapacity of the rest of the spiritual faculties to function effectively when one of them has become over-active and powerful be understood.

Here, the wise, specially praise the equipollence of faith and wisdom and of concentration and energy. He who is very strong in faith and feeble in wisdom becomes a person who believes in foolish people who have no virtue, persons who are not trustworthy. He who has very strong wisdom and feeble faith gets crafty-minded, and is like a drug-produced disease that cannot be cured. Such a person thinks that wholesome karma arises with just the intention to do good. Going along the wrong way, by a species of thought beyond the limits of reason, and doing neither almsgiving nor other similar good deeds, he is born in a state of woe. By the equipollence of faith and wisdom one believes only in those like the Buddha who are worthy of trust because there is a reason for trusting them.

As concentration naturally inclines towards indolence, when there is too much of concentration and too little of energy, indolence overwhelms the mind. As energy inclines naturally towards restlessness or flurry, when there is much energy and little concentration restlessness overwhelms the mind. When concentration is combined well with energy there will be no falling of the mind into indolence. When energy is combined well with concentration there will be no falling of the mind into restlessness.

Discord of faith and wisdom and discord of concentration and energy through functional unevenness are not conducive to success in meditation.

Faith and wisdom should be made functionally even and harmonious. So, too, concentration and energy. With the making even functionally of these pairs full absorption occurs.

Further, to a worker in concentration—*a man pursuing the path of quietude [samatha]*—faith that is *somewhat* strong is meet. With faith that is (rather) strong, the yogi will, by believing in and fixing the mind on the object, reach full absorption.

If for instance the yogi is meditating on the element of earth he will not think thus: "How can absorption arise by the repetition of the word EARTH*?" He will think that the method of meditation taught by the Supreme Buddha will surely succeed, and he will settle in, and leap on to the object by way of firm belief, having, as it were, forced his way into it.*

Concerning concentration and wisdom it is said as follows: For the worker in concentration—*the man pursuing quietude [samatha]*—strong one-pointedness is meet *by reason of the fact that concentration is the principal thing in absorption.* With strong one-pointedness he reaches full absorption. For the man pursuing the path of insight [vipassanā] strong wisdom is meet; if strong wisdom exists he arrives at the penetration of the characteristics. By the equalising of the concentration and wisdom of the worker in concentration, the man pursuing quietude, there is just full absorption.

Owing to the very great strength of the concentration of the man pursuing quietude very great strength of wisdom too should be desired.

FULL ABSORPTION *is mundane full absorption. Supramundane full absorption also is expected through the equalising of these. Accordingly the Master said: " He makes become quietude and insight yoked together."*

Strong mindfulness is meet everywhere since it protects the mind from falling into restlessness belonging to faith, energy and wisdom and from falling into indolence belonging to concentration. Faith, energy and wisdom have a tendency towards excitement and concentration has a tendency towards sloth.

Therefore, mindfulness is to be desired by the yogi always. It is likened to the salt-flavouring which is in all curries, and the minister-of-all-work wanted in every business of the king.

And because of this (universality of application of mindfulness) the commentator made the following statement: " And indeed, it was said by the Blessed One thus: 'Mindfulness is to be desired everywhere.' Why? Because mindfulness is the mind's help, because mindfulness has just protection as its manifestation, and because without mindfulness there is no exerting or restraining of the mind."

Because it is applied always mindfulness is always useful or desirable; and because in all states of elation and depression it should be developed by the man longing for the factors of enlightenment it is necessary.

MIND'S HELP *the help of a wholesome or skilful state of consciousness. It is the support of such a state of mind for attaining the yet unattained.*

Avoiding the ignorant is keeping away from foolish folk not grounded in the knowledge of the divisions of the aggregates and so forth. Association with wise folk is fellowship with persons possessed of the knowledge of rise and fall through the laying hold of all the fifty characteristics.

Reflecting on the profound differences of the profound process of the aggregates and so forth is the analytic reflection according to wisdom of the movement of the hard-to-perceive aggregates and so forth.

Inclining towards the enlightenment factor of the investigation of mental objects is the mental state inclining, tending, and sloping towards the purpose of originating this enlightenment factor in every posture of standing, sitting, walking and lying down.

The yogi understands that the culture of this enlightenment factor arisen thus comes to completion through the path of saintship.

3. Energy

There is the mode (or element) of energy that is inceptive, the mode of energy that is enduring, and the mode of energy that is strong, powerful, courageous, and an abundance of right reflection on these (modes of energy) is the reason conducive to the arising of the non-arisen enlightenment factor of energy, and for the increase, expansion and the completion by culture of that enlightenment factor when it has arisen.

Eleven things lead to the arising of the enlightenment factor of energy : Reflection on the fearfulness of states-of-woe [apāya bhaya] ; the seeing of the benefits of energy ; reflection on the path to be trodden ; the honouring of alms ; reflection on the greatness of the heritage ; reflection on the greatness of the Master ; reflection on the greatness of race ; reflection on the greatness of fellows in the holy life ; the avoiding of lazy folk ; the associating with folk who have begun to exert ; and the inclination towards the development of the enlightenment factor of energy.

Reflection on the fearfulness of the states-of-woe as stated in the Devadūta and other Suttas produces in the yogi the thought: " Now is the time to rouse energy ; it is not possible to be energetic when subject to great suffering."

The seeing of the benefits of energy is the appreciation of the fact that only by one who has begun to exert himself (in the development of the enlightenment factors etc.), could the Supramundane Truth be obtained and not by a lazy person.

" The path trodden by all the Supreme Buddhas, the Paccekabuddhas, and the Great Disciples, has to be trodden by you," says the yogi to himself, " and that path is impossible for an indolent person." That is the reflection on the path to be trodden.

The yogi thinks thus : " Those who support you with alms-food and so forth are not relatives of yours, are not your servants ; they do not give you excellent alms thinking : ' We shall (in the future) live depending on you.' But they give expecting from their offerings great fruit. Also the requisites were not allowed to you by the Master so that you may make use of the requisites and live strong-bodied in comfort, but they were allowed to you so that you may do the duty of the recluse and escape the round of suffering whilst using the requisites. The indolent one does not honour the alms ; only he who has begun to be energetic honours it." Reflection in this way about honouring the alms permitted by the Buddha produces energy, as in the case of the Thera Mahā Mitta (Great Friend).

The Thera lived in Kassaka Leṇa (Cultivator's or Farmer's Cave). In the village to which he resorted for alms there was a certain Mahā Upāsikā (elderly or great female lay devotee) who taking him as a child of hers looked after him.

One day she was preparing to go to the forest, and spoke to her daughter thus : "Here is old rice; here, milk ; here, ghee ; and here, treacle. When your brother the venerable Mitta comes cook the rice and give it to him with milk, ghee, and treacle. You, too, eat of it. I have eaten the cold rice cooked yesterday with gruel." "Mother, what will you take at noon ?" "Cook a sour gruel with herbs and broken rice and put it by (for me)."

Just as the Thera was taking out the bowl (from the bowl-bag), after he had robed himself to go out for alms, he heard that talk of the mother and daughter through his clairaudient power, at the door of his cave, and thought as follows : "The great lay devotee has eaten stale rice with gruel and will take sour gruel at noon. For you she has given old rice, milk, ghee and treacle. She does not expect field or food or cloth from you. Only expecting the three good attainments of the human, divine and hypercosmic planes does she give (alms to you). Will you be able to bestow on her those attainments ? Verily her alms is not fit to be taken by you with (heart of) lust, hatred and ignorance." Then, he put back the bowl into the bowl-bag, unloosened the robe-knot, refrained from going for alms, and returning to the Cultivator's Cave put the bowl under his bed, the robe on the robe pole and sat down resolved on endeavour thinking, "I will not go from here without attaining saintship."

This recluse who had been earnest for a long time, after developing insight, reached the fruit of saintship even before meal-time, and the great destroyer of the corruptions smiling like an opening lotus went out of the cave.

To him the guardian deity of the tree near the cave said this :

Hail to thee man-steed of finest strain,
Hail to thee the best of mortal kind,
Gone are thy cankers, Sorrowless One, and so
Worthy art thou to take a gift of faith.

Having uttered this appreciation, the tree deity said : "Venerable Sir, after giving alms to a saint like you wandering for alms the elderly woman will escape suffering."

When the Thera got up and opened the door to observe what the time was he found that it was still quite early. So he took his bowl and robe and entered the village.

The young girl, having prepared the rice, sat looking towards the door of her house thinking, "Now, my brother will come."

And when the Thera arrived she took the bowl, filled it with milk-rice alms mixed with ghee and treacle and placed it in his hands, and he departed after giving thanks with the words: "May there be happiness," and the girl stood there looking at the departing one. The colour of the Elder at that time was exceedingly clear, and his controlling faculties specially pure and his face was shining like a ripe palm-fruit freed from the foot-stalk.

The mother of the girl on returning from the forest inquired: "Dear, did your brother come?" The daughter told her everything. The Mahā Upāsikā knowing that her son's renunciation-work had that day reached its acme, said, "Dear, your brother delights in the Dispensation of the Buddha. He is not dissatisfied."

There is reflection on the greatness of the heritage when one thinks thus: "Great, indeed, is the heritage of the Teacher, namely the Seven Real Treasures [Satta Ariya Dhanāni]. These are not to be got by the slothful. The indolent man is like a son disowned by his parents. He does not get his parents' wealth when they pass away. So too it is with the Seven Real Treasures. Only the man of energy gets these."

Reflection on the greatness of the Master consists in recalling the great events in the teacher's life, and admonishing oneself thus: "Does it befit you to be slack after entering the Dispensation of such a Teacher?"

Reflection on the greatness of race is carried out by way of the fact that in entering the Buddha's Dispensation one has become the Conqueror's son [spiritually], and that for such a one slacking is not fit.

Reflection on the greatness of fellows in the holy life consists of admonishing oneself thus: "Sariputta, Mahā Moggallāna, and the great disciples penetrated the hypercosmic after much endeavour. Are you following their way of life?"

The avoiding of lazy folk is the avoiding of people without physical and mental energy who are like a rock-snake lying inert after a full feed. And the association with folk who have begun to exert themselves is mixing with those whose minds are turned towards and who are endeavouring for the attainment of Nibbāna. Inclination towards the development of this enlightenment factor is the inclining, sloping and bending of the mind towards right exertion in all postures of sitting, standing and so forth. The enlightenment fact that arises in this way comes to completion by culture through the path of saintship.

4. Joy

There are things which condition the enlightenment factor of joy and an abundance of right reflection on these is the reason that is conducive to the arising of the non-arisen enlightenment factor of joy and for the increase, expansion and completion by culture of the enlightenment factor when it has arisen.

Eleven things lead to the arising of the enlightenment factor of joy: Buddha-recollection, Norm-recollection, Order-recollection, recollection of virtue, of liberality, of the shining ones [devas], and the recollection of subsidence [upasama], the avoiding of coarse folk, association with refined folk, reflection on the discourses inspiring confidence, and the inclination towards joy.

By recollection of the Buddha's qualities, of the qualities of the Dhamma, and of the Sangha, joy arises.

Joy arises also for one who having kept the precepts of fourfold purity unbroken for a long time reflects on one's virtue; to laymen who reflect on their virtue through observing the ten and the five precepts; to one reflecting on liberality and recollecting one's gift of excellent food to one's fellows in the holy life during a time of scarcity and the like; to laymen recollecting their liberality in giving alms to virtuous folk; to one reflecting on one's possession of qualities by which beings have reached the state of shining ones (devas); to one reflecting thus by way of subsidence: "The passions suppressed by the higher attainments do not occur for sixty or seventy years."

The avoiding of coarse folk is the keeping away from rough people who are like dirt on a mule's back, who show a callous nature through irreverence, owing to lack of faith-inspired affection for the Buddha and the like, in worshipping shrines or elders. Refined folk are those who have much faith in the Buddha and the like and are gentle of mind. Discourses which illumine the qualities of and inspire confidence in the Triple Gem are discourses inspiring confidence. The inclination towards joy refers to the mind sloping towards this enlightenment factor in all postures of sitting and the like. The completion by culture of this enlightenment factor is through the path of saintship.

5. Calm

There are things which condition the enlightenment factor of calm of the body (the aggregates of feeling, perception and the conformations) and of the mind (the aggregate of consciousness) and an abundance of right reflection on these things is conducive to the arising of the non-arisen enlightenment factor of calm and for the increase, expansion, and completion by culture of this enlightenment factor when it has arisen.

Seven things lead to the arising of the enlightenment factor of calm: The resorting to fine food, comfortable weather, and comfortable postures; judgment according to the middle way; the avoiding of people who are physically restless; the association with people who are physically calm and the inclination towards the development of the enlightenment factor of calm.

THE RESORTING TO FINE FOOD *is the resorting to excellent, beneficial food that is suitable to one.* THE RESORTING TO COMFORTABLE WEATHER AND POSTURES *means the resorting to weather and postures suitable to one. By resorting to this threefold suitability, well-being of mind comes into existence by way of the basis of bodily well-being and there proceeds then the reason for twofold calm.*

Judgment according to the middle way is reflection on one's own deed as one's own property and another's deed as that other's property.

This is the judgment of things based on the acknowledgment of the law of moral causation avoiding first the extreme view that the suffering and happiness experienced by living beings are causeless, and then the other extreme view of ascribing these to a fictive cause like that of a Creator God, and the knowing of all suffering and happiness as one's own action.

But he who has the nature of a great man is patient of all kinds of weather and postures. Not concerning such a person has the above been said.

The avoiding of people who are physically restless is the keeping away from restless people who go about harassing others with clod and stick. People who are physically calm are those who are quiet because they are restrained of hand and foot. The inclination towards the development of this enlightenment factor is the inclining, sloping, and bending of the mind towards calm in all postures. By the saint's path the completion by culture of this enlightenment factor takes place.

6. Concentration

There is the sign of quietude, and the sign of non-confusion, and an abundance of right reflection on these is the reason conducive to the arising of the non-arisen enlightenment factor of concentration and for the increase, expansion and completion by culture of the enlightenment factor of concentration when it has arisen.

The first stage of tranquillity which arises when an object is being grasped by way of bearing it in mind, the composed manner, is the characteristic sign of quietude.

There the sign of quietude is just the quietude *by way of the composed manner.* And in the sense of non-distraction is the sign of non-confusion to be taken.

Confusion is the state of mind which, because of the whirling in a multiplicity of objects, is jumping from thing to thing, diverse of aim, and not one-pointed. Distraction is the same in character. Unsteadiness is its salient feature, and deviation is its manifestation. By one-pointedness of mind confusion is thrown out.

Eleven things lead to the arising of concentration : Purification of the basis ; the imparting of evenness to the spiritual controlling faculties ; skill in taking up the sign of the object of meditation ; the inciting of the mind on occasion, the restraining of the mind on occasion, the gladdening of the mind on occasion and the regarding of the mind without interfering on occasion ; the avoiding of people who are not collected in mind ; association with people who are collected in mind ; reflection on the absorptions and the emancipations ; and the inclination towards the development of the enlightenment factor of concentration.

Skill in the taking up of the sign which is the cause for the arising of absorption is skill in taking up sign.

The inciting of the mind on occasion is the applying of the mind vigorously by bringing into being the enlightenment factors of the investigation of mental objects, energy and joy, when there is excessive laxity of energy and of the application of wisdom, and a deficiency of delight in the meditation.

The restraining of the mind refers to the checking of the mind that is become excessively energetic, too strong, in the application of wisdom and elated with delight, by bringing into being the enlightenment factors of calm, concentration and equanimity.

The gladdening of the mind means : The enlivening with confidence of the mind become dissatisfied either through weak application of wisdom or the non-attainment of the bliss of restfulness (or of the subsidence of the passions even temporarily). This enlivening is done through reflection on the eight reasons for the upsurge of spiritual feeling, namely, birth, decay, disease, death, the suffering of the four states of woe, the saṁsāric round of suffering in the past, and the suffering rooted in the search for nutriment in the present life, and through contemplation on the qualities of the Triple Gem.

The regarding of the mind without interfering is the absence of the work of inciting, restraining and gladdening the mind which has got to right practice and which proceeds well in the object, free from sloth, free from restlessness, and free from dissatisfaction. It is comparable to the state of a charioteer who looks on uninterfering when the horses are going well.

The keeping away from persons who have not reached partial or full absorption and are distracted of mind is the avoiding of people who are not collected in mind. Association with persons who have reached those states of absorption is association with people who are collected in mind. The mind inclining, sloping, and bending towards concentration-production in all postures of standing, sitting and the like constitutes the inclination for this factor. The completion by culture of the enlightenment factor of concentration is through the path of saintship.

EXCESSIVE LAXITY......OF APPLICATION OF WISDOM *means feeble working of wisdom. As the principal thing in liberality is non-greed, and in virtue non-hate, so in meditation it is wisdom (non-ignorance) that is the principal thing. Therefore, if wisdom is not very strong in the making become of concentration there will be no causing of contemplative attainment (or distinction) As unprepared food gives no pleasure to a man, so, without the application of wisdom, the object of meditation does not give satisfaction to the yogi's mind. To the yogi then there is the pointing out of the remedy for that lack of satisfaction in the stirring up of spiritual feeling and confidence.*

7. Equanimity

There are things which condition the enlightenment factor of equanimity and an abundance of right reflection on these is the reason that is conducive to the arising of the non-arisen enlightenment factor of equanimity and for the increase, expansion and the completion by culture of the enlightenment factor when it has arisen.

Five things lead to the arising of the enlightenment factor of equanimity : The detached attitude towards beings ; the detached attitude towards things ; the avoiding of persons who are egotistical in regard to living beings and things and the inclination for developing the enlightenment factor of equanimity.

The detached attitude towards beings is brought about by reflection on beings as possessors of their own deeds, and by reflection in the highest sense.

Reflection on beings as possessors of their own deeds is there when a person thinks thus : " You have been born here by your own deeds in the past and will depart from here and fare according to your own deeds. Who then is the being you are attached to ? "

Reflection in the highest sense is thinking in the following way : " Really no living being exists. To whom can then you be attached ? "

The detached attitude towards things is brought about by reflection on ownerlessness and temporariness.

A person thinks thus : " This robe will fade, get old, become a foot-cleaning rag and be after that fit only to be taken up at the end of a stick and flung away. Surely, should there be an owner of this he would not let it come to ruin in this way ? " This is the reflection on ownerlessness. To think that this robe cannot last long and that its duration is short is to reflect on the temporariness of it. These two reflections are applicable in a similar way to the bowl and other things.

Persons who are egotistical in regard to living beings are laymen who cherish their own sons and daughters and the like and recluses who cherish their resident pupils, mates, preceptors and the like. And these persons, if for instance, they are recluses do with their own hands for them whom they cherish hair-cutting, sewing, robe-washing, robe-dyeing, bowl-lacquering, and so forth. If even for a short time they do not see their cherished ones they look hither and thither like bewildered deer, and ask, " Where is such and such novice?" or "Where is such and such young bhikkhu." And if these recluses are entreated by others to send a novice or a young bhikkhu so that those others may get some such work as hair-cutting done, the novice or young bhikkhu is not sent on the plea that he is not made to do even his own work, and that if he is made to do the work of others he would get tired. Persons egotistical in this way should be avoided.

A person who is egotistical in regard to things is he who cherishes robes, bowls, beakers, walking sticks, staffs and so forth and does not let another even touch these. When asked for a loan of some article he would say : " Even I do not use it ; how can I give it ? " Persons egotiscal in that way, too, should be avoided.

A person who is neutral, indifferent, as regards both living beings and things is a person who is detached as regards both living beings and things. The company of such a person should be sought.

Inclination for developing this enlightenment factor is the inclining, sloping, and bending of the mind towards equanimity in all postures of standing and so forth.

The completion by culture of the enlightenment factor of equanimity is wrought by the path of saintship.

ITI AJJHATTAṀ = "Thus internally." The yogi lives contemplating mental objects in mental objects (that is, contemplating mental objects only and nothing else) by laying hold of his own enlightenment factors or another's enlightenment factors or at one time his own enlightenment factors and at another time another's enlightenment factors.

Here, origination and dissolution should be known by way of the origination and dissolution of the enlightenment factors.

From here on the exposition is just according to the manner already stated.

The cause of the enlightenment factor of equanimity is the impartial state, the middle state, free from attraction and repulsion. If that freedom from attraction and repulsion exists then there is equanimity; when it does not exist there is no equanimity. This state of freedom from attraction and repulsion is twofold by way of scope: detachment in regard to beings and detachment in regard to things.

Repulsion is thrown away even by the development of the enlightenment factor of calm and in order to show just the way of casting out attraction is the instruction beginning with detachment in regard to beings taught.

Specially, equanimity is an enemy of lust and so the commentator said: Equanimity is the path of purity of one who is full of lust.

The detached attitude towards beings is developed by reflection on the individual nature of moral causation and by reflection on soullessness. By reflection on ownerlessness, the state of not belonging to a soul is brought out and by reflection on temporariness, the impermanence of things is brought out to produce the detached attitude towards inanimate things.

THE FOUR TRUTHS

Having explained thus the contemplation of mental objects by way of the seven factors of enlightenment, the Master said, "And further," and so forth in order to explain the meditation by way of the Four Truths.

IDAṀ DUKKHANTI YATHĀBHUTAṀ PAJĀNĀTI = "A bhikkhu understands: 'This is suffering,' according to reality." He puts aside craving, and understands all things of the three planes of becoming as suffering, according to nature. He understands according to nature the previous craving that produces and makes to arise that very suffering. He understands the non-occurrence of both suffering and its origin, according to nature, as Nibbāna. He understands, according to nature, the Real Path which penetrates suffering, abandons origination, and realises cessation.

The rest of the explanation of the Real Truths is in the Path of Purity [Visuddhi Magga].

ITI AJJHATTAṀ = "Thus, internally." He lives contemplating mental objects in mental objects having laid hold of his own four truths or the four truths of another or at one time his own four truths and at another time another's four truths.

In this explanation of the truths, the origination and dissolution of the four truths should be understood according to nature by way of arising and stopping.

From here on the explanation is according to the manner already stated.

With this have been stated the following twenty-one subjects of meditation : Breathing, Modes of Deportment, the Method of the Thirtytwo Parts of the Body, the Determination of the Four Modes of Materiality (or the Four Elements), the Nine Cemetery Contemplations, Contemplation of Feeling, Contemplation of Consciousness, the Laying Hold on the Hindrances, the Laying Hold on the Aggregates, the Laying Hold on the Sense-bases, the Laying Hold on the Enlightenment Factors, and the Laying Hold on the Truths. The Cemetery Contemplations are counted separately.

The Contemplation on Breathing, the Thirtytwo Parts and the Nine Cemetery Contemplations, these eleven, are subjects of meditation which produce full absorption. The Dīgha-bhāṇaka (Reciter of the Long Collection of Discourses) Mạhā Sīva, however, says that the Nine Cemetery Contemplations are here stated by way of considerations (only productive of partial absorption). Therefore according to his view only two subjects, Breathing and the Thirtytwo Parts, produce full absorption ; the rest produce only partial absorption. Does adherence by way of wrong views arise in regard to all these or not ? It cannot be said that it does not arise, because adherence by way of wrong views does not arise in the Modes of Deportment, the Four Kinds of Clear Comprehension, the Hindrances and the Enlightenment Factors and it arises in the other subjects of meditation. But the Thera Mahā Sīva says : "In these too there is the arising of adherence by way of wrong views (of the self) because the yogi lays hold of the Modes of Deportment and so forth thinking thus : Have I or have I not the Four Modes of Deportment......the Four Kinds of Clear Comprehension.......the Five Hindrances...... the Seven Factors of Enlightenment. Therefore in all subjects of meditation adherence by way of wrong views does arise.

YOHI KOCI BHIKKHAVE IME CATTĀRO SATIPAṬṬHĀNE EVAṀ BHĀVEYYA = " Verily, o bhikkhus should any person make become the Four Arousings of Mindfulness in this manner." If any bhikkhu or bhikkhuni or upāsaka or upāsikā cultivates mindfulness from the beginning according to the method taught here.

TIṬṬHANTU BHIKKHAVE = "O bhikkhus, let alone." This, together with what follows this, was said by way of the average person capable of being trained.

But concerning the person of keen intelligence it was stated as follows : Instructed in the morning, he will attain in the evening; instructed in the evening, he will attain in the morning.

The Blessed One pointed out the teaching thus : " Bhikkhus, my Dispensation leads to Deliverance in this way," closed the instruction that is crowned with Saintship in twenty-one places and uttered the following words : " This is the only way o bhikkhus for the purification of beings, for the overcoming of sorrow and lamentation, for the destruction of suffering and grief, for reaching the right path, for the attainment of Nibbāna, namely the Four Arousings of Mindfulness."

NOTES

Page—xv

*Refer to Paramattha-Dīpanī Iti-Vuttakaṭṭhakathā of Dhammapālācariya, P. T. S. Edition Vol. 1, pages 80—81 for the source of the explanation of appamāda given here.

Page—xix

*Visuddhi Magga translated as The Path of Purity by Pe Maung Tin in three volumes, Pali Text Society Translation series Nos. 11, 17 and 21, Oxford University Press, London E.C.

Page—xx

*In this connection it will be profitable for the practiser of the Way to read the twentieth discourse of the Middle Collection [Majjhima Nikāya], in the translation by Sīlācāra or by Chalmers.

Page—17

*The Land of the Jambu, Sinhala : Mā Daṁ, Eugenia Jambolana, a tree that grows to fairly great proportions and yields a small roundish fruit with purple pulp enclosing a stone.

**Fully enlightened ones.

***Solitarily enlightened ones.

Page—18

*See the story of Kalmāsapāda and its evolution in Indian literature, by Watanabe, Journal of the Pali Text Society, 1909, p. 236 foll. Mahā Sutasoma Jātaka (No. 537) ; and Jayaddisa Jātaka (No. 513). Dictionary of Pāli Proper Names, vol. I. pp. 528—529. Watanabe's study is comprehensive. He believes Jātaka No. 537 to be older than 513. Some said that the converting of Speckled Foot was in No. 537. The Mahā Vihāra teachers said that it was in No. 513.

Page—19

*" The ancient Kuru country may be said to have comprised the Kuruksetra and Thāneswar. The district formerly included Sonepat, Āmin Kernāl and Pāṇipat, and was situated between the Saraswatī (mod. Sarsuti) on the north and the Dṛṣadvatī (mod. Rākshi) on the south."—Cited from G. De by R. Mehta in Pre-Buddhist India p. 382, Bombay, 1939.

" The kingdom of Kuru......was divided into three parts, Kurukshetra, the Kurus (i.e. the country of the Kurus), and Kurujāngala (the forest tract included in the kingdom)." Notes to S. M. Sastri's edition of Cunningham's Ancient Geography of India, p. 701, Calcutta, 1924.

Page—20

*Saṁyutta Nikāya V. Pages 168 and 186. P. T. S. Edition.

**Sutta Nipāta verse 714.

Page—22

*Not found in the Patisambhidā Magga.

**Not found in the Patisambhidā Magga ; these are verses 273—275 of the Dhammapada.

***Saṁyutta Nikāya iii. page 151, P. T. S. Edition. The verse which precedes this passage here resembles a saying attributed to the Porāṇas in Adikāram's Early History of Buddhism in Ceylon, Appendix II. A, page xxii, quotation 77.

****Sutta Nipāta verse 949.

*****Dhammapada verse 288.

Page—26

*Saṁyutta Nikāya i, p. 53 P. T. S. Edition.

**Saṁyutta Nikāya i, page 54. P. T. S. Edition.

Page—31

*An almsman, a mendicant, monk, religious, or recluse. In the Buddhadhamma it indicates generally any person who accepts and follows earnestly the teaching ; but technically it refers to one who has received the higher ordination in the Holy Life.

**Dhammapada Verse 142.

Page—34

*Saṁyutta Nikāya V, page 115. P.T.S. Edition.

Page—39

*Saṁyutta Nikāya, IV, page 207, P. T. S. Edition.

Page—48

*In the explanation of the contemplation on breathing, the passage beginning with "When breathing in long, how does he understand, 'I breathe in long,'?" and ending with the words "non-quaking of the body," consists of extracts from pages 272—277 of the Visuddhi Magga, Part 1. P. T. S. Edition.

Page—54

*Nyāyācārya S. Abhayasinha says that this passage is a statement of the Naiyāyika theory of perception and that it is mentioned in the Siddhānta Candrodaya of Srī Krsṇa Dhūrjati Dīksita, a commentary of Tarkasangraha, thus : Ātmā manasā saṁyujjate mana indriyeṇendriyamarathena tataḥ pratyaksaṁ.

Page—68

*In the highest sense, a living being is a process of consciousness, and consciousness in the highest form is that of the Saint, the Arahanta which is not different from the Norm and within that consciousness the Norm is included.

Page—77

*Material phenomena of bodily or vocal expression which arise and cease together with the thought that motivates expression are ignored as too plain to be misunderstood. Only other phenomena of matter not connected with vocal or bodily expression are mentioned.

Page—78

*One who realises that which one experiences. The person who experiences absorption first realises Nibbāna afterwards. That person should be understood as of sixfold character counting from the state of the fruition of stream-winning to the state of the path of arahatship. Therefore the commentator said : Here a certain person, having experienced by the body the eight emancipations, lives ; in that person the cankers become destroyed owing to his having seen the emancipations with wisdom. Digha Aṭṭhakathā Part III. pages 889—890. seen P. T. S. Edition.

Page—80

*Here, it is necessary to explain further how a course of cognition with moral consequences takes place. Awareness or lack of it in regard to, for instance, the true nature of a visible object is not due to the sensory qualities of the eye. Nevertheless when a visible object becomes clear after existing for the space of a thought-unit in regard to consciousness of the life-continuum without however causing any ruffle in the placid flow of the continuum there arises once and ceases consciousness as life-continuum movement of one thought-unit's duration and once, too, arises and ceases consciousness as life-continuum stoppage of one thought- unit's duration. Then completing the function of adverting or turning to the visible object, consciousness as a barely active mind-process arises once and ceases. After that in regular order arise and cease one thought-unit of eye-consciousness completing the function of seeing the object, one thought-unit of consciousness of a resultant mind-process completing the function of receiving the object, one thought-unit of resultant non-causal process of mind-consciousness completing the function of considering the object and one thought-unit of barely active non-causal mind-consciousness completing the function of determining the object. Immediately after that conscious impulsion impels seven times, that is, during the space of seven thought-units. There, from the state of the life-continuum to that of determining no moral consequences take place. And no very strong moral consequences take place even in the first seven impulsions that follow determining. At the close of those seven impulsions consciousness slides into the life-continuum or in other words consciousness becomes the life-continuum taking up as object the karma, the karmical sign or the destiny-sign which brought about the relinking mind of the present existence. This activity of the life-continuum is repeated very many times and then consciousness regrasps the visible object that was comprehended earlier in the course of sense-door cognition, and exists for the space of one thought-unit by way of life-continuum movement, and for the space of one thought-unit, by way of life-continuum stoppage, at the mind-door. After that consciousness arises once and ceases by way of adverting to the mind-door and arises and ceases seven times by way of impulsion of mind-door cognition. It is even in the fourth impulsion-set beginning with sense-door cognition or in the impulsion-set of the third of the courses of mind-door cognition that very strong moral consequence take place. Cf. Majjhima Nikāya Aṭṭhakathā pp. 75—76 P. T. S. Ed. and the Visuddhi Mārga by Buddhaghosa Thera with commentary of Kalikāla Sāhityas Sarvagjña Pandita Parākrama Bāhu and new explanation by M. Dharmaratne, 1890, Colombo, Part. 1 p. 91. The extract given below is from the Paramattha Mañjūsā Tīkā Part 1, p. 43, edited by M. Dhammānanda Thera, 1928, Colombo : ettha ca cakku dvāre rūpārammaṇe āpāthagate niyamitādi vasena kusalākusale javane sattakkhattuṁ uppajjitvā bhavaṅgam otiṇṇe tadanurūpameva mano dvārika javane tasmiṁ yevārammaṇe sattakkhattuṁ yeva uppajjitvā bhavaṅgaṁ otiṇṇe puna tasmiṁ yeva dvāre tadevārammaṇaṁ nissāya itthī purisoti ādinā vavatthāpentaṁ pasāda rajjanādi vasena sattakkhattuṁ javanaṁ javati.

Page—95

*" Waking=the state of being awake ; there, when there is non-occurrence of the process which makes or is made of action, what is called waking does not exist ; the bhikkhu laying hold (of the matter), thinking, ' waking comes to be when a trace of the process which makes or is made of action occurs ' is called a doer of clear comprehension [Jāgarite ti jāgaraṇe. Tattha kriyāmayapavattassa appavattiyā sati jagaritaṁ nāma na hoti. Kriyāmayapavattavalañje pavattante jagaritaṁ nāma hotīti parigganhanto bhikkhu jāgarite sampajānakārī nāma hoti]. Sāmmoha Vinodanī, Jhāna Vibhanga, p. 364 P. T. S. Ed.

Page—97

*Vibhanga page 250, P. T. S. Edition.

Page—98

*Cp. Jhāna Vibhanga, Sammoha Vinodanī, pp. 363—4, P. T. S. Ed.

Page—99

*The three kinds of wisdom: inclination of mind, Nibbāna, the four fruits of the homeless life [Tisso vijjā: cittassa adhimutti, nibbānaṁ, cattāri sāmaññaphalāni] Paramattha Mañjūsā Ṭikā.

Page—100

*Anguttara i, 256 : the ideas of concentration, energy and equanimity should be applied to the mind, according as they are needed, to check idleness, agitation and non-concentration.

**Anguttara iii, 435 : the bhikkhu should have these six states to reach peace: restraint, energy, interest, equanimity, leaning to the good, love of Nibbāna,

***Saṁyutta v, 112: The bhikkhu should know that when the mind is indolent it is not the time to cultivate the enlightenment-limb of calm.

Page—112

*He, thinking : ' the origination of feeling comes to be through the origination of ignorance,' in the sense of the origin of conditions, sees the arising of the aggregate of feeling.........(Patisambhida Magga P. T. S. Edition Page 55).

Page—120

*Theragāthā Verse 983.

Page—137

*Saṁyutta Nikāya iii, page 120, P. T. S. Edition and Dhammapada Aṭṭhakathā IV pages 117—119, P. T. S. Edition.

Page—138

*Vinaya Mahāvagga. Cammakkhandha, and Anguttara Nikāya III. Pages 374—5 P. T. S. Edition.

Printed at the Daily News Press, Lake House, McCallum Road, Colombo, by Bernard de Silva, for Mrs. B. Moonasinghe, Nelson Place, Wellawatte, Colombo—May 1949

CPSIA information can be obtained at www.ICGtesting.com
233946LV00001B/80/A

9 781417 978618